Table of Contents

Carson-Dellosa Publishing LLC
P.O. Box 35665
Greensboro, NC 27425 USA

ISBN 978-1-62399-101-2

01-002131151

Table of Contents

Table of Contents

Pronunciation Key

As you read, you may find words that you do not know or words that are difficult to pronounce. In this book, the difficult words are respelled the way you say them. A syllable in CAPITAL LETTERS will have the most stress. The key below gives examples of how words are respelled.

Letters	Example	Respelling	Letters	Example	Respelling
a	sat	(sat)	m	moose	(moos)
ah	mop	(mahp)	n	nature	(NAY cher)
ahr	car	(cahr)	oh	no	(noh)
air	fair, pear	(fair), (pair)	oi	foil, toy	(foil), (toi)
aw	law, all	(law, (awl)	oo	moon, blue	(moon), (bloo)
ay	pay, late	(pay), (layt)	or	corn, more	(corn), (mor)
b	bat	(bat)	ow	now, house	(now), (hows)
ch	chin, beach	(chihn), (beech)	ng	sing	(sihng)
d	dime	(dighm)	p	pen	(pehn)
eh	net	(neht)	r	ring	(rihng)
ee	see, eat	(see), (eet)	s	say, cent	(say), (sehnt)
er	fern, stir, turn	(fern), (ster), (tern)	sh	ship, brush	(shihp), (bruhsh)
f	fan, phone	(fan), (fohn)	t	tail	(tayl)
g	gate, dog	(gayt), (dahg)	th	three	(three)
h	hat	(hat)	u	book	(buk)
ih	him	(hihm)	uh	sun	(suhn)
igh	fine, buy	(fighn), (bigh)	v	valley	(VA lee)
j	jeep, gem,	(jeep), (jehm)	w	win	(wihn)
k	kit, can	(kiht), (kan)	y	yes	(yehs)
ks	fox	(fahks)	yoo	few, mule	(fyoo), (myool)
kw	quit	(kwiht)	z	zebra, size	(ZEE bruh), (sighz)
l	lamp	(lamp)	zh	treasure	(TREH zher)

ARCTIC and ANTARCTIC

LAND and SEA ANIMALS

Walrus

Orca

Wolverine

Caribou

Lemming

Ermine

Snowy Owl

Penguin

Seal

Polar Bear

Musk Ox

Caribou

Caribou (CAIR ah boo) are sometimes called "reindeer." They are large animals weighing 136 to 272 kilograms. Both male and female caribou have very large antlers. In fact, the female caribou is the only female member of the deer family able to grow antlers. Caribou have long hair and woolly fur. They are great long-distance runners and can easily outrun a pack of wolves. Their wide hooves help them walk easily through snow. Caribou can also swim.

In summer, caribou feed on grass, leaves and other low-growing plants of the tundra, the flat, treeless land of the arctic. In winter, caribou migrate to wooded areas and feed on small, dry plants that grow on rocks and trees called lichens (LEYE kuhnz).

Think and Learn

1. How much do caribou weigh? _____

2. Caribou are members of the _____ family.

3. Where do caribou migrate in winter? _____

4. What do caribou eat during summer? _____

_____

Ermine

Ermine (ER mehn) are members of the weasel family. They are tiny animals, weighing less than a kilogram. Ermine have huge dark eyes and long whiskers. They have smooth, silky fur. During the spring and summer, their fur is brown. When autumn approaches, ermine grow a new coat of thick, snow-white fur. This white fur helps ermine blend in with their snowy environment.

Ermine live in northern regions of North America along riverbanks and at the edges of forests. They are good hunters and feed on small animals, such as rabbits and rats. In April, ermine have litters of 3 to 13 fuzzy white babies. By late summer, these babies are fully grown.

Think and Learn

1. During spring ermine have _____ fur.

2. What colour fur do ermine have in winter?_____

3. Where do ermine live? _____
   _____

4. What do ermine eat? _____
   _____

Lemming

Lemmings are chubby little animals belonging to the rodent family. They look very much like hamsters and guinea pigs. Lemmings dig in the soil to build their nests, which they line with grass. They eat plants and live in areas where food is often scarce.

An old legend about lemmings says that every few years lemmings march to the ocean, jump in and drown. Scientists have learned that some lemmings will move to a new area when the number of lemmings in an area is too high. Lemmings always migrate in a straight direction, crossing anything in their path. If they come to a river, they jump in and swim across it. When they come to the ocean and jump in, they cannot swim across it, so they drown.

Think and Learn

1. What other animals do lemmings look like?_____
   _____

2. Where do lemmings build their nests? _____

3. What do lemmings eat? _____

4. When do lemmings migrate? _____
   _____

Musk Ox

Musk oxen are huge animals with large heads and short legs. They grow to 1.5 metres tall at the shoulders and weigh up to 400 kilograms. Musk oxen have long dark brown hair that almost touches the ground. Thick woolly fur under the hair keeps them warm and dry. They use their hooves to scratch through the snow to find grass, willows and other plants to eat.

Musk oxen live together on the tundra in herds of 20 to 100. When danger is near, the adult musk oxen gather in a circle, facing outward. The calves stay in the centre of the circle for protection. When the adult oxen lower their heads, showing their enormous horns, even a pack of wolves will not come near.

Think and Learn

1. Musk oxen have _____ legs.

2. Musk ox hair almost touches the _____.

3. How do musk oxen find food? _____
_____

4. How big are herds of musk oxen? _____

Orca (Killer Whale)

The black and white orca (OR kuh) is a large dolphin that is often called a "killer whale." It grows up to 9 metres long and weighs 3,000 to 9,000 kilograms. The orca has 40 to 48 large pointed teeth that it uses to catch and hold its prey. It eats over 45 kilograms of food every day.

Orcas live and travel in family groups called pods. They are affectionate animals and are often seen touching each other. Female orcas give birth to one baby every 3 to 10 years. The baby will stay with its mother for 10 years. Orcas are very intelligent animals. They communicate with each other by making sounds.

Think and Learn

1. Is an orca a dolphin or a whale? _____

2. What colour is an orca? _____

3. How much food does an orca eat each day? _____

4. Orcas travel in family groups called _____.

5. Orcas communicate by making _____.

PENGUINS

Pull-Out Storybook

What animal seems dressed for a fancy party? A penguin, of course. The penguin's black-and-white colouring looks like a tuxedo. There are 17 different kinds of penguins. The emperor penguin is the largest. It can weigh up to 40 kilograms and grow to be 1 metre tall. The little blue penguin is the smallest. It weighs 1 kilogram and is about 0.3 metre tall.

Emperor Penguin

Little Blue Penguin

Penguins have bodies that are built for water. Their short wings serve as flippers. A penguin uses its tail as a rudder to steer. Penguins get their food from the sea. Their favourite foods are krill, which are small shrimplike animals, fish and squid, which they catch and eat underwater.

If there is snow, penguins like to get around by tobogganing. They flop on their bellies and slide, using their wings and feet to paddle forward. Some penguins can leap from the water several metres into the air! Imagine if you could pop out of a pool like a penguin!

King Penguin chicks

Like all other birds, a penguin's feathers wear out. So, each year, the penguin sheds its old feathers and grows new ones. During this time, a penguin cannot go in the cold water because it is no longer waterproof. Therefore, it cannot eat. Penguin chicks shed their downy feathers when they are about a year old. The feathers underneath are waterproof.

Most penguins build nests to keep their eggs safe. Emperor penguins, however, do not build nests. The egg is kept warm on the tops of the parents' feet. The fathers huddle together to keep the eggs warm while the mothers go to the sea to feed. The mothers return after the chicks have hatched, and the fathers go to the sea.

A penguin chick must peck its way out of the eggshell. Both the mother and father penguins will care for the chick. Penguin parents must go to the sea for fish, then come back to feed their hungry chicks. When chicks get older, they gather in groups for warmth and protection. Once a young penguin molts, or sheds its feathers, it grows adult feathers. Then, the penguin is ready to feed and live on its own.

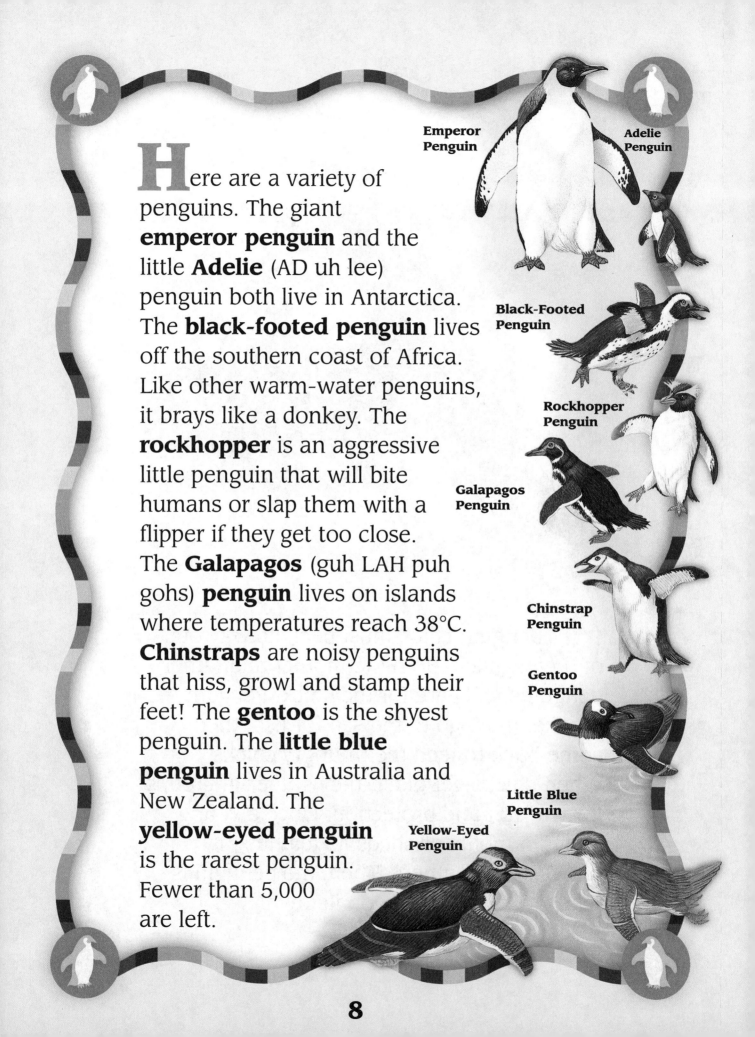

Here are a variety of penguins. The giant **emperor penguin** and the little **Adelie** (AD uh lee) penguin both live in Antarctica. The **black-footed penguin** lives off the southern coast of Africa. Like other warm-water penguins, it brays like a donkey. The **rockhopper** is an aggressive little penguin that will bite humans or slap them with a flipper if they get too close. The **Galapagos** (guh LAH puh gohs) **penguin** lives on islands where temperatures reach 38°C. **Chinstraps** are noisy penguins that hiss, growl and stamp their feet! The **gentoo** is the shyest penguin. The **little blue penguin** lives in Australia and New Zealand. The **yellow-eyed penguin** is the rarest penguin. Fewer than 5,000 are left.

Emperor Penguin

Adelie Penguin

Black-Footed Penguin

Rockhopper Penguin

Galapagos Penguin

Chinstrap Penguin

Gentoo Penguin

Little Blue Penguin

Yellow-Eyed Penguin

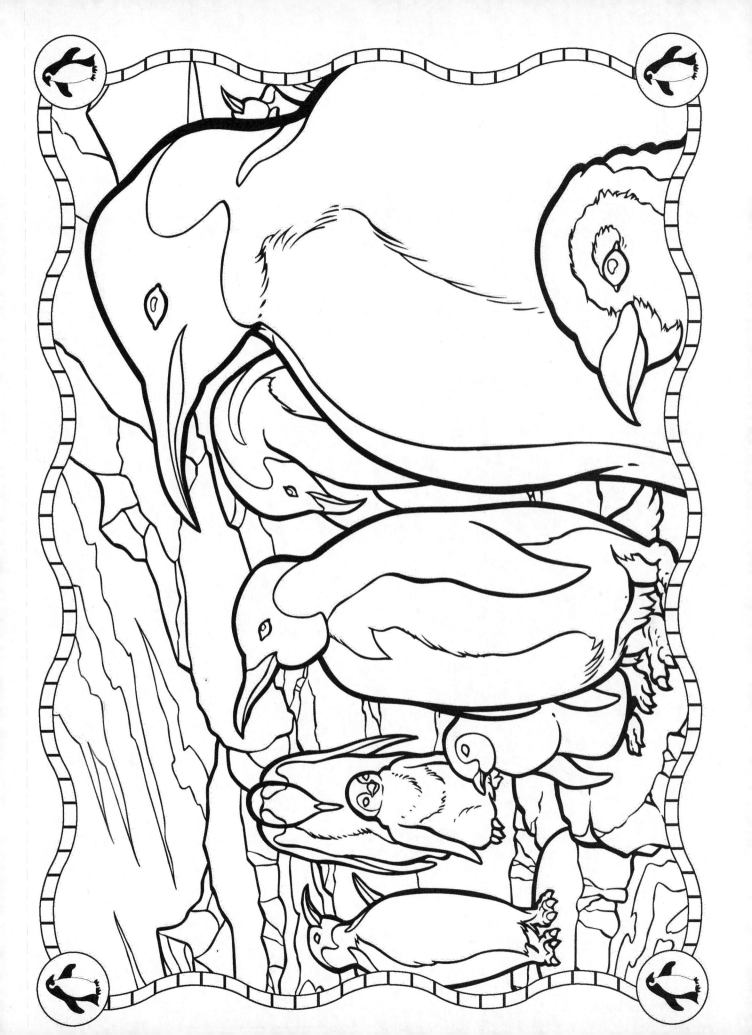

Polar Bear

Polar bears are the world's largest four-legged meat-eating animals—2.7 metres tall and 725 kilograms! They have special features to help them live in the arctic. Their thick fur and a layer of fat keep them warm. Their small ears lose less body heat. Pads on the bottom of their feet keep them from slipping on ice. Polar bears are excellent swimmers. Webbing between their clawed toes helps them swim. Polar bears hunt seals, walruses, small whales and fish. In the summer months, they eat berries and plants.

Female polar bears make dens in ice caves or in snow banks. They give birth to one to three cubs, weighing 0.5 kilogram. The cubs stay with their mother for 2 years.

Think and Learn

1. What features keep polar bears warm?_____

   _____

2. Polar bears have webbed toes to help them _____.

3. What do they eat in the summer? _____

4. How long do polar bear cubs stay with their mother?

   _____

Seal

Seals are animals with special features to live in water. Their flippers move them quickly and gracefully through water. Their bodies are covered with oily fur and a layer of blubber, or fat, to keep them warm. There are two kinds of seals—sea lions and true seals. Sea lions have ears outside their heads, but true seals have no outer ears. While sea lions can move easily on land, true seals must use their chest muscles to move on land. True seals never have to leave the water.

True seals hunt underwater for their food. They eat shrimp, crab, fish and seabirds. Seals give birth to white baby seals, called pups. Their colouring helps hide them from polar bears. As the pup grows, its white fur will turn dark brown like its parents' fur.

Think and Learn

1. Seals are adapted to live in _____.

2. _____ move seals quickly through water.

3. What keeps seals warm? _____

4. Which kind of seal moves easily on land? _____

5. What colour are seal pups? _____

Predator and Prey

Polar bears live along frozen shores and on ice floating in arctic waters. The polar bear is a predator (PRED uh tur) because it hunts other animals for food. The animals hunted by predators are called prey. When hunting for seals, polar bears like to wait by a seal's breathing hole in the ice. The seal may not see the polar bear waiting by the breathing hole. The polar bear's white fur helps it blend in with its snowy environment. When the seal comes up to breathe, the polar bear catches it. Seals are dark brown to help them blend in with their environment. When a polar bear looks down into the water, the water reflects the colour of the ocean bottom, which is dark brown or black. Sometimes the polar bear does not see the seal.

1. Colour the picture to show how the animals blend into the environment.

2. Label the predator and the prey in the picture.

Snowy Owl

The snowy owl gets its name from the snow-white feathers covering its body. It has thick feathers covering its feet and legs for warmth. Like other owls, snowy owls must turn their heads to look around because their eyes cannot move. Their ears are tiny slits on their faces. Owls raise their face feathers when they are listening.

Snowy owls hunt for rats and arctic hares, but lemmings are their main food source. If lemmings are plentiful, snowy owls will lay more eggs. When lemmings are scarce, snowy owls may not lay any eggs. Snowy owls live on the treeless tundra, so they build their nests on the ground in places where they can watch for predators.

Think and Learn

1. Snowy owls have _____ covering their feet and legs.

2. Why must owls turn their heads to look around? _____
   _____

3. What is the main food source for snowy owls? _____

4. Snowy owls build nests on the _____.

Walrus

The walrus is a huge animal, weighing between 1,800 and 2,700 kilograms. Its thick skin and layer of blubber protect it from the cold. Both male and female walruses have ivory tusks. They use their tusks to pull themselves across ice and for protection against polar bears.

Walruses are excellent swimmers. They can stay out at sea for days. They feed on the ocean floor by using their "moustache" bristles to feel for clams. Then, they use their snouts to dig the clams out. Walruses live together in herds containing thousands of walruses. One of their favourite things to do is sleep. When one walrus is awakened, it slaps another walrus. This goes on until the whole herd is awake. In time, they will fall back to sleep.

Think and Learn

1. How much does a walrus weigh? _____

2. Why are the tusks of a walrus important? _____
   _____

3. What do walruses eat? _____

4. Walruses live together in _____.

Wolverine

The wolverine is the largest member of the weasel family. It reaches a height of 0.3 metre at the shoulder and weighs 13 to 23 kilograms. Wolverines are covered with long, shaggy, dark brown hair. Water does not freeze to their fur.

For their size, wolverines are probably the strongest and fiercest animals of the North. Often, wolverines chase away a bear or a mountain lion from its food so they can eat the food. After a wolverine eats a large meal, it will not eat again for a few days. Female wolverines give birth to two or three cubs in a litter. They are born in early summer already covered in woolly fur coats. By winter, the cubs can live on their own.

Think and Learn

1. The wolverine is the largest member of the _____ family.

2. What is special about wolverine fur? _____

3. Why are wolverines thought of as fierce animals?

   _____

   _____

4. When are wolverine cubs born? _____.

NORTH AMERICAN

ANIMALS

Moose

Bald Eagle

Porcupine

Beaver

White-Tailed Deer

Wild Turkey

Grizzly Bear

Grey Wolf

Pronghorn

Otter

Striped Skunk

Bald Eagle

The bald eagle is a bird of prey, or a bird that catches and eats other animals. It is a large bird, with a wingspan reaching 2.5 metres. The bald eagle is well known for its white head and neck. Most bald eagles live near water because they love to eat fish. Their hooked bills and long, curved claws help them to catch fish.

Of all the eagles, bald eagles build the largest nests. Some nests have been measured at 2.5 metres across! Eagles lay two ivory-white eggs. The eaglets are born brown. They do not look like adults until they are three years old. The bald eagle has been the national bird of the United States since 1782.

Think and Learn

1. The bald eagle has a wingspan of _____.

2. What colour is the bald eagle's head? _____

3. What helps bald eagles catch fish? _____

_____

4. The bald eagle is the national bird of _____.

Beaver

The beaver is a member of the rodent family. It grows to a length of 0.6 metre and usually weighs 15 to 18 kilograms. The beaver has dark brown fur that keeps the animal warm and dry. Its strong jaws have two cutting teeth, called incisors. The incisors keep growing all through a beaver's life so that these teeth are never worn down. Beavers use their incisors to cut down trees. Beavers eat twigs and bark from trees that grow near water.

Beavers are graceful swimmers. They move easily through the water with their webbed toes. Their tail helps steer them. Beavers mate for life and live in colonies. All the beavers in a colony work together and build lodges as their homes.

Think and Learn

1. What are the beaver's cutting teeth called?_____

2. What do beavers eat? _____

3. How does a beaver use its tail? _____

4. What is a beaver home called?_____

Beaver Lodges

Beavers in a colony work together to build their lodges. Lodges are made of tree branches and grass. Beavers use mud to keep the branches in place. A lodge can be 1 to 2 metres high and 2 metres across. It has two rooms. The living room is above the water. It is where the beavers sleep and keep warm. The underwater storage room is where they keep their food. If the water level drops, beavers build dams. Dams raise the water level around the lodge so the storage room stays under water.

1. In the beaver lodge above, label the entrance, the living room and the storage room.

2. Is the entrance above water or below water?_____

Grey Wolf

The grey wolf is the largest member of the wild dog family. This animal can reach a length of 1.2 metres and can weigh 45 kilograms. Grey wolves live in northern forests. They hunt for deer, elk and moose in packs of 3 to 24. Wolves, like other members of the dog family, can go for several days without food.

The leader for the wolf pack is the strongest male. Other wolves show respect by lowering their ears and putting their tails between their legs. Wolves mate for life. A female gives birth to a litter of 3 to 13 young, called pups. The pups are helpless at first. Other members of the pack help the parents care for the cubs.

Think and Learn

1. The grey wolf is a member of the _____ family.

2. Where do grey wolves live?_____

3. Grey wolves hunt in _____.

4. How do wolves show respect to the leader?_____

_____

Word Search

Find the names of North American animals in the puzzle. They are written **across** and **down**.

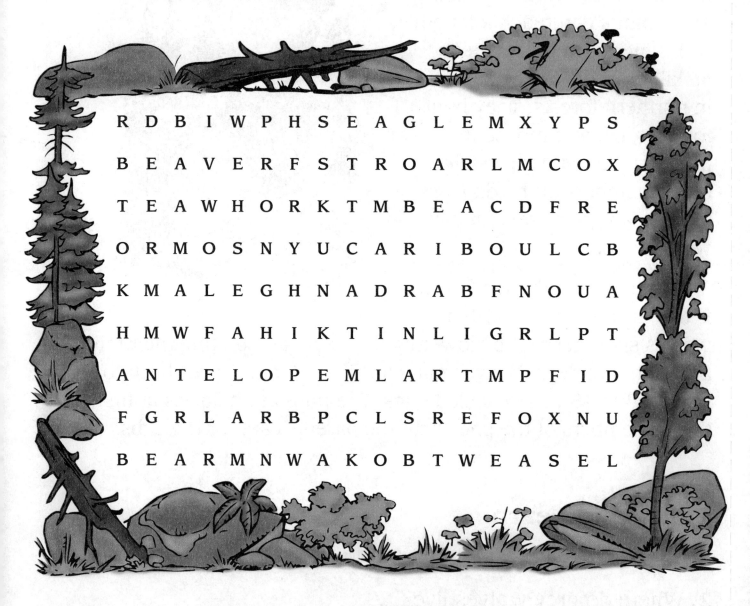

```
R D B I W P H S E A G L E M X Y P S
B E A V E R F S T R O A R L M C O X
T E A W H O R K T M B E A C D F R E
O R M O S N Y U C A R I B O U L C B
K M A L E G H N A D R A B F N O U A
H M W F A H I K T I N L I G R L P T
A N T E L O P E M L A R T M P F I D
F G R L A R B P C L S R E F O X N U
B E A R M N W A K O B T W E A S E L
```

caribou	beaver	eagle	armadillo
fox	skunk	bear	pronghorn
wolf	deer	rabbit	porcupine
bat	weasel	antelope	

WOLVES

Pull-Out Storybook

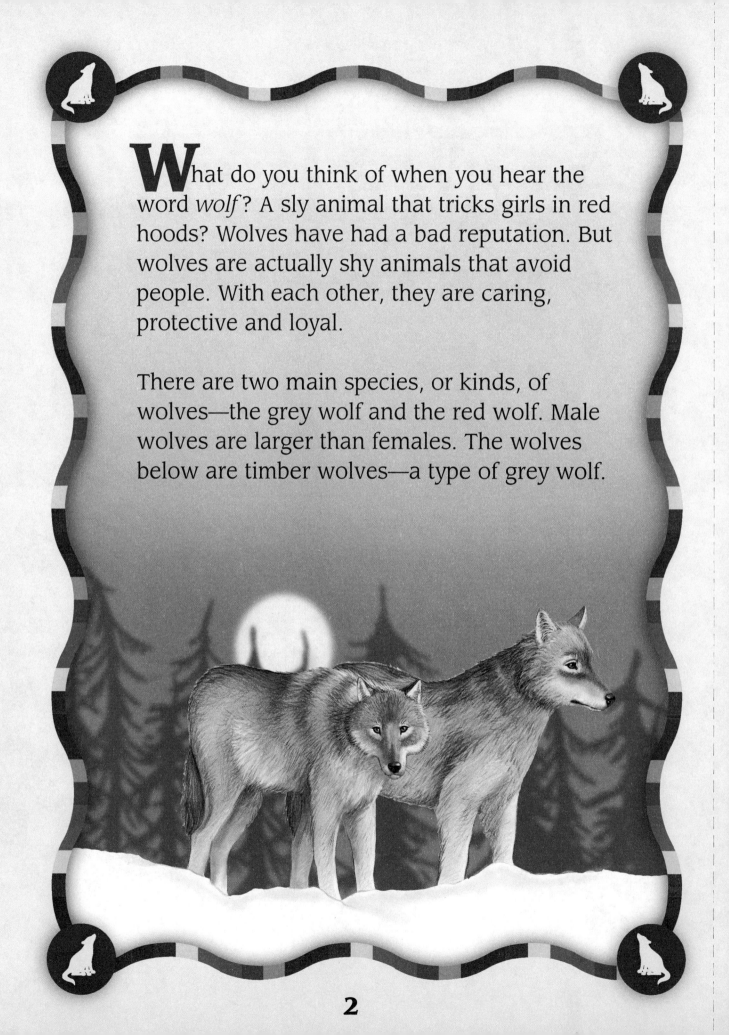

What do you think of when you hear the word *wolf*? A sly animal that tricks girls in red hoods? Wolves have had a bad reputation. But wolves are actually shy animals that avoid people. With each other, they are caring, protective and loyal.

There are two main species, or kinds, of wolves—the grey wolf and the red wolf. Male wolves are larger than females. The wolves below are timber wolves—a type of grey wolf.

Wolves look like large dogs. In fact, they are members of the dog family. Wolves have longer legs and bigger paws than dogs. Their fur is also thicker and bushier. This helps keep them warm in freezing temperatures.

Wolves have excellent eyesight and a keen sense of hearing. They can hear sounds 10 miles away. Wolves also have an excellent sense of smell.

Grey wolves live in family groups called packs. Most packs have between 6 and 20 wolves. Pack members care for and protect each other. They work together to hunt food. They also help raise the wolf pups.

Wolves are curious, intelligent animals. They sometimes remind us of dogs. But as friendly as wolves may look, they are wild animals and do not make good pets.

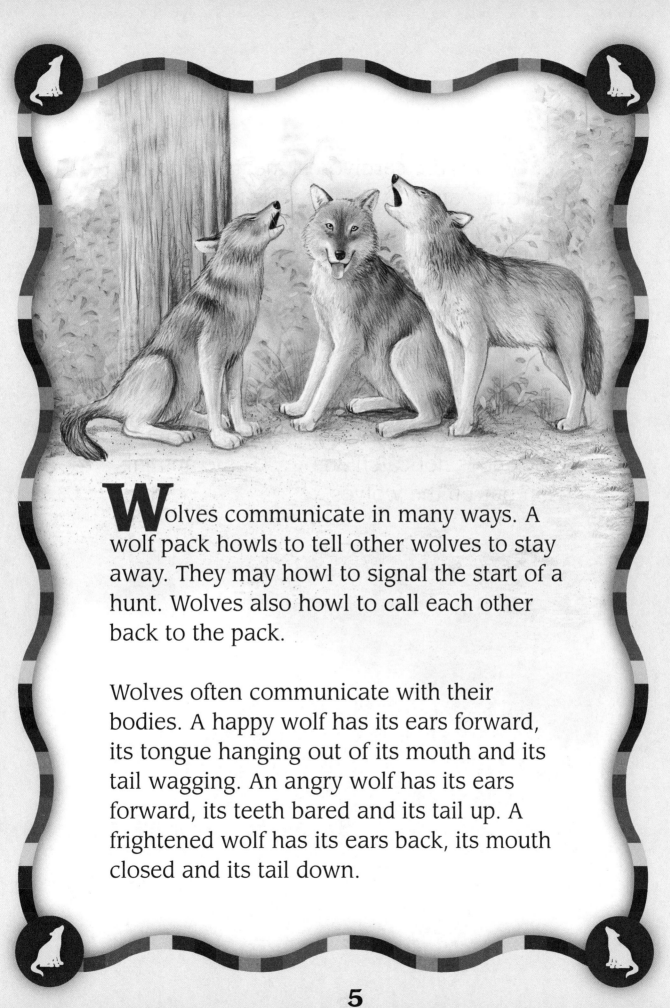

Wolves communicate in many ways. A wolf pack howls to tell other wolves to stay away. They may howl to signal the start of a hunt. Wolves also howl to call each other back to the pack.

Wolves often communicate with their bodies. A happy wolf has its ears forward, its tongue hanging out of its mouth and its tail wagging. An angry wolf has its ears forward, its teeth bared and its tail up. A frightened wolf has its ears back, its mouth closed and its tail down.

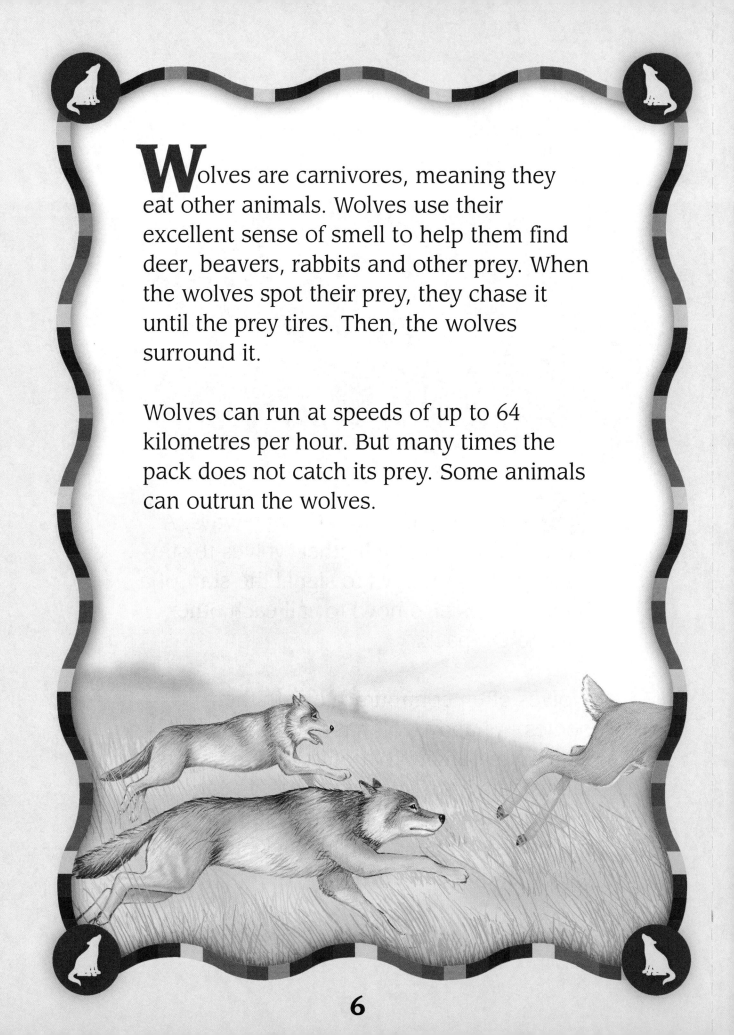

Wolves are carnivores, meaning they eat other animals. Wolves use their excellent sense of smell to help them find deer, beavers, rabbits and other prey. When the wolves spot their prey, they chase it until the prey tires. Then, the wolves surround it.

Wolves can run at speeds of up to 64 kilometres per hour. But many times the pack does not catch its prey. Some animals can outrun the wolves.

Wolves are caring parents. The mother wolf finds or digs a den before her pups are born. Wolf pups are born blind and helpless. The mother cares for the pups inside the den for a few weeks. She feeds them milk from her body. In the meantime, the father wolf brings food for the mother.

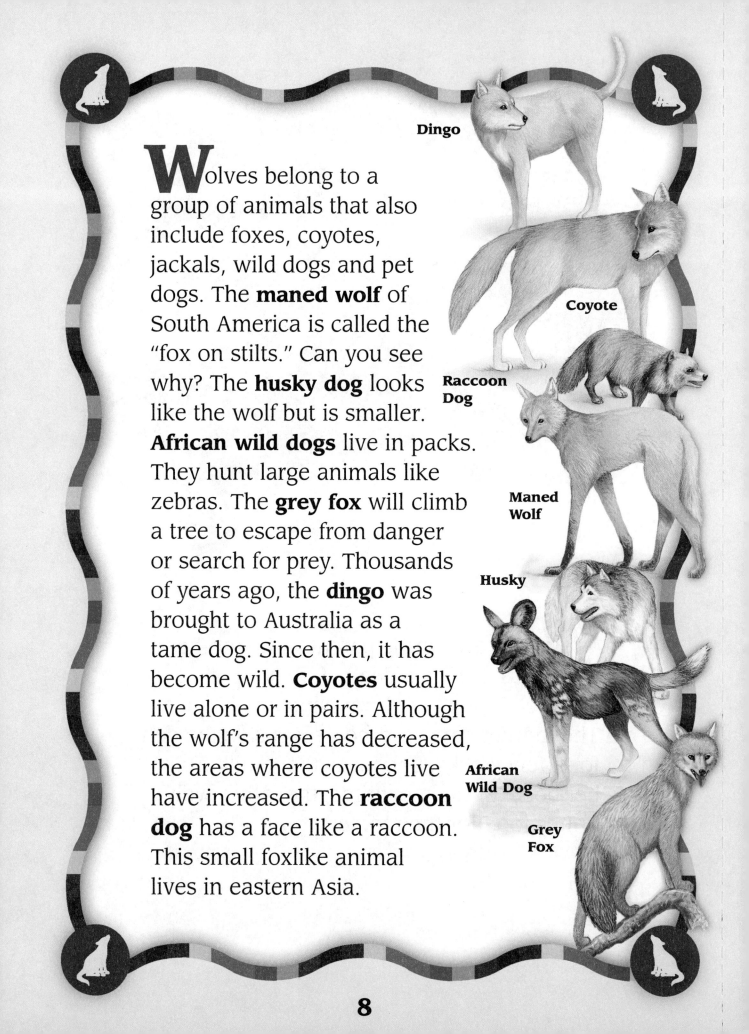

Dingo

Coyote

Raccoon Dog

Maned Wolf

Husky

African Wild Dog

Grey Fox

Wolves belong to a group of animals that also include foxes, coyotes, jackals, wild dogs and pet dogs. The **maned wolf** of South America is called the "fox on stilts." Can you see why? The **husky dog** looks like the wolf but is smaller. **African wild dogs** live in packs. They hunt large animals like zebras. The **grey fox** will climb a tree to escape from danger or search for prey. Thousands of years ago, the **dingo** was brought to Australia as a tame dog. Since then, it has become wild. **Coyotes** usually live alone or in pairs. Although the wolf's range has decreased, the areas where coyotes live have increased. The **raccoon dog** has a face like a raccoon. This small foxlike animal lives in eastern Asia.

Grizzly Bear

Grizzly bears once lived in large numbers from Canada to Mexico. Now, most grizzly bears live in national parks. Male grizzly bears stand 2.5 metres tall and weigh 360 to 450 kilograms. Grizzly bears have very good senses of smell and hearing. These senses make up for their poor eyesight.

Grizzly bears are omnivores— they eat both plants and animals. Their favourite foods are berries, leaves, fish and small animals. In autumn, grizzly bears spend a lot of time eating. They are fattening up to get ready for their winter sleep, or hibernation. Grizzly bears hibernate differently from other animals. Their body functions do not slow down, and they are easily awakened.

Think and Learn

1. Where do most grizzly bears live today? _____

2. Which senses make up for the grizzly bear's poor eyesight?

_____

3. What do omnivores eat?_____

4. How do grizzly bears get ready for hibernation?_____

_____

Dot-to-Dot

Connect the dots. Colour the picture.

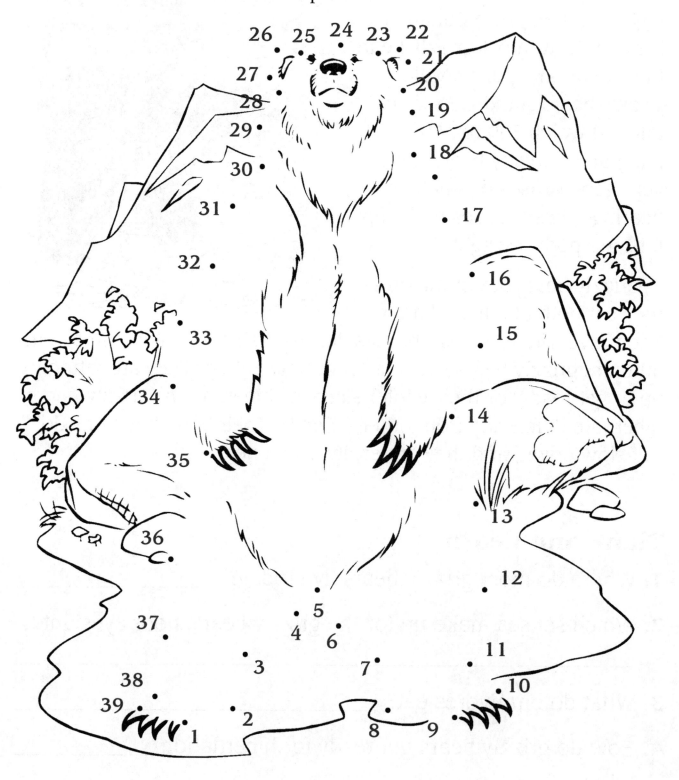

BEARS

Pull-Out Storybook

Have you ever seen a live bear? A bear's shape makes it easy to recognize. Bears have big bulky bodies with short legs and short tails. They have small round ears and small eyes.

The **sun bear** is the smallest bear. It is about the size of an eight-year-old child, but it weighs more. The **polar bear** is the largest bear. One male polar bear measured over 3.5 metres in length. An **American black bear** is not always black. It may also be white, cinnamon, brown or bluish-black.

Polar Bear

Sun Bear

American Black Bears

Bears may look big and clumsy, but they can move fast. Some run faster than 48 kilometres per hour. Many bears are strong climbers and most are good swimmers. A **polar bear** has webbed feet and a long shape that make it a champion swimmer. **Grizzly bears** can climb trees when they are cubs. But as adults, most are too big and heavy. The **spectacled bear** lives in trees in the Andes Mountains of South America.

Spectacled Bear

Grizzly Bears

Polar Bear

A hungry polar bear will wait patiently at a hole in the ice until a seal comes up for air.

Bears are omnivores, meaning they eat both plants and animals. A bear's diet depends on where it lives. Polar bears eat more meat than other bears since there are few plants in the Arctic. Brown bears and black bears eat many different foods, including grass, nuts, berries, insects, fish and deer.

The sloth bear does not have front teeth. This helps it catch its favourite food—termites. After digging up a termite nest, the bear sticks its mouth in and sucks up the termites like a vacuum cleaner.

Bears spend most of their time alone. Mother bears with cubs are the exception. They spend between 1 and 3 years together.

Bears are generally peaceful animals. A bear may make a warning sound if another animal comes too close. When bears meet, the younger or smaller bear often runs away.

When a grizzly bear stands tall and shows its teeth, few animals will challenge it.

Sometimes adult polar bears will wrestle and play together.

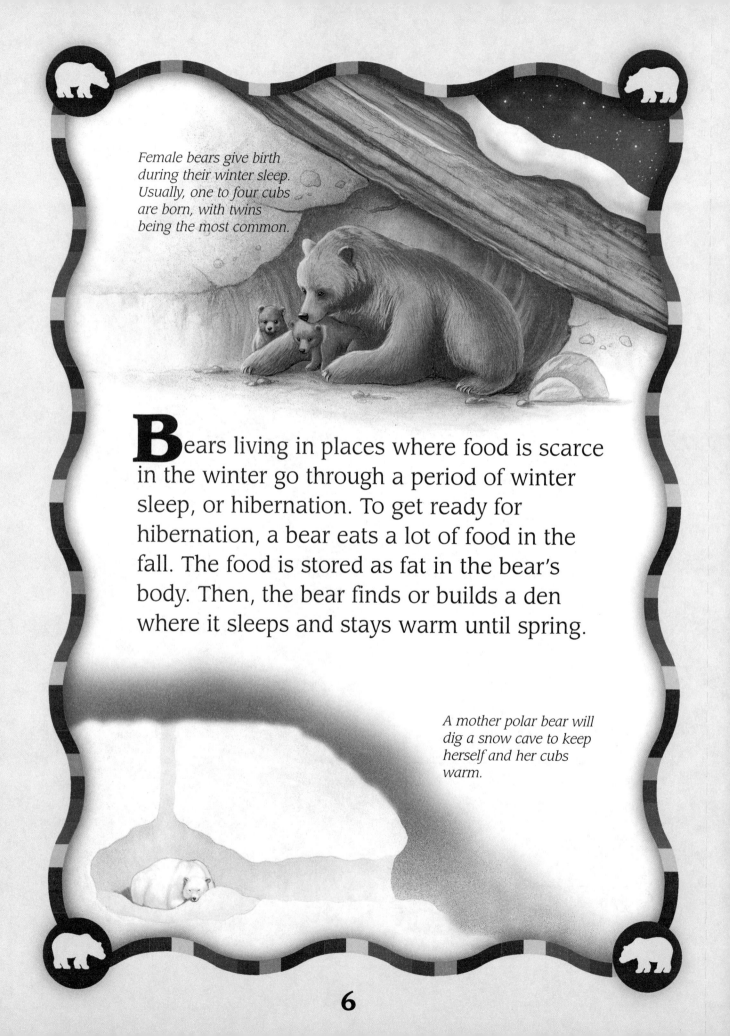

Female bears give birth during their winter sleep. Usually, one to four cubs are born, with twins being the most common.

Bears living in places where food is scarce in the winter go through a period of winter sleep, or hibernation. To get ready for hibernation, a bear eats a lot of food in the fall. The food is stored as fat in the bear's body. Then, the bear finds or builds a den where it sleeps and stays warm until spring.

A mother polar bear will dig a snow cave to keep herself and her cubs warm.

Most bear cubs are born in dens. They are tiny and helpless at birth but are soon able to nurse on their own. A mother bear is devoted to her cubs. She cleans them and keeps them warm. Like other mammals, she feeds the cubs milk from her body. The cubs are ready to leave the den in spring. Mother bears teach their cubs many things—how to find food, how to swim, how to escape from danger and more. Bear cubs are playful! They enjoy running, wrestling, climbing and swimming.

There are eight main groups of bears. They are found only on four continents—North America, South America, Europe and Asia. Some species of bears are endangered, such as the giant panda and the spectacled bear.

The giant panda lives in a small area of bamboo forest in China.

Sun bears live in the lowland forests of Southeast Asia.

The American black bear is one of the most numerous bears in North America.

Asiatic black bears live in the mountain forests of southern and eastern Asia. They are sometimes called "moon bears" because of the moon-shaped markings on their chests.

Brown bears live primarily in the northern regions of North America, Europe and Asia. There are several different kinds, including the grizzly.

The scraggly sloth bear makes its home in the jungle areas of India, Pakistan and Sri Lanka.

The polar bear lives in areas bordering the Arctic Ocean.

The spectacled bear is South America's only bear. It gets its name from the markings around its eyes that look like glasses.

Most bear cubs are born in dens. They are tiny and helpless at birth but are soon able to nurse on their own. A mother bear is devoted to her cubs. She cleans them and keeps them warm. Like other mammals, she feeds the cubs milk from her body. The cubs are ready to leave the den in spring. Mother bears teach their cubs many things—how to find food, how to swim, how to escape from danger and more. Bear cubs are playful! They enjoy running, wrestling, climbing and swimming.

There are eight main groups of bears. They are found only on four continents—North America, South America, Europe and Asia. Some species of bears are endangered, such as the giant panda and the spectacled bear.

The giant panda lives in a small area of bamboo forest in China.

Sun bears live in the lowland forests of Southeast Asia.

The American black bear is one of the most numerous bears in North America.

Asiatic black bears live in the mountain forests of southern and eastern Asia. They are sometimes called "moon bears" because of the moon-shaped markings on their chests.

Brown bears live primarily in the northern regions of North America, Europe and Asia. There are several different kinds, including the grizzly.

The scraggly sloth bear makes its home in the jungle areas of India, Pakistan and Sri Lanka.

The polar bear lives in areas bordering the Arctic Ocean.

The spectacled bear is South America's only bear. It gets its name from the markings around its eyes that look like glasses.

Moose

The largest member of the deer family is the moose. These huge animals are 3 metres long and weigh about 816 kilograms. Male moose have very large, flattened antlers. Every year they shed their antlers and grow a new pair in spring. Moose enjoy water and are excellent swimmers. They usually live near marshes, lakes or in moist forests.

During the summer months, moose eat water plants, roots, leaves and grass. In winter, moose walk easily through the deep snow. They find tree shoots and twigs to eat. Moose live alone in the summer. When winter arrives, it is common for small bands of moose to stay together in the woods for warmth and protection.

Think and Learn

1. The moose is a member of the _____ family.

2. Each year moose shed their _____, then grow a new pair.

3. Where do moose usually live? _____
_____

4. Why do moose stay together in small bands in winter?
_____

Otter

Otters are members of the weasel family. Their long bodies have special features, or adaptations, that allow them to live most of the time in water. Otters have flat tails and webbed feet that help them swim. Their coarse, outer fur is waterproof. They also close their nostrils and ears when underwater.

Otters make their homes by digging burrows or finding caves near water. They mainly eat fish that they catch while swimming. But they also eat crayfish, frogs, snails and insects. Otters are fun to watch because they are so playful. They love to slide on their bellies down banks of mud or snow and splash into the water. They communicate with each other by barking, chirping and growling.

Think and Learn

1. Where do otters spend most of their time? _____

2. Otters have _____ feet.

3. What do otters eat?_____

_____

4. How do otters communicate with each other?_____

_____

Wild Turkey

Wild turkeys are large birds that live mainly on the ground. Males, or toms, may weigh as much as 10 kilograms. Females, or hens, weigh only 5 kilograms. Tom turkeys look different from hens. They have a flap of skin, called a snood, that falls over the beak. They also have a wattle, a flap of skin that grows from the throat. Both toms and hens have short rounded wings and heavy bodies. They fly for only short distances. They also have strong feet with four toes. This makes them very fast runners.

Wild turkeys live in woods near water. They eat seeds and insects but sometimes eat frogs or lizards. When threatened, they usually run away and hide. Wild turkeys sleep in tree branches at night.

Think and Learn

1. Where do wild turkeys live? _____

2. What features do toms have that hens do not? _____

_____

3. What makes turkeys fast runners? _____

_____

4. Where do wild turkeys sleep?_____

Porcupine

The porcupine (POR kyoo pighn) is a gnawing animal that is best known for its strong, sharp quills. Quills are bunches of hair that have grown together. The quills are white with black tips. They cover a porcupine's tail, sides and back. Porcupines are rather small, weighing between 6 and 9 kilograms. They are also peaceful and never attack other animals.

Porcupines are nocturnal. This means they sleep during the day and are active at night. They spend most of the night in trees looking for food. They might climb 18 to 21 metres up a tree to reach young leaves. In summer, they eat seeds, fruits and leaves. In winter, they eat twigs, leaves, bark and pine needles.

Think and Learn

1. What are quills? _____

2. Why don't porcupines attack other animals? _____

_____

3. Porcupines are _____ , they sleep during the day.

4. What do porcupines eat during the summer? _____

_____

Colour Me

I am a _____.

Striped Skunk

The skunk is known for its black and white fur and its horrible odour. The striped skunk is the most common kind of skunk. It gets its name from the white stripes running down its back. Skunks are about the size of a small cat, measuring 38 centimetres long. They weigh 2 to 3 kilograms. Skunks have short legs, an arched back, a long bushy tail and a patch of white fur on the forehead.

Skunks make their dens in burrows, hollow trees and under buildings. They are found in forests, grasslands and in towns. Even though skunks annoy people with their odour, skunks are very helpful animals. Skunks eat harmful insects, rats, mice and other small animals that damage crops and fields.

Think and Learn

1. What two things are skunks known for? _____

_____

2. A skunk is about the same size as a small_____.

3. Where are skunks found?_____

4. How are skunks helpful to people?_____

_____

Animal Defences

Skunks and porcupines have adaptations that help them defend themselves. Because of their colouring, skunks do not blend in with their environment. If an animal threatens a skunk, the skunk warns the animal by stomping its feet. If the animal does not leave, the skunk sprays the animal with a bad-smelling liquid.

Porcupines ignore most animals. However, if a porcupine feels threatened, it raises the quills on its sides and back. Then, it swings its quill-covered tail at the animal. The quills are barbed. They get stuck in the skin of the animal and are very painful.

Think and Learn

1. How does a skunk warn an animal to go away?_____
_____

2. What does a porcupine do when it feels threatened?

_____
_____
_____

White-Tailed Deer

The white-tailed deer is easy to recognize by its snow-white tail. White-tailed deer are found throughout North America, but they are most common in southern Canada and northern United States. Only the males, called bucks, grow antlers. These antlers are shed each winter. White-tailed deer eat nuts and berries, as well as the buds and twigs from trees.

White-tailed deer are fast runners and great jumpers. Bucks frequently fight during mating season. They use their antlers and hooves as weapons. Female deer, called does, give birth to one to three fawns in the spring. The fawns are covered with white spots that disappear in six months.

Think and Learn

1. What are white-tailed deer recognized by? _____

2. Only bucks grow_____.

3. What do deer eat? _____

4. How is a fawn's colouring different from an adult deer?

_____

Pronghorn

The pronghorn is North America's fastest animal. It can run about 64 kilometres per hour and jump very high. The pronghorn is mostly covered with reddish-brown fur and has white fur on the lower parts of its body, including the tail. The pronghorn lifts its fur straight up to cool its body in hot weather. In cold weather, it holds its fur flat against its body for warmth. The pronghorn has long horns that it never sheds.

Pronghorn live in the grasslands of western United States and Canada. They eat shrubs, sagebrush, grass and twigs. In summer, they live in small groups. As winter comes, they form large herds of 100 or more.

Think and Learn

1. The pronghorn is North America's _____ animal.

2. How does a pronghorn keep cool in hot weather?

_____

3. Where do pronghorn live? _____

_____

4. What do pronghorn eat?_____

Compare and Contrast

Read about the white-tailed deer and the pronghorn. Then, use the Venn diagram and the facts you have learned to compare and contrast these two animals. Write facts that tell only about the white-tailed deer on the left, facts that tell only about pronghorn on the right and facts that tell about both in the middle.

White-Tailed Deer

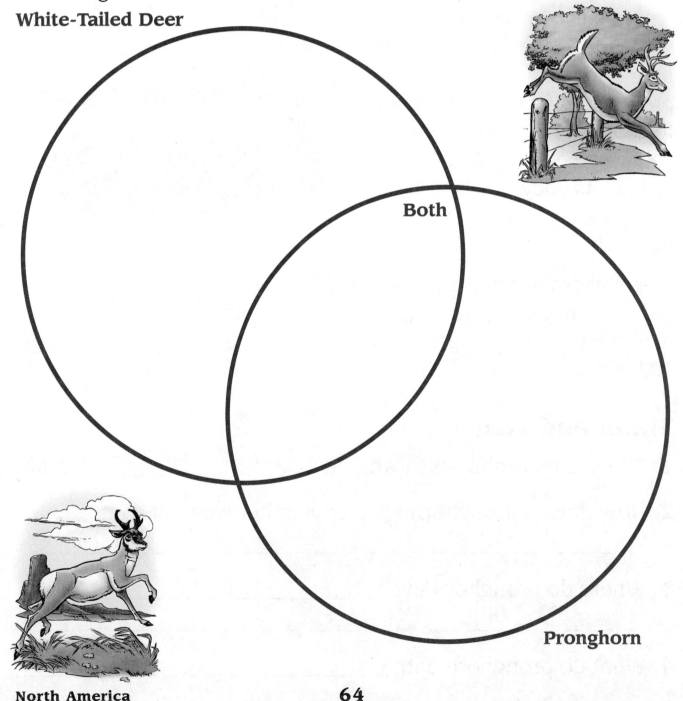

Both

Pronghorn

ASIAN
ANIMALS

Snow
Leopard

Gibbon

Giant Panda

Tiger

Malayan Tapir

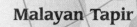

Sloth Bear

Chevrotain

Orangutan

Wild Boar

Water Buffalo

Chevrotain

Chevrotains (SHEHV ruh taynz) are very small animals with cowlike hooves. They are sometimes called "mouse deer" because they look like tiny deer. Chevrotains have two long tusklike teeth and no other upper teeth. They use their long upper teeth to defend themselves from other animals.

Chevrotains live in the tropical forests of India and Southeast Asia. They eat at night, keeping hidden in the underbrush. They feed on fruit, leaves, twigs and grass. During the day, chevrotains hide behind rocks or in the bushes. They are quiet, timid animals. Chevrotains live alone except during the mating season. A female chevrotain usually gives birth to two babies, called fawns.

Think and Learn

1. Chevrotains are also called _____.

2. What do chevrotains use to defend themselves?_____
_____

3. Where do chevrotains live? _____
_____

4. When do chevrotains eat? _____

Giant Panda

The giant panda is a very large black and white furry animal. Scientists used to classify pandas as part of the raccoon family. Now, they classify pandas as bears. The giant panda is found in bamboo forests in the mountains of west central China.

Pandas reach a height of 1.5 metres and weigh about 90 kilograms. They easily climb trees and spend most of their time eating bamboo plants. They eat every part of the plant. Pandas have a special thumblike toe on their front feet used for holding bamboo stems. Their teeth are large and wide to help them grind up the bamboo.

Think and Learn

1. Scientists now classify the giant panda as a _____.

2. Where do giant pandas live?_____

3. Pandas eat all parts of the _____ plant.

4. How do pandas use the thumblike toe on their front feet?

_____

A Vanishing Act

The panda is one of many endangered animals. Endangered animals may soon disappear from Earth. That's what happened to dinosaurs, dodo birds and passenger pigeons. They disappeared, or became extinct.

Write the letter that comes before each letter in the alphabet to decode the names of some endangered animals.

A B C D E F G H I J K L M N O P Q R S T U V W X Y Z

_ _ _ _ _ _ _ _   _ _ _ _ _ _ _
N P V O U B J O   H P S J M M B

_ _ _ _ _ _ _   _ _ _ _ _ _ _
B G S J D B O   F M F Q I B O U

_ _ _ _ _ _ _ _   _ _ _ _ _
X I P P Q J O H   D S B O F

_ _ _ _ _   _ _ _ _ _
C M B D L   S I J O P

_ _ _ _ _   _ _ _ _ _
H J B O U   Q B O E B

_ _ _   _ _ _ _
T F B   M J P O

_ _ _ _   _ _ _ _
H S F Z   X P M G

_ _ _ _ _ _ _ _
D I F F U B I

PANDAS

Pull-Out Storybook

Giant pandas live in China. They look like teddy bears with their large heads and chubby, furry bodies. Whenever pandas are shown off at a zoo, crowds of people come from everywhere to see them. The Chinese people have made the giant panda a symbol for their country.

Giant pandas are easy to recognize with their black-and-white colouring. A panda's fur looks soft, but it is actually stiff and coarse. The thick, waterproof fur keeps the animal warm in cold weather and dry in the rain.

Giant pandas can spend 12 to 16 hours a day eating! They feed mainly on bamboo, which grows in the forests where they live. They prefer to eat the tender shoots and leaves. But, they will eat the thick, large stems, too. The panda uses its strong teeth to strip away the stem's outer covering to eat the soft insides.

A female panda has one or two cubs at a time. The mother panda gives birth in a den. The den is usually in a cave or hollow tree. As soon as a cub is born, the mother cuddles it in her arms. For the first few days, she holds her baby day and night, not leaving the den even to eat. Panda cubs are helpless for the first few months of their lives. Their eyes don't open for 40 days. They don't start crawling until they are about 3 months old.

A panda cub grows quickly. By 5 months, it starts to eat bamboo. At 7 months, the cub can run and climb trees. As the cub grows, its mother takes it along on feeding trips. She carries the cub by the neck and places it in a safe spot. Most young pandas stay with their mothers until they are 18 months to 2 years old. During that time, the mother teaches her cub the skills it needs to survive.

Giant pandas, both young and old, have flexible bodies that they can bend and twist in many directions. A giant panda can stand on its head. It can turn somersaults, and will often roll over again and again. Touching its head with its foot is easy for a panda. It's easy for a giant panda to stand on its head. While lying on its back, a giant panda can scratch one foot with the other.

Giant pandas are endangered, or could die out. Hunting pandas and destroying bamboo forests have greatly reduced the panda population. Today, fewer than 1,000 giant pandas live in the wild. The Chinese government is working to save the pandas. Hunting pandas in China is against the law. Also, nature reserves have been set up to protect the panda's habitat, or home. These reserves also protect the bamboo that pandas need for food.

Gibbon

Gibbons (GIHB uhnz) are the smallest members of the ape family. Gibbons are built for swinging through the trees. In fact, it is awkward for them to walk on the ground. Their long arms enable them to "fly" from branch to branch, with leaps over 9 metres.

Gibbons are found in the rainforests of Southeast Asia. They live in the trees, where they get most of their food. They eat seeds, leaves, fruits, young birds and insects. Gibbons live in family groups made up of a male, a female and their young. Gibbons mate for life. At night, the gibbon family huddles together for safety.

Think and Learn

1. Gibbons are the smallest member of the _____ family.

2. How are gibbons built for swinging through trees?

_____

3. Where are gibbons found? _____

4. Gibbons live in _____ groups.

Rainforest Maze

Help the gibbon swing through the maze.

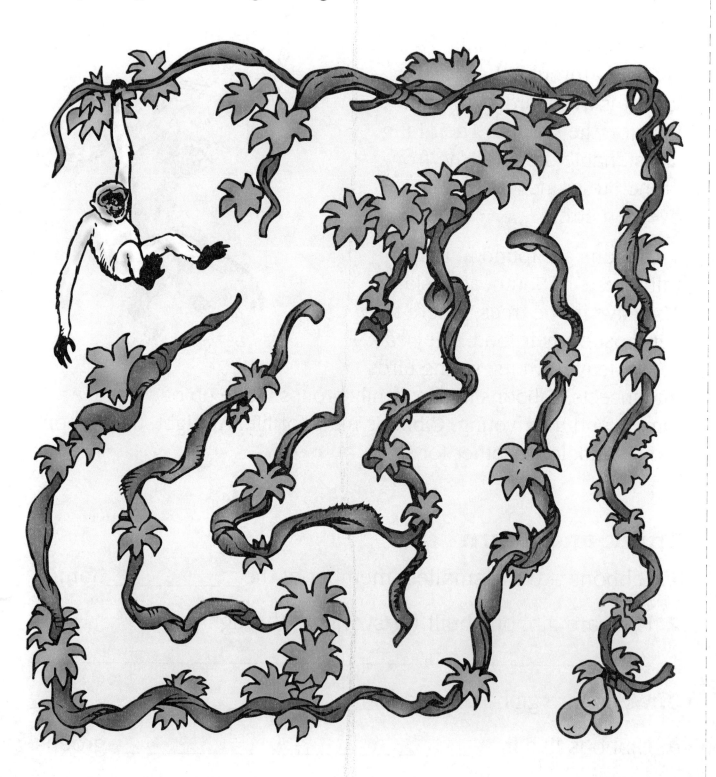

Malayan Tapir

The Malayan tapir (muh LAY uhn TAY per) is related to the horse and the rhinoceros. It canters and gallops like a horse. Its snout is an upper lip that works much like an elephant trunk. It has a pig-shaped body and weighs about 295 kilograms. Its coat is brownish-black and cream-coloured.

Malayan tapirs are found in Sumatra and Malaysia in tropical rainforests near rivers and lakes. At night, they look for leaves, grass and water plants to eat. Malayan tapirs love to dive and swim in the water. They lie in mud holes where they get relief from ticks and insects.

Think and Learn

1. To what animals are the Malayan tapirs related?

   _____

2. Describe the tapir's snout. _____

   _____

3. When do Malayan tapirs find food? _____

4. What do tapirs do in water? _____

Orangutan

Orangutan (oh RANG uh tan) is a Malay word that means "forest man." Do you think an orangutan looks like a person? It is a large animal that grows to be 1.5 metres tall. Its arms, hands and feet help the orangutan to live in the trees. An orangutan is easily identified by its long, shaggy, reddish-brown hair.

Orangutans are found in Borneo and Sumatra. They eat fruits, nuts, seeds and leaves, as well as lizards, tree frogs, eggs, young birds and insects. Orangutans build sleeping platforms in the trees. They sometimes use large leaves as blankets when it rains. Orangutans do not live in family groups like other apes.

Think and Learn

1. What does the word "orangutan" mean? _____

2. Where do orangutans live? _____

3. What colour is orangutan hair? _____

4. What do orangutans build for sleeping? _____

5. How do orangutans sometimes use leaves? _____

Sloth Bear

The sloth bear is a huge, shaggy bear. It has a mane of fur around its neck. Sloth bears have very long snouts. They live in the rocky canyons and hills of India and Sri Lanka. They hunt for termites and bee nests at night. A sloth bear can climb any tree to find food. It uses its long claws to rip open a termite or bee nest. The sloth bear is so noisy when it eats that people can hear it 182 metres away!

Sloth bears sleep in caves during the day. They are also very noisy sleepers. They snore as loud as they eat! Sloth bears live in family units. Both parents care for the cubs. The cubs stay with their parents for 3 years.

Think and Learn

1. Sloth bears have very long _____.

2. Where do sloth bears live?_____

   _____

3. What do sloth bears eat? _____

4. What do sloth bears do during the day? _____

Snow Leopard

The snow leopard (snoh LEHP erd) is large cat that lives in the mountains of central Asia. It is 1.5 metres long and weighs about 40 kilograms. The snow leopard is known for its beautiful fur. Its dense undercoat is covered with long grey and cream-coloured hair and speckled with black spots. The snow leopard's large paws are padded for warmth.

The fierce snow leopard does not roar like a lion but purrs like a house cat. Like most cats, snow leopards hunt animals for food. The snow leopard is endangered. It has been overhunted for its fur. It has also lost its natural prey due to the clearing of land for farming.

Think and Learn

1. Where do snow leopards live? _____

2. The snow leopard's paws are padded for _____.

3. What sound do snow leopards make?_____

4. Why are snow leopards endangered? _____

_____

Tiger

The tiger is the largest member of the cat family. It is known by its orange and black stripes. Tigers are found only in Asia. They live in different environments—from cold regions to rainforests. Tigers live alone. Every tiger claims its own territory. Tigers, like all cats, stalk their prey and swiftly attack. Tigers hunt at night. They hunt deer, antelope and wild pigs.

Female tigers, called tigresses, give birth every 2 years to a litter of three or four cubs. The tigress is a loving mother. She teaches her young how to hunt and care for themselves. The cubs stay with their mother for 2 years.

Think and Learn

1. The tiger is the largest member of the _____ family.

2. Tigers are found only in _____.

3. What animals do tigers hunt? _____
_____

4. What do tigresses teach their cubs? _____
_____

Hidden Pictures

The tiger's stripes help keep it well hidden in the jungle. Find the tigers hidden in the picture. Colour the picture.

Water Buffalo

The water buffalo is a gigantic animal that is 3 metres long and 1.8 metres tall. It has thick, greyish-black skin. Water buffalo have large horns. The horns grow out of each side of the head and curve upward. Water buffalo love water. They are often found resting in water up to their noses. Water buffalo also roll in mud until they are covered with it. This helps protect them from insects.

Water buffalo are wild cattle. Some have been tamed and help with rice farming. Rice is grown in flooded fields. Water buffalo can easily pull a plow through water that is knee deep. Although they look like gentle animals, water buffalo can become very fierce. However, they are friendly to people they know.

Think and Learn

1. Large _____ grow out of a water buffalo's head.

2. What do water buffalo like to rest in? _____

3. Why do water buffalo roll in mud? _____
_____

4. How do water buffalo help with rice farming? _____
_____

Wild Boar

The wild boar is a wild hog found in forests throughout Asia. It can reach a length of 1.2 to 1.5 metres and weighs an average of 136 kilograms. Its long piglike snout is used for lifting, pushing and digging. The wild boar has two long tusks that grow out of its lower jaw. These tusks are 30 centimetres long. Wild boars use their tusks to protect themselves.

Wild boars like to eat almost anything. They use their snout to search for leaves, fruit, roots, worms and insects. Wild boars can see and hear well. However, they rely mainly on their sense of smell. Male and female boars travel in separate herds. The female boars raise their young alone.

Think and Learn

1. Where are wild boars found? _____

2. How do wild boars use their snouts? _____

_____

3. Wild boars use their _____ for protection.

4. Which sense do wild boars rely on most? _____

CENTRAL and SOUTH AMERICAN

ANIMALS

Jaguar

Spider Monkey

Giant Armadillo

Giant Anteater

Chinchilla

Woolly Monkey

Llama

Two-Toed Sloth

Macaw

Toucan

Chinchilla

Chinchillas (chihn CHIHL uhz) look like large mice, but they are actually related to squirrels. They have thick, soft fur. Their blue-grey colour is beautiful. In the 1500s, Spanish explorers brought chinchillas back to Europe. The demand for chinchilla fur nearly caused this animal to be killed off. Today, a small chinchilla population lives in the Andes Mountains.

Chinchillas eat roots and grass. Water is scarce high in the Andes. However, chinchillas get enough water from the plants they eat. Chinchillas are nocturnal, or active at night. They sleep during the day. At sundown, they begin looking for food.

Think and Learn

1. Chinchillas are related to _____.

2. Describe chinchilla fur. _____

   _____

3. Where do chinchillas live? _____

4. How do chinchillas get water? _____

   _____

Giant Anteater

The giant anteater is an animal that eats ants and termites. Giant anteaters have three large claws on each paw. They use their claws to rip open ant nests. Giant anteaters have a sticky tongue that is 0.6 metre long. They push their tongue into an anthill to get the ants. Giant anteaters cannot see well. Instead, they find ants with their sharp sense of smell.

Giant anteaters are found only in Central and South America. They never dig burrows or make homes. Instead, they wander alone looking for food until they tire. Then, they lie down in a hidden place, cover their heads with their long bushy tails and fall asleep.

Think and Learn

1. What do giant anteaters eat? _____

2. How do giant anteaters use their claws? _____

   _____

3. Giant anteaters have _____ tongues.

4. Where do giant anteaters sleep? _____

   _____

Giant Armadillo

The giant armadillo (ahr muh DIHL oh) is the largest of all armadillos. It can reach a length of 1.5 metres and weigh as much as 59 kilograms. Giant armadillos are found only near rivers in the eastern part of South America. Early Spanish explorers named the armadillo. The name means "little armored one."

Armadillos are covered with hard bony plates called scutes.

Giant armadillos use their long curved claws for digging burrows and for finding food. They eat termites, worms, snakes and insects. Armadillos are quiet animals that prefer to live alone. When threatened, they either run away or crouch low. Their scutes protect their soft undersides.

Think and Learn

1. Where are giant armadillos found?_____

_____

2. What does the word "armadillo" mean? _____

3. What are scutes? _____

4. What do armadillos use their claws for?_____

_____

Jaguar

The jaguar (JAG wahr) is a member of the cat family. It is 1.8 metres long and weighs about 136 kilograms. This beautiful animal has yellowish-tan fur with black dots encircled by black rings. Some jaguars are almost entirely black. The jaguar is found throughout Central and South America in many different habitats. It can live in shrub country, rainforests, mountains and woods.

Jaguars like to hunt almost any kind of animal, including fish, turtles, deer and wild pigs. They often lie on tree branches and wait until they can pounce down on their prey. Not only are jaguars skilled climbers, they are also great swimmers. They will often hunt in the water, especially when the rivers have flooded.

Think and Learn

1. The jaguar is a member of the _____ family.

2. In what habitats do jaguars live?_____
_____

3. Where do jaguars often wait for prey? _____

4. Jaguars are skilled _____ and great _____.

Llama

Llamas (LAH muhz) belong to the camel family. They are 1.2 to 1.5 metres tall and weigh over 90 kilograms. Llamas come in many colours—white, tan, brown and black. Llamas live in the semi-desert region near the Andes Mountains. They eat shrubs and other plants. Like the camel, a llama can live for weeks without water. The llama gets the water it needs from the plants it eats.

Llamas have been tamed for centuries. Their wool is used for making clothing, ropes and blankets. Llamas are useful pack animals. They travel easily through mountains carrying heavy loads. However, if a llama thinks it has worked long enough for one day, it sits down and refuses to move.

Think and Learn

1. Llamas belong to the _____ family.

2. What do llamas eat? _____

3. Llamas can live for weeks without _____.

4. Why are llamas useful pack animals? _____

_____

Macaw

Macaws (muh KAWZ) are the largest members of the parrot family. They come in many bright colours. All macaws have powerful hooked bills. They use their bills to help them climb and to break open nuts and seeds. Macaws have four toes on each foot. Their feet are well suited for perching, climbing and holding objects. Macaws are only found in rainforests. They live in holes that they make in tree trunks.

Macaws are in danger of extinction, or dying out. They are losing their homes as the rainforest is destroyed. Laws protect these birds, but people still capture them to sell as pets. Macaws are not good pets because they like to scream and bite.

Think and Learn

1. Macaws are members of the _____ family.

2. All macaws have powerful, hooked _____.

3. What do macaws use their feet for? _____

_____

4. Why are macaws in danger of extinction? _____

_____

Spider Monkey

Spider monkeys are small monkeys well suited for living in trees. In fact, they rarely come down to the ground. These monkeys move quickly through trees by swinging and jumping from branch to branch. Spider monkeys have tails that are longer than their bodies. These tails can easily grab and pick up things.

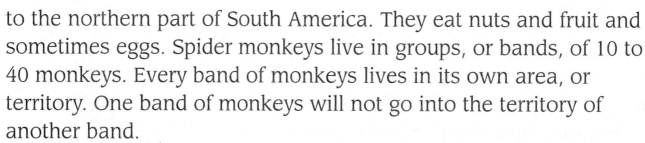

Spider monkeys are found in rainforests from southern Mexico to the northern part of South America. They eat nuts and fruit and sometimes eggs. Spider monkeys live in groups, or bands, of 10 to 40 monkeys. Every band of monkeys lives in its own area, or territory. One band of monkeys will not go into the territory of another band.

Think and Learn

1. How do spider monkeys move quickly through trees?

_____

2. Their _____ can grab and pick up things.

3. What do spider monkeys eat?_____

4. Spider monkeys live in groups called _____.

Dot-to-Dot

Spider monkeys live in rainforests. They usually run away and hide if another animal scares them. Connect the dots to find the hidden monkey. Then, colour the picture.

97

Toucan

Toucans (TOO kanz) are birds with large colourful bills. Although a toucan bill looks heavy, it is really very light. The bill is hollow. It is made from a hornlike material. Toucans live in the rainforests of Central and South America. Toucans eat fruit, large insects, lizards and young birds. A toucan sits on a branch and reaches for fruit with its long bill. The curved end of the bill helps the toucan pick the fruit and hold on to it.

Toucans make their nests in the holes of trees. Both the male and female take turns sitting on the eggs. Newly hatched toucans are blind and have no feathers. After 6 to 7 weeks, the young toucans are ready to live on their own.

Think and Learn

1. Toucans have large colourful _____.

2. Where do toucans live?_____
   _____

3. What do they eat? _____
   _____

4. Where do toucans make nests? _____

Two-Toed Sloth

A sloth (slawth) is an animal that lives in trees. Sloths rarely go down to the ground. In fact, they cannot walk at all. The two-toed sloth has two long, curved claws on its front legs. Sloths use their claws to hold onto tree trunks and branches. They often hang upside down. Sloths move very slowly along tree branches, paw over paw, while hanging upside down.

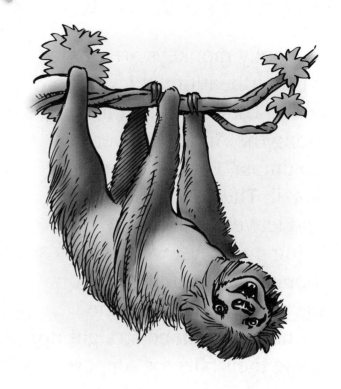

Two-toed sloths are found from the southern part of Central America to central Brazil and Peru. They eat leaves, twigs and buds. Sloths are nocturnal, or active at night. It is hard to see sloths sleeping in the trees during the day. Green algae often grow on the sloths' fur, so the sloths blend in with the leaves.

Think and Learn

1. Sloths cannot _____ at all.

2. What do sloths use to hold onto branches? _____

3. When are sloths active? _____

4. How do sloths blend in with tree leaves? _____

_____

Woolly Monkey

Woolly monkeys are named for their beautiful thick, woolly coats. They are found in forests along the Amazon River in Columbia, Ecuador, Peru and Brazil. They eat fruit, flowers and leaves. Unlike other tree-living monkeys, woolly monkeys are often found on the ground. While on the ground, they stand straight up, using their tails for support.

Woolly monkeys live in groups, or bands, of 10 to 30 monkeys. They move more slowly than other monkeys. When frightened, they swing through tree branches and hide. Woolly monkeys are friendly. They are often seen in the company of other kinds of monkeys.

Think and Learn

1. Woolly monkeys are named for their _____.

2. How do woolly monkeys stand while on the ground?_____

   _____

3. Woolly monkeys live in groups called _____.

4. Woolly monkeys move more_____ than other monkeys.

AUSTRALIAN
ANIMALS

Wallaby

Giant Grey Kangaroo

Koala

Dingo

Tasmanian Devil

Kookaburra

Echidna

Dugong

Wombat

Platypus

Dingo

The dingo (DIHNG goh) is the only wild member of the dog family found in Australia. Dingoes are about the same size as medium-sized dogs. Their ears stand up, and they have bushy tails. Dingoes cannot bark but can yelp and howl. Dingoes are excellent hunters. They hunt alone or in family groups for small animals to eat. Scientists think Aborigines, native Australians, brought dingoes to Australia thousands of years ago.

Dingoes give birth only once a year to three to six puppies. Both parents care for the puppies and keep them hidden. The Aborigines search for the puppies to train them for hunting. Adult dingoes cannot be trained.

Think and Learn

1. The dingo is a member of the _____ family.

2. Dingoes cannot _____, but they can yelp and howl.

3. What do dingoes hunt for?_____

4. Why do Aborigines look for dingo puppies? _____

_____

Dugong

The dugong (DOO gahng) is related to the manatee. Dugongs are mammals, or animals that feed their young with their mothers' milk. Even though dugongs breathe air, they spend their entire life in water. They surface only to breathe about every 1 to 10 minutes. They have an unusual snout. It is rounded, with a large whiskered upper lip. Only male dugongs grow tusks.

Dugongs are found in the Indian Ocean, the Red Sea and off the northern coast of Australia. Dugongs eat only sea grass. They are often called sea cows because they graze on sea grass just as cows graze on field grass.

Think and Learn

1. What are dugongs related to?_____

2. Only male dugongs grow _____.

3. Where are dugongs found? _____

   _____

4. Dugongs are often called _____.

Echidna

The echidna (ih KIHD nuh) is sometimes called a spiny anteater. It is found throughout Australia in open forests. The echidna's body is covered with coarse hair and pointed spines. Echidnas sleep in hollow logs during the day. At night, they use their sharp claws to scratch up insects. They eat the insects by licking them up with their long sticky tongues. Echidnas do not have teeth.

Echidnas are mammals that lay eggs. Mammals are animals whose young feed on the mother's milk. Female echidnas lay one egg each year. The mother keeps the egg in her pouch, where it hatches. The baby stays in the pouch for several weeks, drinking the mother's milk and growing.

Think and Learn

1. What is another name for an echidna? _____

2. When do echidnas sleep? _____

3. How do echidnas eat insects? _____

_____

4. Echidnas are _____ that lay eggs.

Giant Grey Kangaroo

The giant grey kangaroo is the largest of all kangaroos. It grows to 2 metres tall. Kangaroos have huge feet and long, powerful tails. When kangaroos stand, they lean on their tails for balance. Kangaroos are found in the open forest and bush country of Australia. They eat fruit, leaves and roots. Kangaroos travel in groups called mobs.

Kangaroos have excellent hearing, vision and sense of smell. They are gentle, timid animals. Their senses and speed help them escape from danger. Kangaroos are marsupials. This means that they carry their babies, called joeys, in pouches. At birth, a joey is the size of a bee. It lives in its mother's pouch for 1 year.

Think and Learn

1. What does a kangaroo use its tail for? _____

2. Where do kangaroos live? _____
_____

3. Kangaroos travel in groups called _____.

4. A baby kangaroo is called a _____.

Australian Animal Scramble

Unscramble the words below to find the names of Australian animals. The words below will help you.

1. R A O K A O R B U K

_____

2. A L K O A

_____

3. L A B W Y A L

_____

4. D I H A C E N

_____

5. G O U D G N

_____

dingo
wombat
dugong
echidna
platypus
Tasmanian devil
kangaroo
kookaburra
wallaby
koala

6. O G N I D

_____

7. B W O T A M

_____

8. M A S T A N N A I   V L I E D

_____

9. G N A K A O O R

_____

10. S Y P A L T P U

_____

Koala

Although many people call the koala (koh AW luh) a koala bear, it is not a bear. The koala is a marsupial—a mammal with a pouch for carrying its young. The koala has beautiful grey, woolly fur. If threatened, koalas defend themselves with their sharp claws.

Koalas eat the leaves of eucalyptus trees. Koalas are found in the eucalyptus forests on the east coast of Australia. The only time a koala climbs down from a tree is to move to another tree. They get the water they need from the leaves they eat. Koalas are nocturnal and sleep 18 hours during the day. Female koalas have one baby at a time. The baby crawls into the mother's pouch, where it stays for 6 months. Then, the mother carries the baby on her back for 4 or 5 months.

Think and Learn

1. What is a marsupial? _____

_____

2. What do koalas eat?_____

3. When do koalas climb down a tree? _____

4. How long does a baby koala stay in its mother's pouch?

_____

Kookaburra

The kookaburra (KOOK uh ber uh) is a bird that lives in forests in the southern parts of Australia. It is best known for its loud screaming laughter. The kookaburra screams its laughing sounds at dawn and at dusk. Kookaburras make their homes in holes in trees. They eat a wide variety of foods, such as caterpillars, fish, small mammals, frogs and worms. Insects, however, are their favourite food.

Kookaburras usually lay one to four eggs in spring. Male kookaburras protect the nest. Young kookaburras stay in their parents' territory for up to 4 years. The young kookaburras even help to feed their parents' new babies.

Think and Learn

1. The kookaburra is known for its loud screaming_____.

2. Where do kookaburras make their homes?_____

_____

3. A kookaburra's favourite food is _____.

4. How do young kookaburras help their parents? _____

_____

Platypus

The platypus (PLAT ih pus) is a mammal that has a bill like a duck and a flat, beaverlike tail. It is found near rivers and streams in eastern Australia and Tasmania. The platypus is awkward on land but swims gracefully. It has claws under its webbed toes. It uses its claws for digging burrows and getting food. The platypus eats large amounts of snails, worms, shrimp and small fish.

The male platypus is poisonous. It has a poison gland attached to a hollow claw on each hind leg. A scratch from this claw can kill an animal or make a human very sick. The female platypus lays her eggs in a burrow lined with leaves. When the babies hatch, she holds them with her tail. The babies drink milk from her body.

Think and Learn

1. The platypus has a _____ like a duck.

2. What does a platypus use its claws for? _____
_____

3. The male platypus is _____.

4. How does a mother platypus hold her babies?_____
_____

Tasmanian Devil

The Tasmanian devil is a marsupial—a mammal with a pouch to raise its young. It is found only on the island of Tasmania, off the southern coast of Australia. The Tasmanian devil looks somewhat like a small bear. It has a large head, stocky body and strong jaws and teeth. It is named for its bad temper and loud throaty growl.

The Tasmanian devil is nocturnal. It rests during the day in a hollow log or between rocks. At night, it hunts for food. It is a scavenger—it eats the remains of dead animals. It also eats sheep, chickens, reptiles and other small animals. The female Tasmanian devil keeps her young in her pouch for 15 weeks. When the furry babies come out, they still need their mother's milk for several months.

Think and Learn

1. The Tasmanian devil looks like a small _____.

2. What is the Tasmanian devil named for? _____

   _____

3. What does the Tasmanian devil do at night? _____

4. A _____ eats the remains of dead animals.

Wallaby

Wallabies (WAHL uh beez) belong to the kangaroo family. Like kangaroos, they stand on their hind legs and use their tail for balance. Wallabies are found in Australia, New Guinea and Tasmania. They live in grasslands or in woods. They graze on plants in the early morning and late afternoon. During the heat of the day, they rest in the shade. When the weather is very hot, wallabies lick their forearms and paws to cool themselves. Wallabies do not drink much water. They get enough water from the plants they eat.

Like other marsupials, wallabies carry their young in a pouch. The baby crawls through its mother's fur and climbs into the pouch after it is born. There, it drinks milk and grows.

Think and Learn

1. Wallabies belong to the _____ family.

2. During the heat of the day, wallabies rest in the _____.

3. How do wallabies cool themselves in hot weather?

_____

4. Wallabies get water from the _____ they eat.

Wombat

A wombat (WAHM bat) is a marsupial that looks like a small bear. However, it acts more like a rabbit or a mouse. Wombats have two upper and two lower front teeth that never stop growing. They use their strong legs and claws for digging and burrowing. Adult wombats weigh up to 34 kilograms.

Wombats live in dry climates in southern Australia and Tasmania. They can go without water for a long time. Wombats stay in underground burrows all day. At night, they come out to eat roots and leaves. A wombat builds a nest of leaves and bark, where it gives birth to one baby. The baby spends the first part of its life in its mother's pouch. A wombat can live up to 25 years.

Think and Learn

1. What do wombats use their claws for? _____

_____

2. Wombats live in _____ climates.

3. When do wombats eat?_____

4. How long can a wombat live? _____

African Elephant

The African elephant is the world's largest land animal. A male, or bull, can grow to 3 metres tall and 7 metres long. It can weigh as much as 6,350 kilograms. Females, called cows, are smaller. Elephants have trunks that they use like hands. They can easily pick up small fruits or lift tree branches with their trunks. Elephants spend most of the day eating leaves, grass, small branches, bark, coconuts and berries. They also drink large amounts of water every day.

African elephants are found in the warm grasslands and forests of Africa. They live with other animals, such as lions, hyenas, giraffes and zebras. Lions and hyenas will attack baby elephants and sick elephants. Adult elephants are safe from most predators.

Think and Learn

1. The female elephant is called a _____ .

2. Elephants use their _____ like hands.

3. What do elephants eat? _____

_____

4. Adult elephants are safe from most _____ .

Elephant Adaptations

Adaptations (ad ap TAY shuhnz) are special body parts or behaviours that animals have to survive in their environment. Some elephant adaptations help them live in hot places. They flap their large ears to cool off. They also do not have a thick layer of fat, like arctic animals have.

The most unusual elephant adaptation is its trunk. Elephants use their trunks to get food and water, cool off, breathe, touch things, smell, make sounds and "talk" to other elephants. Small "fingers" at the end of the trunk can pick up very small objects.

Think and Learn

1. Label the elephant adaptations in the picture.

2. How do elephants use their trunks?_____

_____

_____

_____

Elephant Facts

Fill in the blanks on this page to make a fact sheet on African elephants.

What Elephants Look Like

1. Height _____

2. Length _____

3. Weight of an adult _____

4. What does an elephant look like? _____

_____

_____

Where Elephants Live

1. Where do elephants live? _____

_____

2. What other animals are found where elephants live?

_____

Eating Habits

1. What do elephants eat?_____

_____

_____

2. What eats elephants?_____

_____

_____

ELEPHANTS

Pull-Out Storybook

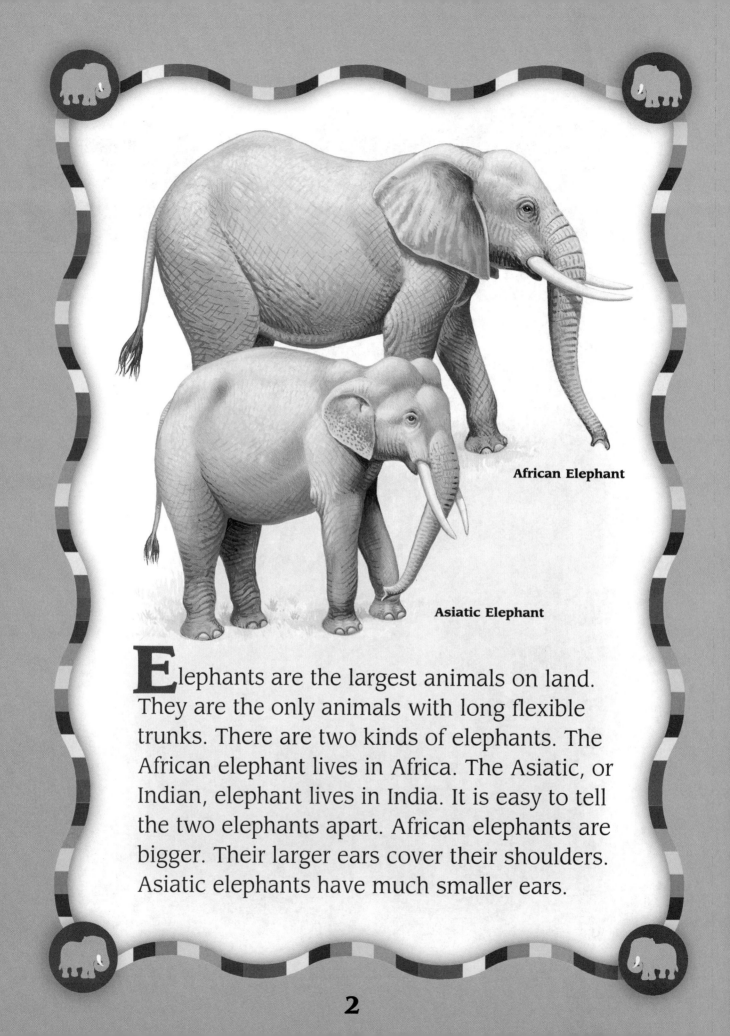

African Elephant

Asiatic Elephant

Elephants are the largest animals on land. They are the only animals with long flexible trunks. There are two kinds of elephants. The African elephant lives in Africa. The Asiatic, or Indian, elephant lives in India. It is easy to tell the two elephants apart. African elephants are bigger. Their larger ears cover their shoulders. Asiatic elephants have much smaller ears.

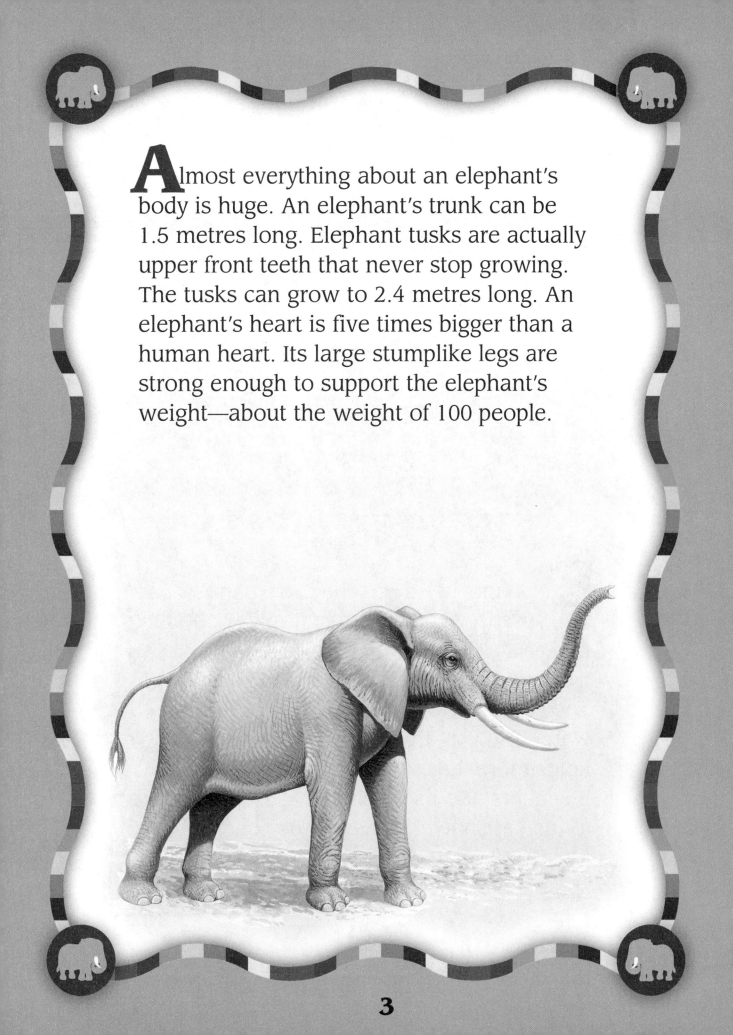

Almost everything about an elephant's body is huge. An elephant's trunk can be 1.5 metres long. Elephant tusks are actually upper front teeth that never stop growing. The tusks can grow to 2.4 metres long. An elephant's heart is five times bigger than a human heart. Its large stumplike legs are strong enough to support the elephant's weight—about the weight of 100 people.

Elephants use their trunks in many ways. They use them to sniff the air and ground to find food. They use them to reach into treetops and pull down branches and leaves. They even use them like straws to drink water. Did you know that an elephant's trunk holds more than 7.5 litres of water? Elephants also use their trunks to take a "shower." They fill up their trunks with water and spray themselves.

Elephants give birth to one baby at a time. When the baby is born, the other females in the herd sniff it and touch it gently. Later, they help look after the baby as it grows. A baby elephant stands about 1 metre at birth and weighs about 90 kilograms. The baby grows quickly, gaining 13 kilograms a month. Baby elephants stay with their mothers until they are 12 to 14 years old.

Baby elephants love to play. They chase and push one another. They grab each other's tail with their trunks. They also climb on top of each other and have "play fights." As the young elephants play, an older sister or aunt usually watches them. Playing helps young elephants learn the rules of the herd. It also teaches them how to get along with other elephants.

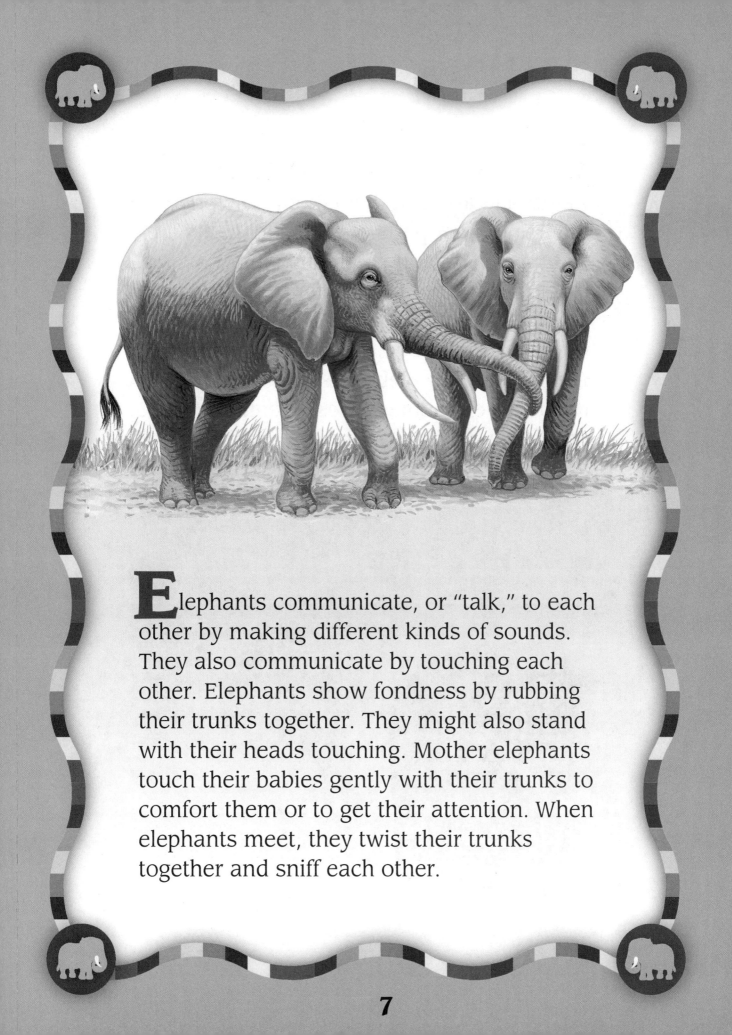

Elephants communicate, or "talk," to each other by making different kinds of sounds. They also communicate by touching each other. Elephants show fondness by rubbing their trunks together. They might also stand with their heads touching. Mother elephants touch their babies gently with their trunks to comfort them or to get their attention. When elephants meet, they twist their trunks together and sniff each other.

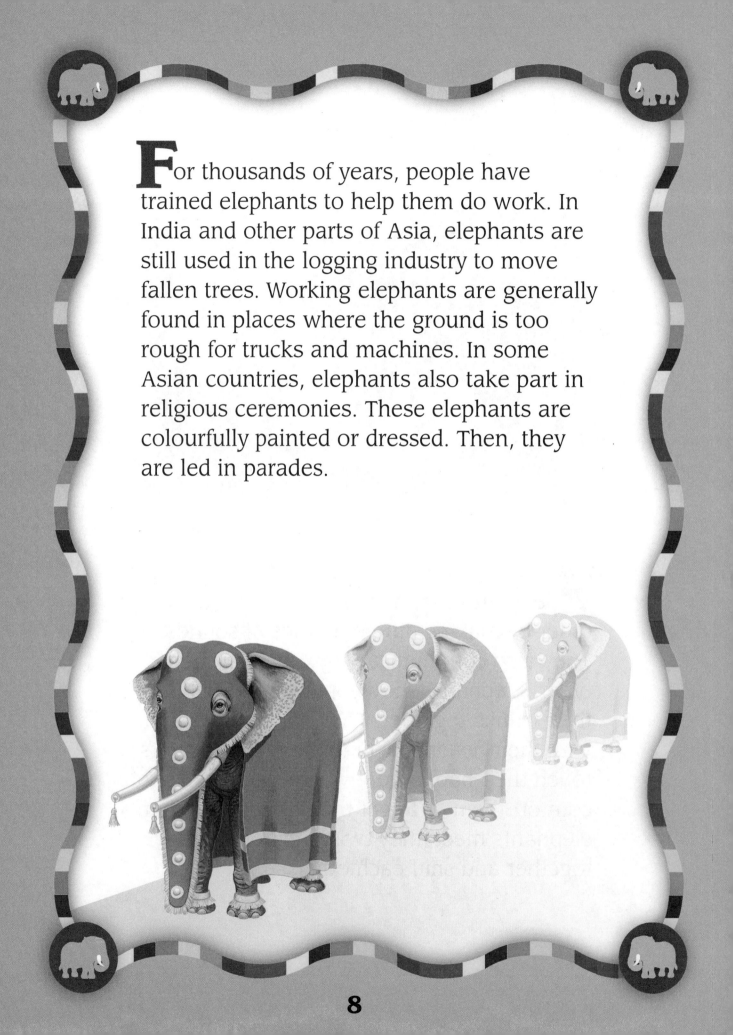

For thousands of years, people have trained elephants to help them do work. In India and other parts of Asia, elephants are still used in the logging industry to move fallen trees. Working elephants are generally found in places where the ground is too rough for trucks and machines. In some Asian countries, elephants also take part in religious ceremonies. These elephants are colourfully painted or dressed. Then, they are led in parades.

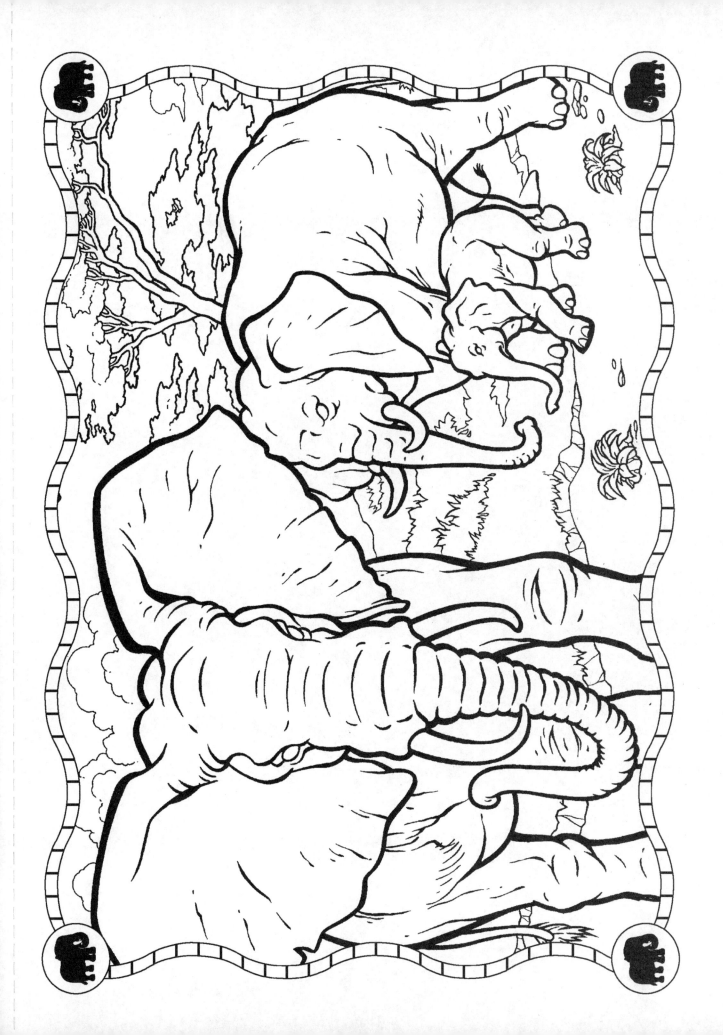

Giraffe

Giraffes are the tallest of all animals. They stand over 5.4 metres tall and weigh over 1,800 kilograms pounds. Even though their necks are so long, they have the same number of neck bones as other animals. Giraffes have sharp eyesight. They can see in all directions without moving their heads. Every giraffe has a different pattern of patches, just as every human has different fingerprints.

Giraffes live in herds on the dry grasslands in Africa. They mainly eat leaves from acacia (uh KAY shuh) trees, which are the most common trees in the area. Giraffes can go weeks without water. When they drink, giraffes spread apart their front legs and lower their long necks to reach the water.

Think and Learn

1. Giraffes are the _____ of all animals.

2. Compare the number of neck bones in giraffes to other animals. _____

3. What do giraffes eat? _____

4. How do giraffes bend down to get a drink?_____

_____

Dot-to-Dot

Connect the dots. Colour the picture.

Chimpanzee

Chimpanzees (chihm pan ZEEZ) belong to the ape family. They are found in rainforests in Africa. Like apes, they can walk on two feet. However, they prefer to move about on all four legs like monkeys do. Chimpanzees have hands that look like human hands, but their thumbs are shorter. Chimpanzees eat fruit, leaves and insects.

Chimpanzees are one of the few animals that make and use tools. To get termites, chimpanzees trim sticks and put them inside termite hills. Then, they eat the termites that cling to the stick. Chimpanzees also build platforms in trees for sleeping. To communicate, or "talk," to each other, chimpanzees use different sounds.

Think and Learn

1. Is a chimpanzee a monkey or an ape? _____

2. Where are chimpanzees found?_____
   _____

3. What do chimpanzees eat? _____

4. What can chimpanzees do that most other animals cannot do? _____

Gorilla

The gorilla is the largest member of the ape family. Adult males grow to 1.8 metres in height and weigh 181 kilograms. Females are smaller. Gorillas have broad chests, wide shoulders, long arms and short legs. Their entire body, except for the face, is covered with dark fur. Gorillas are peaceful animals that live in family groups. An adult male always leads the group. Females and their babies make up the rest of the group.

Gorillas are found in different parts of central Africa. Some live in mountain forests. Others live in forests on low ground. Gorillas spend most of the day eating leaves and fruit. At night, gorillas build sleeping platforms on the ground or in trees.

Think and Learn

1. Gorillas belong to the _____ family.

2. What makes up a gorilla family group?_____
_____

3. Where are gorillas found? _____

4. Where do gorillas sleep?_____
_____

Apes and Monkeys

Apes and monkeys are the animals most closely related to humans. Apes and monkeys are different. Monkeys have tails. Apes do not. Apes have larger brains than monkeys. Larger brains allow for more difficult actions.

Even though they are different, apes and monkeys are alike in some ways. Both monkeys and apes can stand up on two legs. This keeps their hands free to do some kind of task. They both have hands and metres that look like human hands. Their hands and metres have "thumbs" that move in opposite directions to their fingers. This action lets apes and monkeys use their hands and metres to pick up things and hold them.

Think and Learn

1. Label the monkey and the ape in the picture.

2. In what ways are monkeys and apes different? _____

_____

3. How are monkeys and apes similar? _____

_____

_____

Compare and Contrast

Read about the chimpanzee and the gorilla. Then, use the Venn diagram and the facts you have learned to compare and contrast these two animals.

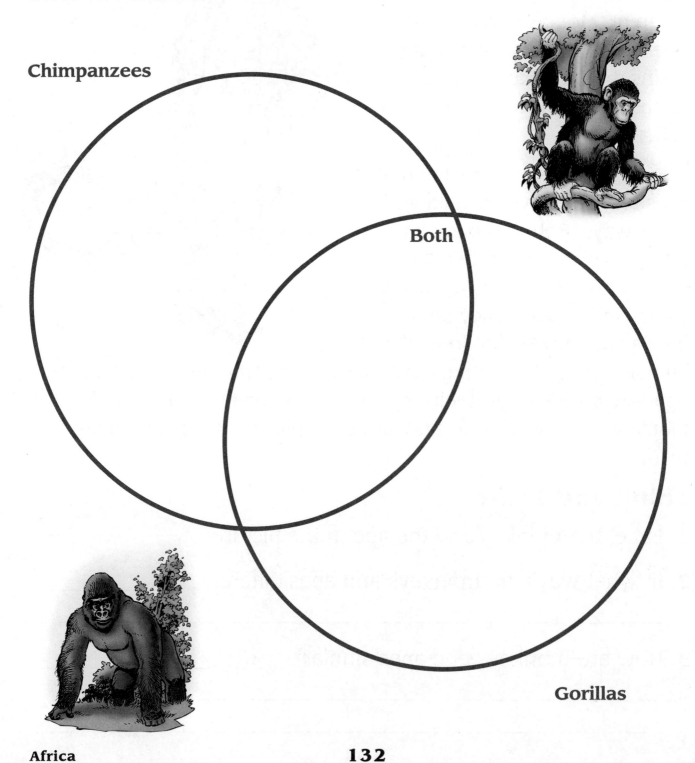

Chimpanzees

Both

Gorillas

Hippopotamus

The hippopotamus (hihp uh PAHT uh muhs) is second only to elephants in size. Hippos are about 3.5 metres long and weigh up to 3,600 kilograms. Hippos have very thick, bluish-grey skin. They have small eyes and ears on their large heads. Their enormous mouths can open 1 to 1.2 metres wide.

Hippos live by streams and marshes in many parts of Africa. During the day, they rest and sleep in the water. They keep their entire body under water, except for their eyes, ears and nose. Hippos are very graceful swimmers. At night, they leave the water to eat grass. They spend up to 6 hours a night eating. Hippos live in herds with 15 to 30 members.

Think and Learn

1. Hippos have very thick _____.

2. Where do hippos live? _____
_____

3. What do hippos do during the day? _____
_____

4. Hippos are very graceful _____.

Africa

Lion

The lion is one of the largest and fiercest members of the cat family. Lions range in size from 120 to 225 kilograms. Only male lions have a mane, the thick fur around the head. The mane protects lions when they fight to defend their territory, or area in which they live.

Lions sleep during the day and hunt at night. They hunt for antelope, zebras, young elephants and other smaller animals. Lions are social animals. They live in groups called prides. A pride is usually made up of one to six males and four to twelve females with their cubs. Each pride has its own territory. The members of a pride hunt only in their territory.

Think and Learn

1. Why do male lions have manes? _____

_____

2. When do lions hunt? _____

3. Lions live in groups called _____.

4. Each pride hunts in its own _____.

Lion Maze

Complete the maze to help the lion cub find its way back to its pride.

Africa

Ostrich

The ostrich (AHS trihch) is the world's largest bird. It stands 2.5 metres tall. Ostriches cannot fly. Their wings are too small. However, ostriches run very fast. They can run as fast as 72 kilometres per hour. Ostriches have very good eyesight. Their large eyes and long necks help them to see for several kilometres.

Ostriches live on dry, grassy plains and sandy deserts in Africa. They can go for a long time without water. Ostriches eat leaves, seeds, flowers, insects and small animals. Ostriches live and travel in flocks. A flock is usually made up of one male and several females. The male ostrich digs a hole as a nest. Each female lays as many as ten eggs in the nest.

Think and Learn

1. How tall is an adult ostrich? _____

2. How fast can an ostrich run? _____

3. Where do ostriches live?_____

_____

4. Ostriches live and travel in_____.

Hidden Pictures

Find the ostriches hidden in the picture. Colour them.

Black Rhinoceros

The black rhinoceros (righ NAHS er uhs) has tough, wrinkled skin and a two-horned snout. A rhinoceros grows to 3.6 metres long and weighs about 1.8 metric tonnes. It is a relative of the horse. Surprisingly, it can run as fast as a horse for short distances. Rhinoceros horns grow from the same material as hair and claws. Rhinos use the longer front horn to dig and to defend themselves. They use the smaller back horn to dig up bushes and small trees to eat.

The black rhino stays hidden during the day. It comes out at night to search for food and water. Rhinos have very poor eyesight. They rely mostly on their sense of smell. A new odour or sound can cause a rhinoceros to charge.

Think and Learn

1. The black rhinoceros is related to the _____.

2. How does a rhinoceros use its front horn? _____

_____

3. What do rhinoceroses eat? _____

4. What sense do rhinoceroses rely on most? _____

Vulture

Vultures (VUL cherz) are large birds of prey, or birds that eat animals. Their wingspan can reach 1.8 to 2.7 metres. Vultures have bare, wrinkled skin on their heads and necks. Their bills are slightly hooked. Vultures live in mountains, grasslands and deserts. They generally do not live in forests or in areas that receive a lot of rain.

Vultures are scavengers. Scavengers feed on the remains of dead animals. Vultures use their sharp eyesight and keen sense of smell to find dead animals. When one vulture finds food, other vultures are quick to follow. Vultures are strong fliers. They come from miles away when food is found.

Think and Learn

1. Vultures are large birds of _____.

2. Where do vultures live?_____

_____

3. What do vultures eat? _____

4. How do vultures find food? _____

_____

Zebra

The zebra is a striped animal related to the horse. The zebra's stripes help the animal blend in with its surroundings. A zebra standing in tall grass is very hard to see. Each zebra has its own stripe pattern, like each human has his or her own fingerprints.

Zebras are found in the deserts and grasslands of eastern and southern Africa. They mainly eat grass, and they spend most of their time eating. Zebras live in herds made up of a male, several females and their babies. Zebras protect themselves by staying together in a herd. If they are in danger, they try to run away. Zebras can run as fast as 72 kilometres per hour.

Think and Learn

1. A zebra's _____ help it blend in with its surroundings.

2. Where are zebras found? _____
_____

3. Zebras live in _____.

4. What do zebras do when they are in danger? _____

Zebra Stripes

Every zebra has a unique pattern of stripes. Design your own pattern on this zebra.

Word Search

Find the names of African animals hidden in the puzzle. The animal names are written **across** and **down**.

```
B Z C L H C H I M P A N Z E E
L E U P I M S E K R A N L P O
C B R A P K S A E M O E L E V
M R A F P O G O R I L L A M U
H A L M O R H E F X A L W J L
P E E Z P A E S D G H A L O T
R H I N O C E R O S M K I W U
M A G K T S A D R L E Z O P R
S O I R A E E N Z E D F N K E
L A R M M J K S E W Z R V U K
T U A L U M E L E P H A N T A
Y M F D S G O P M S A U Y O A
H S F U Y O S T R I C H Z E B
G C E N B E R A L M S Y R E W
```

gorilla   lion   chimpanzee
vulture   ostrich   rhinoceros
giraffe   zebra   hippopotamus
elephant

INSECTS

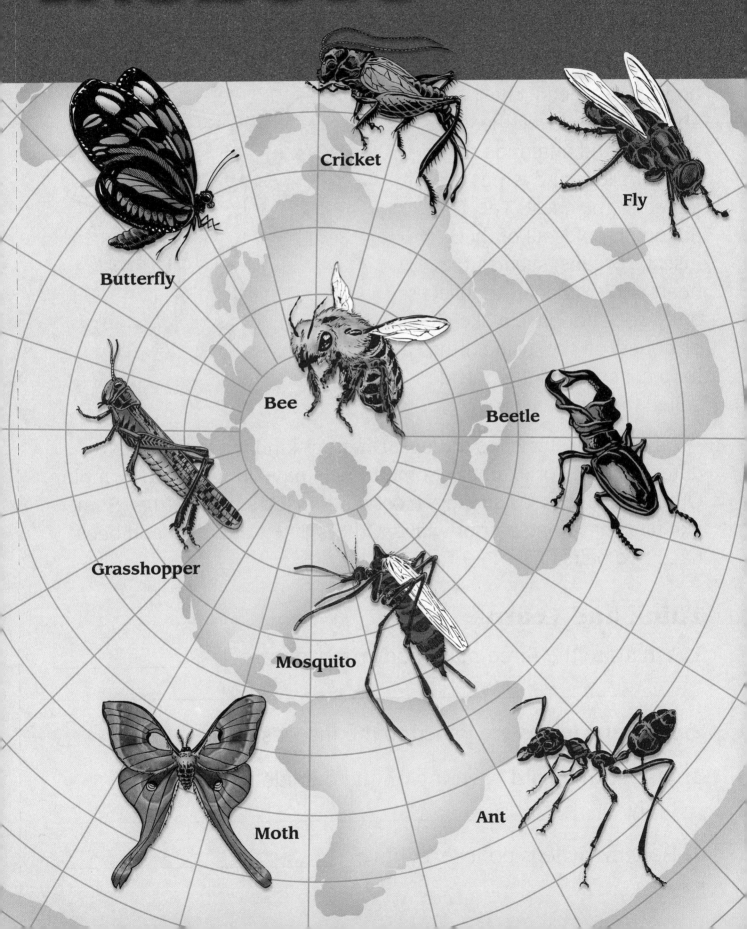

Cricket

Fly

Butterfly

Bee

Beetle

Grasshopper

Mosquito

Moth

Ant

What Is an Insect?

All insects have three main body parts—head, chest and abdomen. An insect has eyes, a mouth and antennae on its head. Its legs and wings are joined to the chest. The abdomen holds all of the insect's organs, such as the heart and stomach. An insect's body does not have a skeleton, or bones, on the inside. It has a hard covering on the outside called the exoskeleton.

All adult insects have six legs. Different kinds of insects have different legs. For example, some insects have long legs for jumping. Others have legs for digging. Most adult insects have wings. Some, like flies, have one pair of wings. Others, like butterflies and bees, have two pairs.

Think and Learn

1. What are the three main body parts of insects?_____

_____

2. Legs and wings are joined to the insect's _____.

3. What is the hard covering on the outside of an insect's body? _____

4. How many legs do insects have? _____

Ant

Ants are social insects that live and work together in large groups. Ants have two bent antennae on top of their heads. The antennae are used to taste, touch and smell. An ant is helpless if its antennae are damaged. Ants have very strong jaws that are used for digging and for getting food.

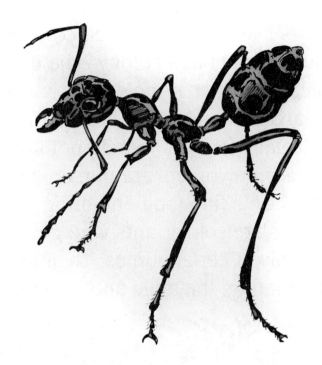

Ants are found all over the world, except for the North and South poles. Ants build different kinds of homes. Some ants live in trees. Some build nests in wood or under leaves. Others burrow under rocks. It is common for ants to dig homes in the dirt. Some dig underground tunnels and rooms in the dirt. Others build large anthills that look like tall mounds of dirt.

Think and Learn

1. Why are ants called social insects?_____

_____

2. Ants have two bent _____ on top of their heads.

3. Ants use their jaws for_____ and for getting food.

4. Where do ants NOT live? _____

Ant Colonies

Ants live in groups called colonies. There are three different groups of ants in a colony—the queen ants, the workers and the males. Each ant in the colony has a special job. The queen ants are the largest females. Their only job is to lay eggs. The worker ants are usually females that do not lay eggs. The workers have many jobs. Some workers are nursery ants who care for the eggs. Other worker ants find food and bring it back to the colony. The largest workers are soldier ants who guard the nest. Male ants live in the nest only at certain times. Their job is to mate with the queen ants. After mating, the male ants soon die.

1. Label the ant in the colony that is a nursery ant. Label the soldier ant.

2. What are the three different groups of ants living in an ant colony? _____

_____

Bee

Bees are the only insects that make a food that people eat. Bees have a special stomach, called a honey stomach, where they store nectar, the sugar from flowers. Their long, hollow tongues work like straws to suck up nectar. Female bees have a stinger that they use for defence.

Bees live all over the world, except for the North and South poles. Bees build their homes in hollow trees or in beehives. Some bees live in social groups like ants. The queen bee lays eggs. The worker bees build the hive, care for the eggs, find nectar and pollen and defend the hive. The drones are male bees that mate with the queen.

Think and Learn

1. What is a honey stomach? _____

_____

2. Female bees have a _____ they use for defence.

3. Where do bees build their homes? _____

_____

4. What are drones? _____

Honeybees

Some farmers build wooden hives for honeybees. Then, the bees move in and make honeycombs. Honeycombs look like a wall with many six-sided rooms. Worker bees build the honeycomb out of beeswax, which they make in their stomach. The rooms in the honeycomb are used for storing eggs, young bees and honey.

Worker bees make honey from the nectar they collect from flowers. As bees collect nectar from flowers, they spread pollen from one flower to another. Pollen grains are the male sex cells of a flowering plant. A flower needs pollen to form fruit and seeds. Farmers often keep bees to help spread the pollen on their fruit trees. Then, the fruit trees will have a lot of fruit. Farmers also collect the honey.

Think and Learn

1. What are honeycombs made of ? _____

2. Why do farmers keep bees? _____

_____

_____

_____

Bzzz, Bzzz, Bzzz

Complete the sentences below by filling in the missing words. Then, write each word in a cell of the honeycomb with the matching number.

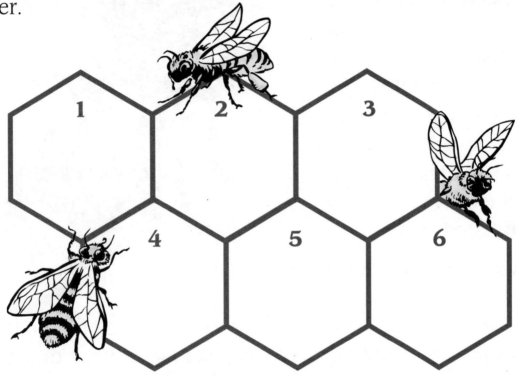

1. Bees collect nectar to make _____.

2. The bees that take care of the hive and make honey are called _____.

3. The bee that lays all the eggs is called the _____.

4. Male bees are called _____.

5. A honeycomb cell has _____ sides.

6. Honeycombs are made out of _____.

Beetle

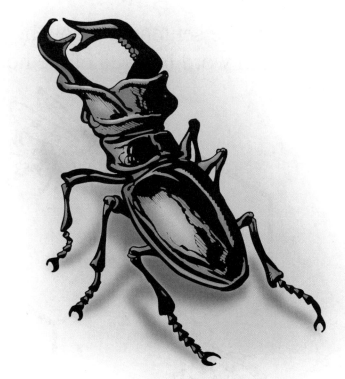

Beetles are the largest group of insects and come in every colour of the rainbow. All beetles have two pairs of wings. The outer wings are hard. They protect the inner, or flight, wings. The flight wings are thin and clear. They stay folded under the outer wings until needed for flight. Beetles have very strong jaws to grab and chew food.

Beetles are found all over the world. Beetles make their homes in many different places, from in water to under the ground. Beetles can be harmful or helpful to people, depending on what they eat. Some beetles damage the plants in gardens and farmers' fields. Other beetles eat harmful insects.

Think and Learn

1. Beetles are the _____ group of insects.

2. Which wings do beetles use for flight? _____
_____

3. Beetles have strong _____ to grab and chew food.

4. How are beetles helpful to people?_____
_____

Butterfly

Butterflies are beautiful insects. The body of a butterfly is long and slender. They have knobs at the ends of their antennae, which are used for smelling. Their wings are covered with tiny scales that give the wings their colour. All butterflies hatch as caterpillars, which look like worms. The caterpillars change to adult butterflies in a cocoon, or paperlike case.

Butterflies are found everywhere. They live on mountains and in deserts. As caterpillars, they eat leaves and fruit, often damaging crops. As butterflies, they cannot bite or chew. For food, they drink nectar, the sugary liquid, from flowers. Butterflies fly only during the day. When resting, they fold their wings straight up.

Think and Learn

1. What do butterflies use their antennae for? _____

2. Tiny _____ give butterfly wings their colour.

3. What do caterpillars eat? _____

4. When do butterflies fly? _____

Cricket

Crickets are jumping insects. Most crickets are either black or brown in colour and are about 2.5 centimetres long. Crickets have two pairs of wings. Both pairs of wings lie flat over the cricket's back. Only male crickets make the chirping sound that crickets are known for. They make the sound by rubbing their wings together. They make this sound to attract female crickets. Crickets hear sounds with a special body part on their front legs.

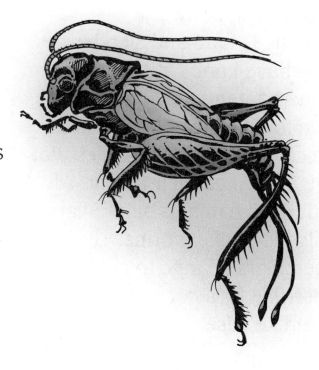

Crickets are found in many parts of the world. They hide during the day and are active at night. This is when they chirp and search for food. Crickets eat grain and the remains of other insects.

Think and Learn

1. Crickets are _____ insects.

2. How do male crickets chirp? _____
_____

3. How do crickets hear? _____
_____

4. When do crickets search for food? _____

Fly

Flies are very common insects. People see and hear them everywhere. There are many different kinds of flies, such as house flies, fruit flies, gnats and deer flies. Flies have only one pair of wings. The buzzing sound you hear when a fly flies by is the sound of its wings beating together. Flies use their antennae to touch and smell things. Flies have tiny, hairy pads on the bottoms of their metres. These help flies cling to walls and walk upside down on ceilings.

Although flies look harmless, they can carry and spread germs. Some flies, however, are helpful. They spread pollen from flower to flower like bees do.

Think and Learn

1. What are some kinds of flies?_____

_____

2. Flies have _____ pair of wings.

3. Flies use their_____ to touch and smell things.

4. Flies can carry and spread _____.

Grasshopper

Grasshoppers are built for jumping. Grasshoppers have long thin legs with powerful muscles. Most grasshoppers have large fragile wings that are protected by a second pair of wings. Like crickets, male grasshoppers make sounds by rubbing their wings together. Although grasshoppers can fly, they fly for only short distances. They move mainly by leaping and jumping.

There are two kinds of grasshoppers—long-horned grasshoppers and short-horned grasshoppers. Long-horned grasshoppers have long antennae. They eat plants and, sometimes, the remains of animals. Short-horned grasshoppers are locusts. They have short antennae and eat only plants. Some locusts damage crops.

Think and Learn

1. Grasshoppers are built for _____.

2. How far do grasshoppers fly? _____

_____

3. Long-horned grasshoppers have _____ antennae.

4. Locusts are _____-horned grasshoppers.

Mosquito

The mosquito is a kind of fly. Like all flies, mosquitoes have only one pair of wings. Mosquito wings can beat 1,000 times each second. The mosquito's head is almost entirely covered by its two large eyes. The antennae, used for hearing and smelling, are located between the eyes. Female mosquitoes have thin antennae. Male mosquitoes have feathery antennae.

Mosquitoes are found in all parts of the world. Some mosquitoes in tropical parts of the world spread diseases. Mosquitoes are most annoying because their bites hurt and itch. Only female mosquitoes bite. They bite to get the blood they need for their eggs to grow.

Think and Learn

1. The mosquito is a kind of _____.

2. Mosquito wings can beat _____ times each second.

3. What do mosquitoes use their antennae for? _____
_____

4. Why do female mosquitoes bite?_____
_____

Moth

Moths are closely related to butterflies. Butterflies and moths are so much alike that it is sometimes hard to tell them apart. Unlike butterflies, moths have chubby bodies and usually fly only at night. Moth antennae look feathery. The antennae give moths their senses of touch and smell. Moths cannot bite or chew. They have a mouth that looks and works like a drinking straw. Moths eat sap and nectar.

Moths are found everywhere. They have many enemies, such as frogs, birds, snakes and spiders. Some moths protect themselves by flying away. Others blend into their surroundings. Some moths taste so awful that other animals leave them alone.

Think and Learn

1. Moths are closely related to _____.

2. When do moths fly? _____

3. Moth antennae look _____.

4. What are some enemies of moths? _____

_____

INSECTS

Pull-Out Storybook

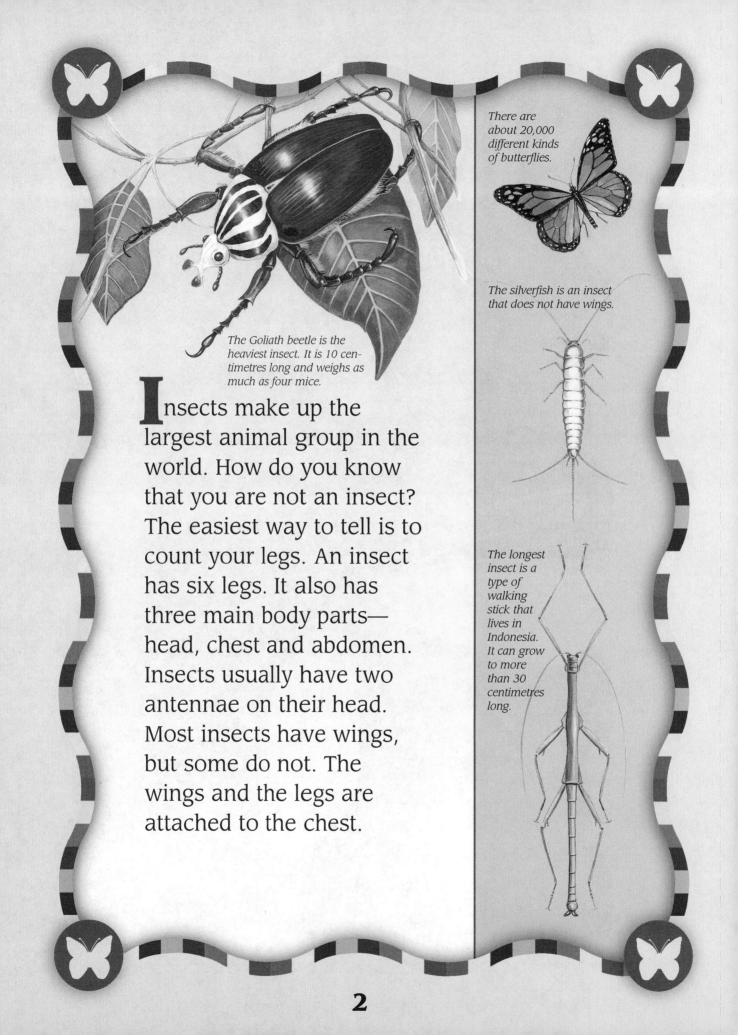

The Goliath beetle is the heaviest insect. It is 10 centimetres long and weighs as much as four mice.

Insects make up the largest animal group in the world. How do you know that you are not an insect? The easiest way to tell is to count your legs. An insect has six legs. It also has three main body parts—head, chest and abdomen. Insects usually have two antennae on their head. Most insects have wings, but some do not. The wings and the legs are attached to the chest.

There are about 20,000 different kinds of butterflies.

The silverfish is an insect that does not have wings.

The longest insect is a type of walking stick that lives in Indonesia. It can grow to more than 30 centimetres long.

The wings of moths and butterflies are made up of tiny overlapping scales.

Most insects have two pairs of wings for flying. Insects fly for many reasons—to find food, to look for a place to live, to escape from danger and to find mates. Insects need to warm up their flight muscles before they can fly on cold days. Some insects open their wings to let the sun heat them. Others move their muscles very fast to get them going.

Dragonflies are the fastest insects. They can fly at speeds of up to 96 kilometres per hour.

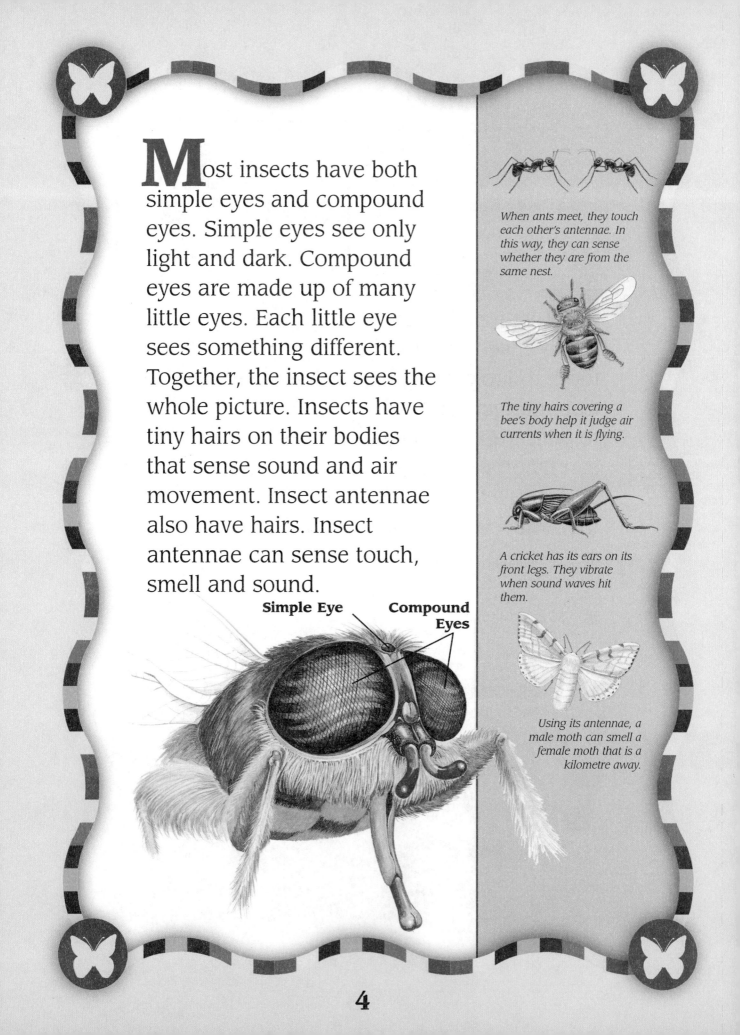

Most insects have both simple eyes and compound eyes. Simple eyes see only light and dark. Compound eyes are made up of many little eyes. Each little eye sees something different. Together, the insect sees the whole picture. Insects have tiny hairs on their bodies that sense sound and air movement. Insect antennae also have hairs. Insect antennae can sense touch, smell and sound.

Simple Eye

Compound Eyes

When ants meet, they touch each other's antennae. In this way, they can sense whether they are from the same nest.

The tiny hairs covering a bee's body help it judge air currents when it is flying.

A cricket has its ears on its front legs. They vibrate when sound waves hit them.

Using its antennae, a male moth can smell a female moth that is a kilometre away.

4

Some termites feed on wood and can damage buildings.

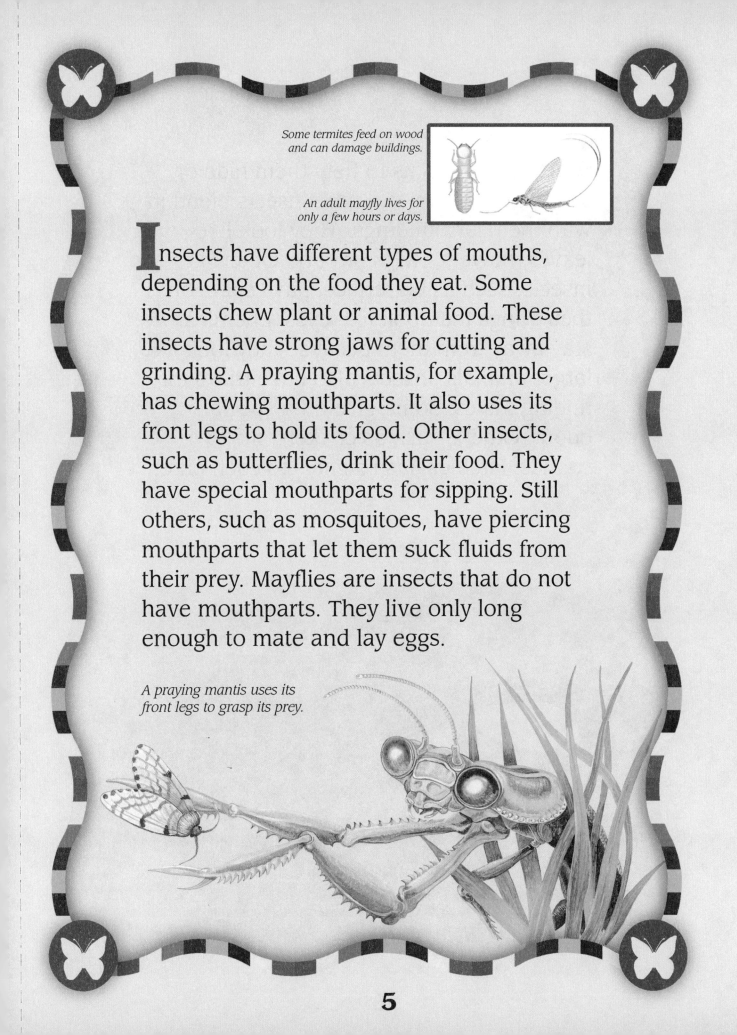

An adult mayfly lives for only a few hours or days.

Insects have different types of mouths, depending on the food they eat. Some insects chew plant or animal food. These insects have strong jaws for cutting and grinding. A praying mantis, for example, has chewing mouthparts. It also uses its front legs to hold its food. Other insects, such as butterflies, drink their food. They have special mouthparts for sipping. Still others, such as mosquitoes, have piercing mouthparts that let them suck fluids from their prey. Mayflies are insects that do not have mouthparts. They live only long enough to mate and lay eggs.

A praying mantis uses its front legs to grasp its prey.

Insects have tricks to help them hide or scare away enemies. Some insects blend in with their surroundings. They look like leaves, flowers, twigs or bark. Other insects, such as butterflies, have spots on their wings that look like eyes. Enemies stay away from them because they look like larger animals. Insects also have tricks for finding mates. Some give off a special odour. Others, such as crickets, make sounds. Fireflies flash signals to each other.

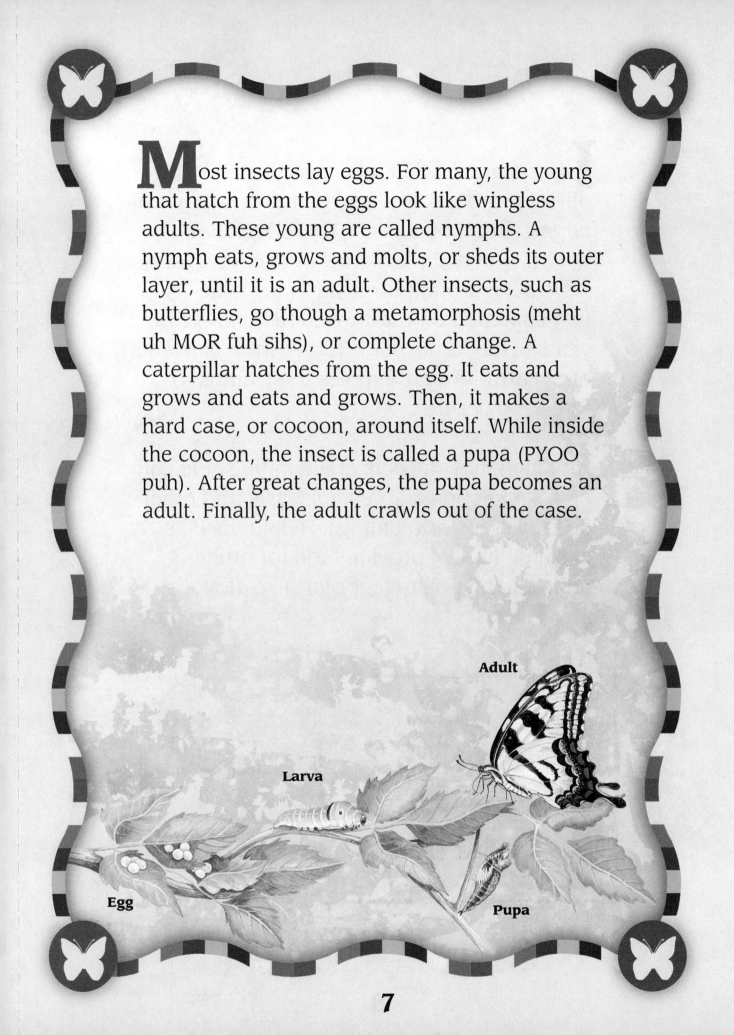

Most insects lay eggs. For many, the young that hatch from the eggs look like wingless adults. These young are called nymphs. A nymph eats, grows and molts, or sheds its outer layer, until it is an adult. Other insects, such as butterflies, go though a metamorphosis (meht uh MOR fuh sihs), or complete change. A caterpillar hatches from the egg. It eats and grows and eats and grows. Then, it makes a hard case, or cocoon, around itself. While inside the cocoon, the insect is called a pupa (PYOO puh). After great changes, the pupa becomes an adult. Finally, the adult crawls out of the case.

Adult

Larva

Egg

Pupa

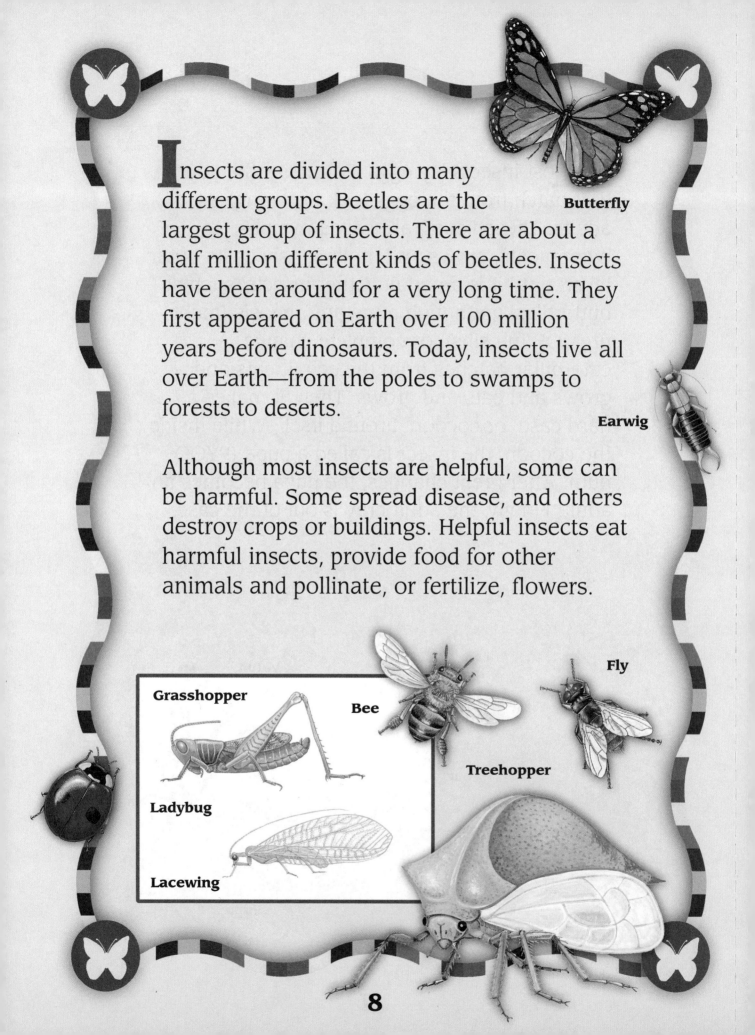

Insects are divided into many different groups. Beetles are the largest group of insects. There are about a half million different kinds of beetles. Insects have been around for a very long time. They first appeared on Earth over 100 million years before dinosaurs. Today, insects live all over Earth—from the poles to swamps to forests to deserts.

Although most insects are helpful, some can be harmful. Some spread disease, and others destroy crops or buildings. Helpful insects eat harmful insects, provide food for other animals and pollinate, or fertilize, flowers.

Butterfly

Earwig

Fly

Grasshopper

Bee

Treehopper

Ladybug

Lacewing

8

REPTILES

Chameleon

Tuatara

Alligator

Garter Snake

Turtle

Rattlesnake

Sea Turtle

Lizard

Crocodile

What Is a Reptile?

Reptiles are cold-blooded animals with scaly skin. Cold-blooded animals cannot control their body temperature. Their body temperature is the same as the temperature of their surroundings. However, many reptiles keep their body temperature even by moving to sunny or shady spots during the day.

The scales on the reptile's skin keep the skin from drying out. As reptiles grow, they shed their skin. Snakes shed their entire skin, while other reptiles have skin that flakes off. Most reptiles lay hard-shelled eggs. However, some reptiles give birth to live young. Scientists divide reptiles into four groups—tuataras, crocodiles, snakes and lizards, and turtles.

Think and Learn

1. _____ are cold-blooded animals with scaly skin.

2. How do some reptiles keep their body temperature even?

_____

3. What keeps a reptile's skin from drying out? _____

4. Most reptiles lay hard-shelled _____.

Tuatara

The tuatara (too uh TAW ruh) looks like a lizard but is actually the last remaining animal in its group. Tuataras lived during the time of the first dinosaurs, about 220 million years ago. They have not changed since that time. Tuataras have a third eye on top of their head. They also have two rows of upper teeth. A row of horny plates runs along their back. These plates rise straight up when tuataras are frightened.

Tuataras are found only on some islands near New Zealand. They live in burrows made by seabirds. They can dig their own burrows but seem to prefer ones already made. Tuataras lay hard-shelled eggs that take 15 months to hatch.

Think and Learn

1. Tuataras lived during the time of the first _____ .

2. How many eyes do tuataras have? _____

3. Where are tuataras found? _____

_____

4. How long do tuatara eggs take to hatch? _____

Reptiles

Crocodile

Crocodiles (KRAHK uh dighlz) are the largest reptiles. They can reach 7.5 metres in length. Of all the animals belonging to the crocodile group, crocodiles are the most dangerous. Crocodiles have long narrow snouts. When their mouths are closed, their lower teeth show.

Crocodiles are found in the tropical parts of the world. They catch fish and small land animals for food. Like alligators, crocodiles are most active at night. During the day, they rest in the sun. Often a crocodile lies with its mouth open to help cool its body. When its mouth is open, the crocodile lets birds go in it and peck out leftover pieces of food.

Think and Learn

1. Crocodiles are the _____ reptiles.

2. Describe the shape of a crocodile's snout._____
   _____

3. What do crocodiles eat? _____

4. How does a crocodile cool its body? _____
   _____

Alligator

Alligators (AL ih gay terz) belong to the crocodile group of reptiles. Although they are members of this group, alligators and crocodiles are two different animals. Alligators have wide rounded snouts. When their mouths are closed, their lower teeth are inside. Alligators are smaller than crocodiles. They grow up to 3.5 metres long.

Alligators are found in southeastern United States and in parts of China. They eat frogs, fish, snakes, turtles and small mammals. Like crocodiles, alligators are good swimmers. Alligators move through the water by moving their tails from side to side. Female alligators lay as many as 50 eggs and guard the eggs until they hatch. Mother alligators care for their young for up to a year.

Think and Learn

1. Alligators belong to the _____ group of reptiles.

2. Describe the shape of an alligator's snout. _____
_____

3. How do alligators move through water?_____
_____

4. Mother alligators care for their young for up to a _____.

Compare and Contrast

Read about crocodiles and alligators. Then, use the Venn diagram and the facts you have learned to compare and contrast these two animals.

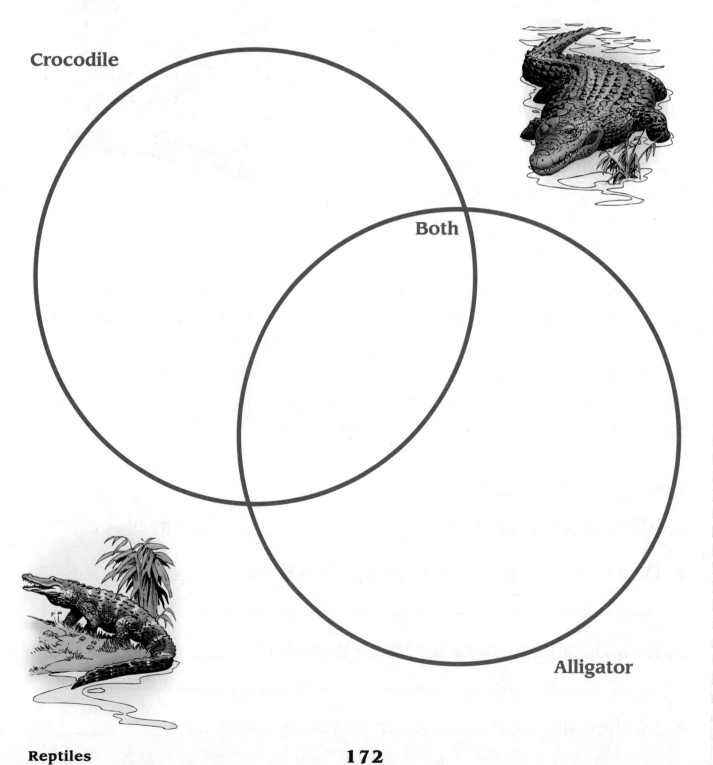

Crocodile

Both

Alligator

Lizard

Lizards and snakes make up the largest group of reptiles. Most lizards have four legs with five clawed toes on each leg. Some lizards do not have legs. Lizards have movable eyelids and good eyesight. They do not have ears, but they have ear openings on the sides of their head. Lizards use their tongue for smelling.

Lizards are found in all parts of the world, except the North and South poles. Most lizards eat insects and small mammals. Some lizards eat plants. Lizards protect themselves by blending in with their surroundings, making their bodies look bigger, or making hissing sounds. Some lizards have tails that break off and keep wiggling, while the lizard escapes. Later, it grows a new tail.

Think and Learn

1. Lizards have _____ eyelids.

2. What do lizards use their tongues for? _____

3. What do most lizards eat? _____

_____

4. Some lizards protect themselves by losing their _____.

Chameleon

Chameleons (kuh MEEL yuhnz) are lizards that can change their body colour to match their surroundings. They can blend in so well that they actually look invisible! Chameleon bodies are flat on the sides. Their eyes are large and bulging. Each eye works separately from the other. They can look in different directions at the same time.

Chameleons are slow-moving lizards. They do not chase down their food. Instead, a chameleon sits quietly and waits for food to come to it. When a chameleon sees an insect, it shoots out its sticky tongue and catches the insect. Chameleons are found only in Africa and Madagascar.

Think and Learn

1. What changes on chameleons? _____

2. How can chameleons look in different directions at the same time? _____

3. Chameleons catch insects with their sticky _____.

4. Where are chameleons found? _____

Snake

Snakes are reptiles that have long bodies and no legs. Snakes move by sliding on their belly. Snakes cannot shut their eyes, because they do not have eyelids. Their eyes are covered with clear scales. Snakes do not have ear slits. Instead, they "hear" sounds by feeling the movement of air around them. Snakes have a long forked tongue that helps them smell.

Snakes eat other animals. The size of animal they can eat depends on the size of their mouth. A snake swallows its food whole. Snakes do not eat often. Most snakes eat only a few times a year. Snakes, like all other reptiles, lay eggs or give birth to live young. They do not take care of their young.

Think and Learn

1. How do snakes move? _____

2. What covers a snake's eyes?_____

3. Snakes use their long, forked _____ to help them smell.

4. How often do most snakes eat?_____

_____

Garter Snake

Garter snakes are harmless snakes found in Central and North America. Female garter snakes grow 50 to 75 centimetres long. Males are slightly smaller. Garter snakes living in different areas look different from each other. They come in many different colours. However, most garter snakes have three stripes running along their body.

Garter snakes are most active in the spring and autumn. That is when most people see them in their yards or in parks. Garter snakes catch and eat small animals, such as frogs, salamanders and fish. Garter snakes do not lay eggs. Instead, they give birth to live young.

Think and Learn

1. Garter snakes are _____ snakes.

2. What feature do most garter snakes have? _____
_____

3. When are garter snakes most active? _____

4. Garter snakes do not lay _____.

Rattlesnake

Rattlesnakes are poisonous snakes with "rattles" on their tails. The rattles are pieces of bone that are loosely connected. Each time a rattlesnake grows enough to shed its skin, a new section of the rattle forms. Many people believe that a rattlesnake will shake its rattle before striking. That is not always true.

Rattlesnakes are most commonly found in the desert areas of the United States and in the mountains of Mexico. Rattlesnakes eat small animals. They catch animals by pouncing on them and biting them. The poison in their fangs, or long front teeth, kills the animal. All rattlesnakes give birth to live babies. Young rattlesnakes can take care of themselves right away.

Think and Learn

1. Where are rattlesnakes found?_____

   _____

2. Their rattles are pieces of loosely connected _____.

3. What do rattlesnakes eat? _____

4. Rattlesnakes have _____ in their fangs.

Turtle

Turtles are reptiles with shells. Turtle shells are made of either horny plates or tough leathery skin. The shell protects the turtle's body. Many turtles can pull their legs and head inside their shell. Turtles do not have teeth. They cut their food with their hard sharp beak. They also breathe air with lungs. All turtles lay eggs and bury them in soil. The warmth from the sun helps the eggs hatch.

Turtles are found all over the world. Some turtles spend most of their time in water. Other turtles spend some time both in the water and on land. There are also turtles that live only on land. Turtles eat both plants and animals.

Think and Learn

1. Turtles are reptiles with _____.

2. How do turtles cut their food? _____

   _____

3. All turtles lay _____.

4. What do turtles eat? _____

Sea Turtle

Sea turtles are turtles that live in the ocean. Sea turtles are very large. They range in size from 0.6 to 2.4 metres and weigh from 45 to 816 kilograms. Instead of claws, sea turtles have flippers to help them swim easily through water. Sea turtles have flat shells instead of rounded shells like land turtles. Flat shells also help them move more easily through water.

Sea turtles are found in warm oceans throughout the world. They eat fish, shrimp, crabs, jellyfish and plants. Sea turtles dig holes and lay their eggs on sandy beaches. The eggs lay buried in the sand for a couple of months before they hatch. When the eggs hatch, the babies dig out of the sand and head for the ocean.

Think and Learn

1. Flippers and _____ shells help sea turtles move in the water.

2. Where are sea turtles found? _____

3. Sea turtles eat fish, shrimp, crabs, jellyfish and _____.

4. Sea turtles lay their eggs on sandy _____.

Reptile Puzzle

Fill in the spaces of the puzzle with the correct animal name.

| R | A | T | T | L | E | S | N | A | K | E |

snake   tuatara   chameleon

turtle   alligator   sea turtle

lizard   crocodile   garter snake

ANIMALS THAT LIVE IN THE WATER

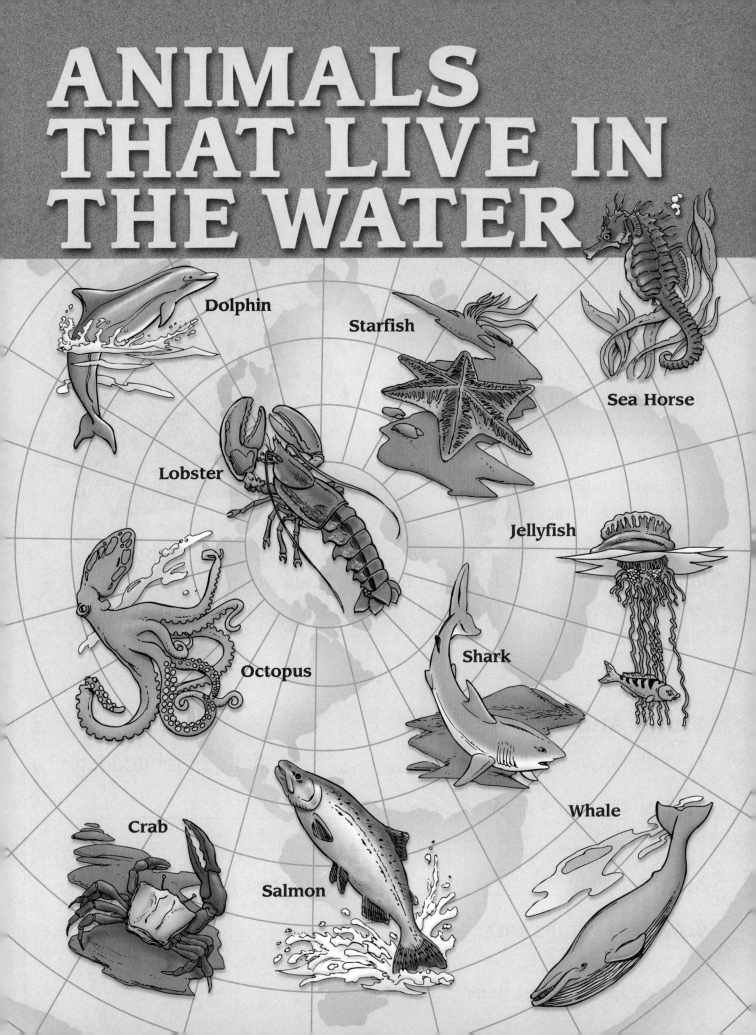

Dolphin

Starfish

Sea Horse

Lobster

Jellyfish

Octopus

Shark

Crab

Whale

Salmon

Crab

A crab is a sea animal covered by a hard shell. Crabs have five pairs of jointed legs. The first pair of legs has large claws. Crabs use their claws to attract mates, defend themselves and get food. On crabs that swim, the last pair of legs is shaped like flippers. On land, crabs often walk sideways on their last four pairs of legs. Crabs come in all sizes, from less than 3 centimetres long to 3.5 metres long.

Crabs are found in oceans all over the world. Some crabs live on land but must lay their eggs in the sea. Their young grow in the sea until they are adults. Then, they move to the land. Crabs eat both plants and animals.

Think and Learn

1. Crabs have _____ pairs of jointed legs.

2. How do crabs use their claws?_____

_____

3. Crabs walk _____ on their last four pairs of legs.

4. What do crabs eat? _____

Dolphin

Dolphins (DAHL fihnz) are small toothed whales that live in the ocean. They are mammals, not fish. A mammal is an animal whose young feed on its mother's milk. Dolphins also breathe with lungs, not gills like fish. They must come to the surface of the water to breathe. Dolphins have bodies well suited for living in water. They have long narrow bodies, flippers and fins on their backs.

Dolphins are social animals.
They live together in groups.
They also "talk" to each other using many different sounds. Dolphins are very smart animals. Many have been trained by humans to do different jobs and to entertain people. Dolphins mainly eat fish and squid.

Think and Learn

1. Dolphins are _____ , not fish.

2. Dolphins breathe with _____.

3. How are dolphin bodies suited for living in water?

_____

4. What do dolphins eat?_____

Dot-to-Dot

Connect the dots. Colour the picture.

DOLPHINS

Pull-Out Storybook

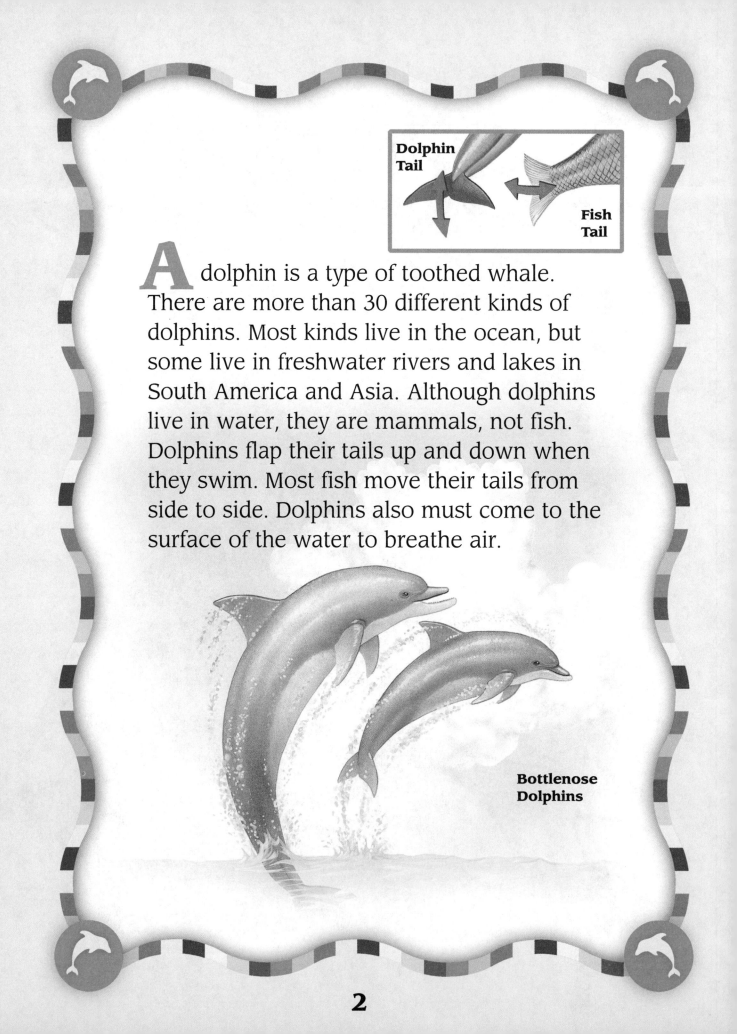

Dolphin Tail

Fish Tail

A dolphin is a type of toothed whale. There are more than 30 different kinds of dolphins. Most kinds live in the ocean, but some live in freshwater rivers and lakes in South America and Asia. Although dolphins live in water, they are mammals, not fish. Dolphins flap their tails up and down when they swim. Most fish move their tails from side to side. Dolphins also must come to the surface of the water to breathe air.

Bottlenose Dolphins

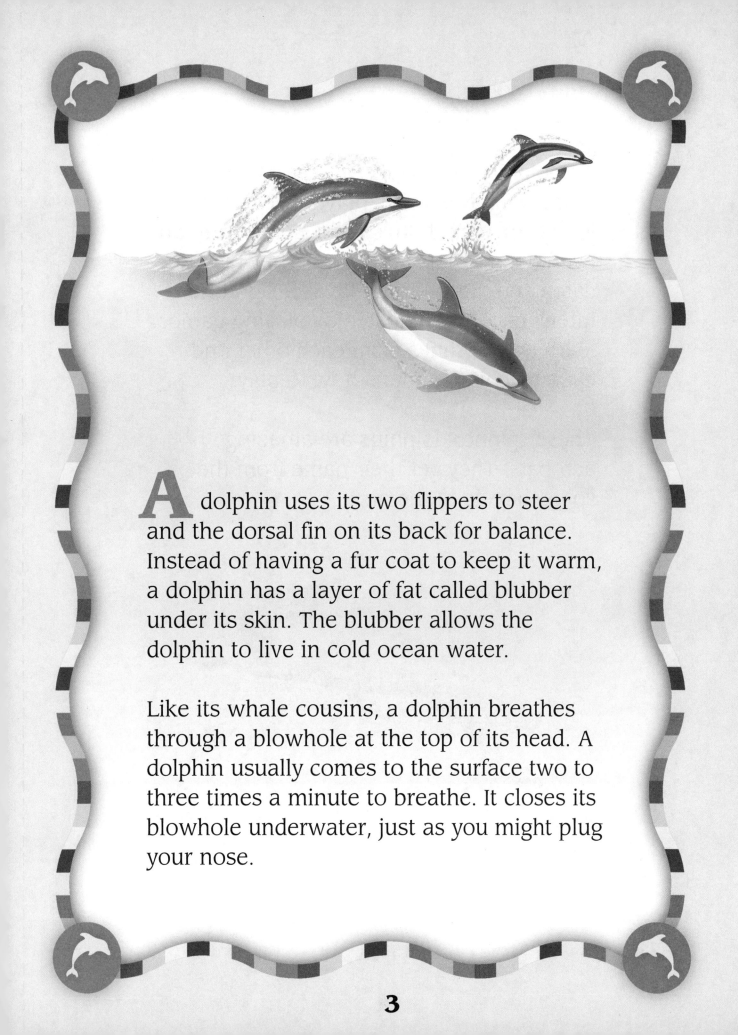

A dolphin uses its two flippers to steer and the dorsal fin on its back for balance. Instead of having a fur coat to keep it warm, a dolphin has a layer of fat called blubber under its skin. The blubber allows the dolphin to live in cold ocean water.

Like its whale cousins, a dolphin breathes through a blowhole at the top of its head. A dolphin usually comes to the surface two to three times a minute to breathe. It closes its blowhole underwater, just as you might plug your nose.

If dolphins could talk, their most common words might be "Let's play!" They race, leap, surf, spin, flop, splash, somersault and even do back flips in the air. They play tag, catch and tug-of-war. Play is a sign of intelligence. Dolphins enjoy playing games, learning new ones from each other and even teaching humans how to play.

These spinner dolphins are amazing acrobats. They get their name from the spins they do in the air.

Dolphins are social animals that live in groups called pods or schools. Living in groups helps dolphins hunt for food and protect themselves from enemies, like sharks. And of course, it's more fun to play with a buddy. Dolphins "talk" to each other by making many different sounds. They also slap their tails on the water.

Dolphins will help another dolphin that is sick or hurt. They sometimes lift the dolphin in need to the surface so it can breathe.

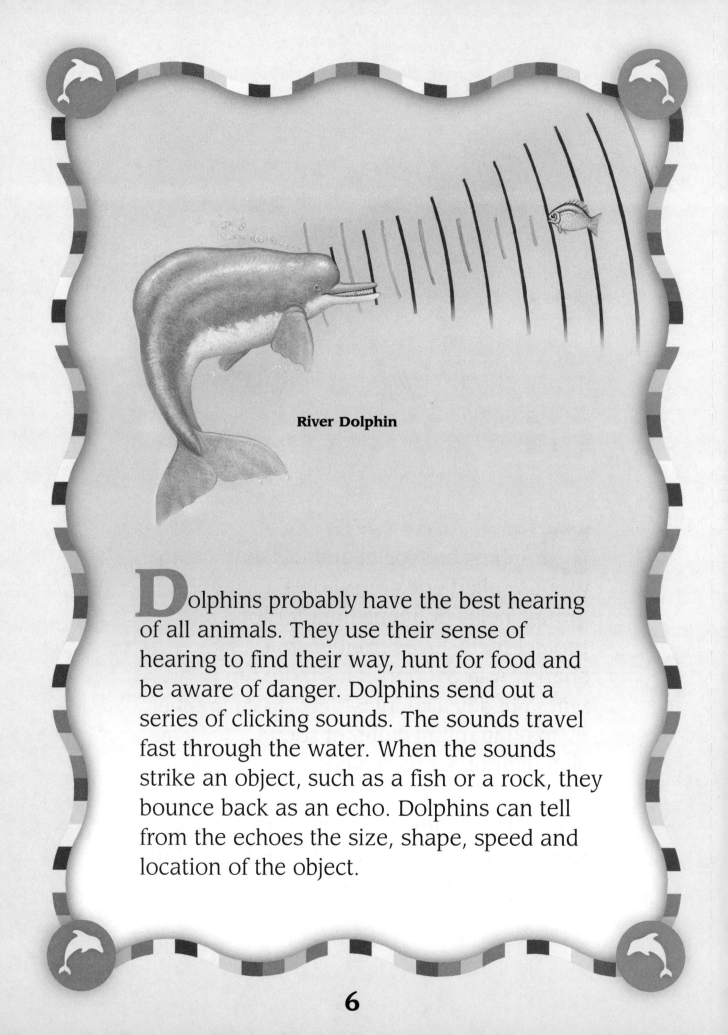

River Dolphin

Dolphins probably have the best hearing of all animals. They use their sense of hearing to find their way, hunt for food and be aware of danger. Dolphins send out a series of clicking sounds. The sounds travel fast through the water. When the sounds strike an object, such as a fish or a rock, they bounce back as an echo. Dolphins can tell from the echoes the size, shape, speed and location of the object.

Mother dolphins are very good parents. A baby dolphin grows inside its mother for about 1 year. The mother dolphin, often with the help of another female dolphin, guides her newborn calf up to the surface for air. A baby dolphin can swim quite well within 30 minutes of birth.

A mother dolphin is very protective of her baby. When the calf is about 6 months old, it begins to eat fish scraps left by adults. Later, its mother teaches it to hunt. Dolphin calves stay with their mothers for up to 3 years.

Dolphins face many dangers throughout the world. Some are accidentally caught in nets set by fishermen searching for tuna and other fish. Other dolphins are hunted as food. In the past 30 years, efforts have increased to protect dolphins and their habitats.

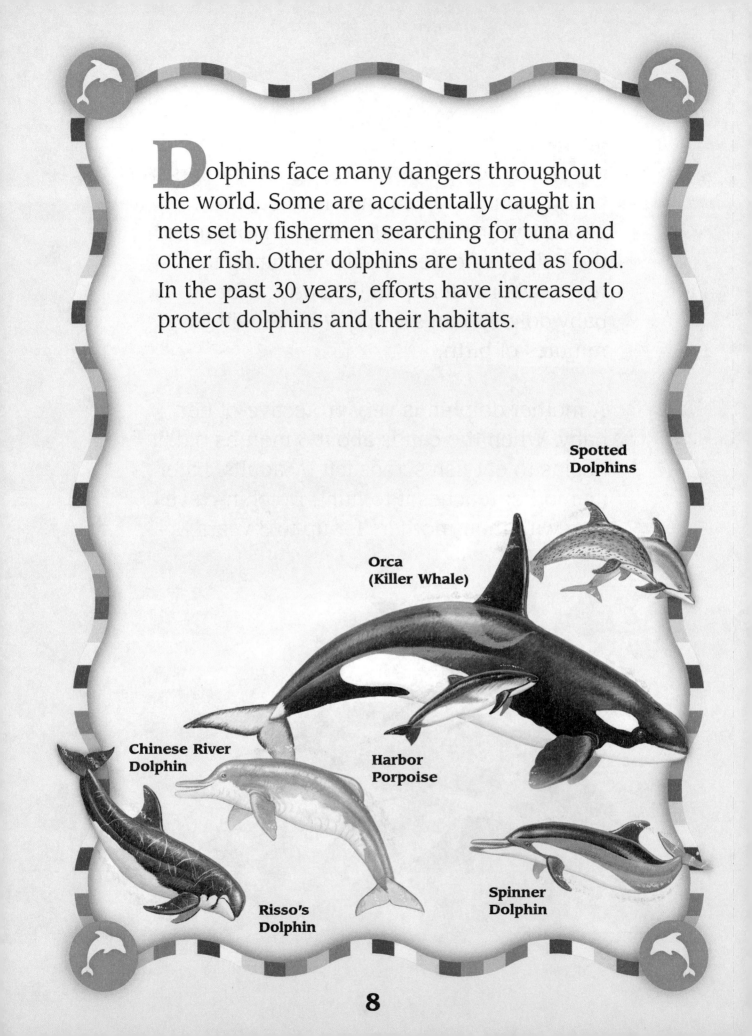

Spotted Dolphins

Orca (Killer Whale)

Chinese River Dolphin

Harbor Porpoise

Risso's Dolphin

Spinner Dolphin

Jellyfish

Jellyfish are soft-bodied animals that live in oceans. Jellyfish get their name from the stiff, jellylike material that makes up their body. Jellyfish have no bones. Their body is shaped like an open umbrella. Their mouth hangs down from the center of their body. Long tentacles hang down around the outside of their body. These tentacles are poisonous.

Jellyfish swim by opening and closing their body. This action pushes the jellyfish through the water. To get food, jellyfish first swim upward. Then, as they float down to the bottom, they catch fish and other small animals by stinging them with their poisonous tentacles.

Think and Learn

1. What are jellyfish named for? _____

   _____

2. What are jellyfish shaped liked?_____

3. Jellyfish have_____ tentacles.

4. How do jellyfish swim? _____

   _____

Animals That Live in the Water

Lobster

Lobsters (LAHB sterz) are sea animals that are related to crabs. Like crabs, lobsters have hard shells and five pairs of jointed legs. The first pair of legs has claws. Lobsters use their claws to grab food and tear it apart. Lobsters have long bodies divided into three parts—the head, the thorax or middle, and the abdomen or tail.

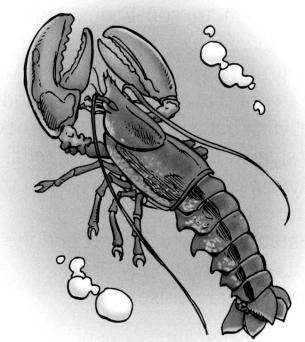

Lobsters live on the ocean floor near the shore. They usually hide in holes or under rocks and wave their antennae outside. Lobsters have eyes on the ends of the stalks near their antennae. When a lobster senses that an animal is passing by, it pounces on the animal and grabs it with its claws. Besides small animals, lobsters also eat plants.

Think and Learn

1. Lobsters are related to _____.

2. How do lobsters use their claws? _____
_____

3. Lobster bodies are divided into _____ parts.

4. Where do lobsters live?_____

Octopus

An octopus (AHK tuh puhs) is a sea animal with a soft body and eight arms. These arms are called tentacles. The bottom sides of the tentacles are lined with suckers. Suckers are round and help octopuses stick to rocks. An octopus uses its arms and suckers to catch food and to move along the ocean floor.

Octopuses are found in oceans all over the world. They eat crabs, lobsters, clams and snails. Many other sea animals eat octopuses. An octopus defends itself by squirting a dark cloud to hide itself. It can also change colours to either scare an enemy or help the octopus blend in with its surroundings. An octopus can shoot out a jet of water from its body and move quickly away.

Think and Learn

1. An octopus has _____ tentacles.

2. How does an octopus use its tentacles? _____
_____

3. What do octopuses eat? _____
_____

4. Octopuses can change_____ to scare away enemies.

Animals That Live in the Water

Salmon

Salmon are large fish that are born in freshwater streams. After birth, the young fish swim to the saltwater ocean. Some kinds of salmon go to the ocean right away. Other kinds stay in the streams for several years. Salmon live most of their lives in the ocean. When salmon are ready to lay eggs, they swim back to the freshwater stream where they were born. The return trip is not easy. Salmon must swim against strong river currents and jump up waterfalls.

Salmon are found in the Pacific and Atlantic oceans. They eat shrimp, squid and small fish. When they return to freshwater rivers and streams to lay eggs, they do not eat. They live off the fat that is stored in their bodies.

Think and Learn

1. Where are salmon born? _____

2. Where do salmon live most of their lives?_____

3. Why is the return trip to lay eggs not easy?_____

_____

4. What do salmon living in the ocean eat? _____

_____

Sea Horse

A sea horse is a small fish with a head that looks like a horse's head. Its body is only about 12 centimetres long. Sea horses have long tails. They use their tails to hold onto plants. Their spiny coat protects them like armor. Sea horses are not strong swimmers. They swim in an upright, or "standing up," position. They move through the water by moving their dorsal, or back, fin back and forth.

Sea horses are found in shallow ocean water in warm climates. They feed by sucking in small animals through their long snout. Female sea horses lay eggs in a pouch on the male sea horse's body. The male sea horse carries the eggs until they hatch.

Think and Learn

1. A sea horse is a small _____.

2. How do sea horses use their tails? _____

3. Sea horses swim in an _____ position.

4. Where do female sea horses lay eggs? _____

_____

Shark

Sharks are fish that feed on other animals. Unlike most fish, sharks do not have bones. Instead, their bodies are supported with cartilage (KART l ij). Cartilage is a tough, bendable material. You have cartilage at the tip of your nose. Most sharks have mouths on the bottom side of their head. Some kinds of sharks have grinding teeth. Others have tearing teeth.

Sharks come in all sizes. Some are as small as 15 centimetres long. Others can grow to 12 metres long. Sharks are found in all parts of oceans. They are very good swimmers. Their long narrow bodies help them move easily through water. Their curved tails help them swim fast.

Think and Learn

1. Sharks are _____ that feed on other animals.

2. Sharks have _____ instead of bones.

3. Where are sharks found? _____

4. How do curved tails help sharks? _____

_____

Starfish

Starfish are sea animals with spines on their skin. Starfish are sometimes called sea stars because they are shaped like stars. Many starfish have five "arms" pointing out from their body. However, some starfish have as many as 40 arms. Starfish have rows of tiny tube-shaped feet along their arms. These tube feet help starfish move and get food.

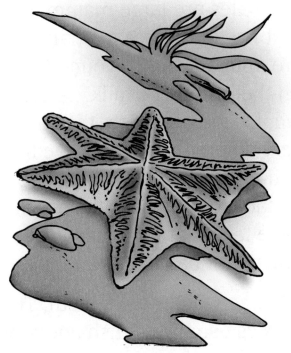

Starfish are found in oceans all over the world. They eat animals with shells, such as clams and oysters. A starfish opens up a shell by attaching its tube feet to both halves of the shell. Then, it pulls apart the shell and pushes its stomach through the opening in the shell.

Think and Learn

1. Starfish have _____ on their skin.

2. Starfish have a body shaped liked a _____.

3. How do starfish use their tube feet?_____

_____

4. What do starfish eat? _____

_____

Whale

Whales are large mammals that live in the ocean. Mammals are animals whose young feed on their mother's milk. Although whales look like fish, they are very different. Whales have lungs and must come to the water's surface to breathe. Whales also have tails that move up and down, not back and forth.

Some whales have teeth. These whales usually eat fish and other animals. Other whales do not have teeth. These whales feed on tiny plants and animals that float in the water. Whales are social animals that live in groups. Whales "talk" to each other by making many different sounds. Whales have a keen sense of hearing and can hear sounds from far away.

Think and Learn

1. Whales are_____ that live in the ocean.

2. How are whales different from fish? _____
_____

3. What do whales without teeth eat? _____
_____

4. Whales have a keen sense of _____.

WHALES

Pull-Out Storybook

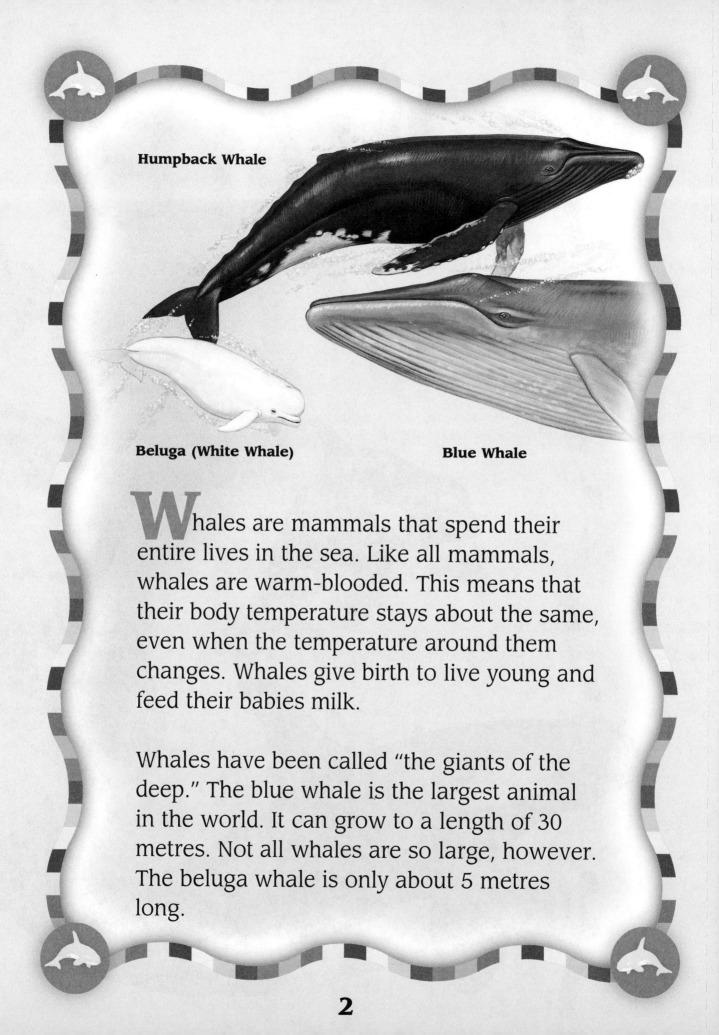

Humpback Whale

Beluga (White Whale)

Blue Whale

Whales are mammals that spend their entire lives in the sea. Like all mammals, whales are warm-blooded. This means that their body temperature stays about the same, even when the temperature around them changes. Whales give birth to live young and feed their babies milk.

Whales have been called "the giants of the deep." The blue whale is the largest animal in the world. It can grow to a length of 30 metres. Not all whales are so large, however. The beluga whale is only about 5 metres long.

At first glance, whales look a lot like fish. Both have tails and fins. But there are some differences between the two. Whales have smooth firm skin. Fish have scales. Whales have tails, called flukes, that they move up and down when they swim. Fish have tails that they swing from side to side. Whales breathe with lungs and must hold their breath underwater. They come to the water's surface to breathe in fresh air. Fish, on the other hand, breathe underwater by using gills.

Pigmy Sperm Whale

Bluefin Tuna

Whales are divided into two groups—toothed whales and baleen whales. Toothed whales have teeth. These whales feed on fish. Baleen (buh LEEN) whales do not have teeth. Instead, they have long fringed plates, called baleen, that hang down from the roof of their mouth. The baleen traps tiny plants and animals, called plankton.

The killer whale, or orca, is a toothed whale.

The finback whale is a baleen whale.

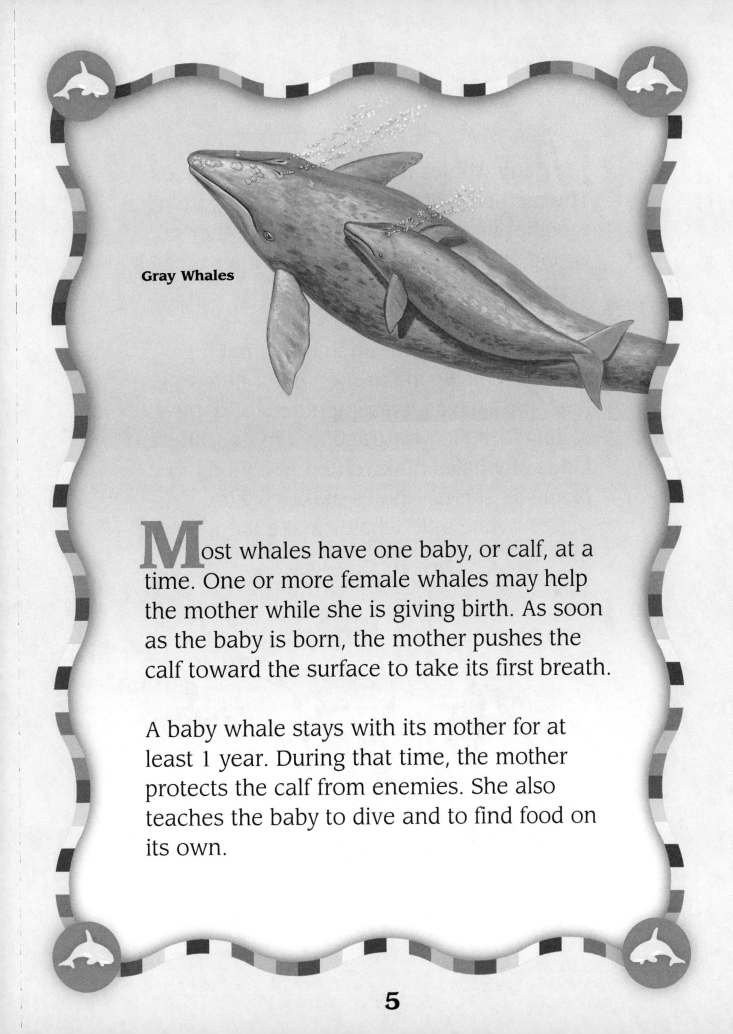

Gray Whales

Most whales have one baby, or calf, at a time. One or more female whales may help the mother while she is giving birth. As soon as the baby is born, the mother pushes the calf toward the surface to take its first breath.

A baby whale stays with its mother for at least 1 year. During that time, the mother protects the calf from enemies. She also teaches the baby to dive and to find food on its own.

Many whales live in groups called pods. The members of a pod feed together, travel together and help look after each other's young. If a whale gets sick, the other whales in the pod help it.

Whales "talk" to one another by making sounds. Whales make sounds for different reasons, such as warning others of danger, calling for help or attracting a mate. Different kinds of whales make different sounds. For example, sperm whales make clicking noises, while blue whales make loud, moaning sounds.

A pod may have as many as 40 or more members.

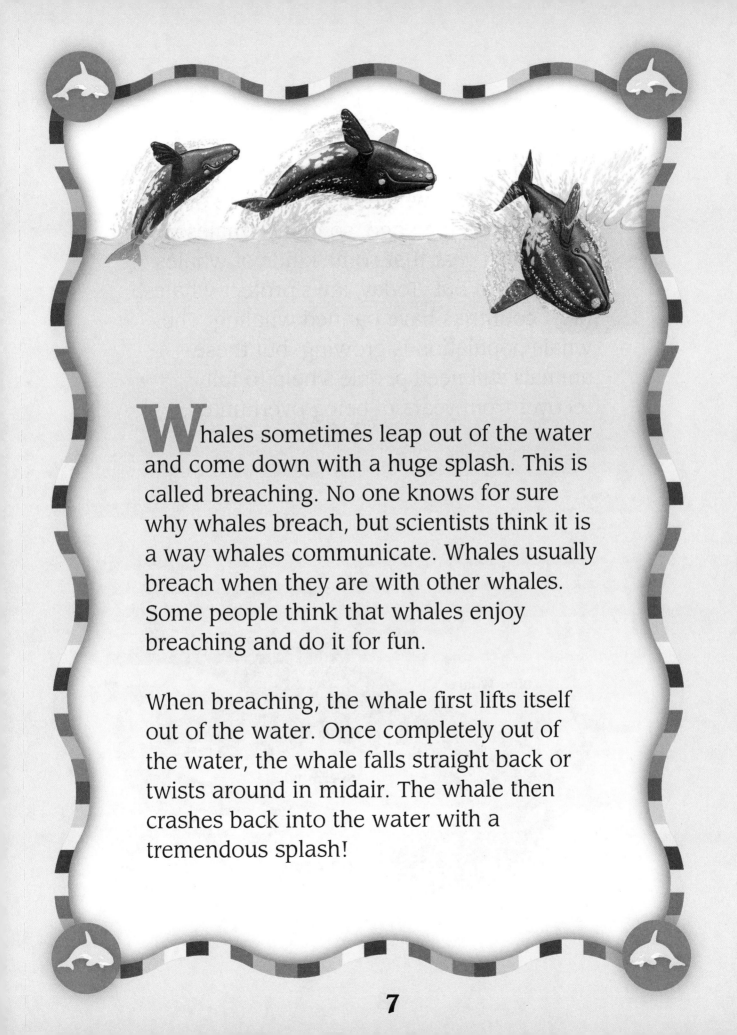

Whales sometimes leap out of the water and come down with a huge splash. This is called breaching. No one knows for sure why whales breach, but scientists think it is a way whales communicate. Whales usually breach when they are with other whales. Some people think that whales enjoy breaching and do it for fun.

When breaching, the whale first lifts itself out of the water. Once completely out of the water, the whale falls straight back or twists around in midair. The whale then crashes back into the water with a tremendous splash!

Whales are found in every ocean, but there are fewer whales now because of whaling. Not long ago, so many whales were killed each year that some kinds of whales almost died out. Today, laws protect whales. Most countries have banned whaling. The whale population is growing, but these animals still need people's help to fully recover from years of being overhunted.

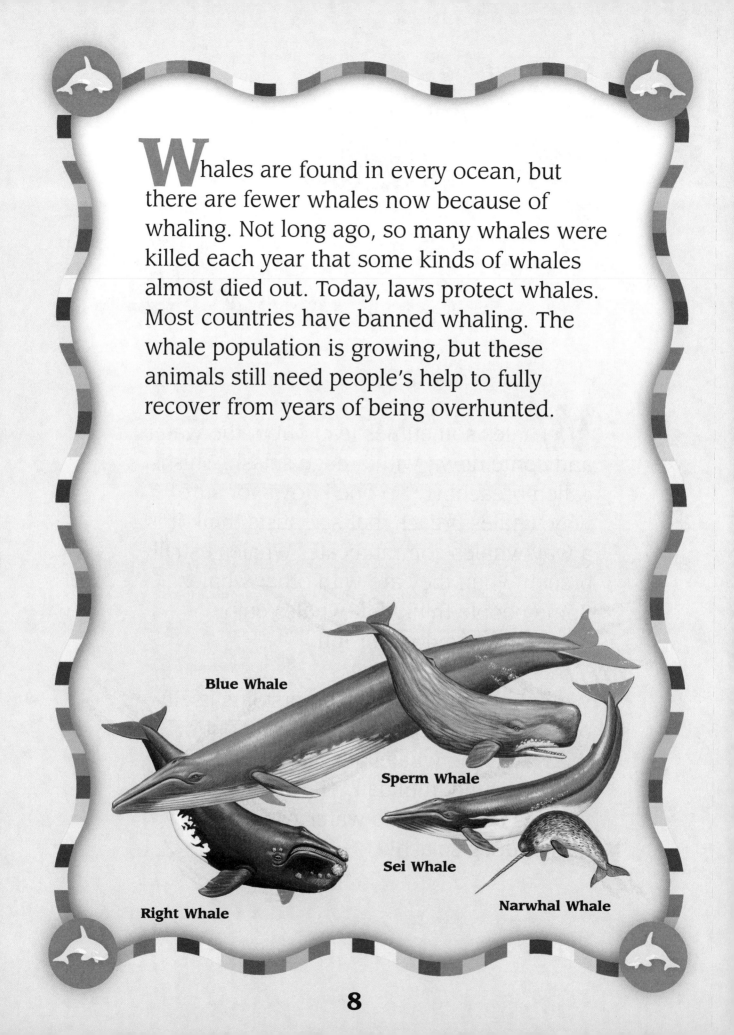

Blue Whale

Sperm Whale

Sei Whale

Right Whale

Narwhal Whale

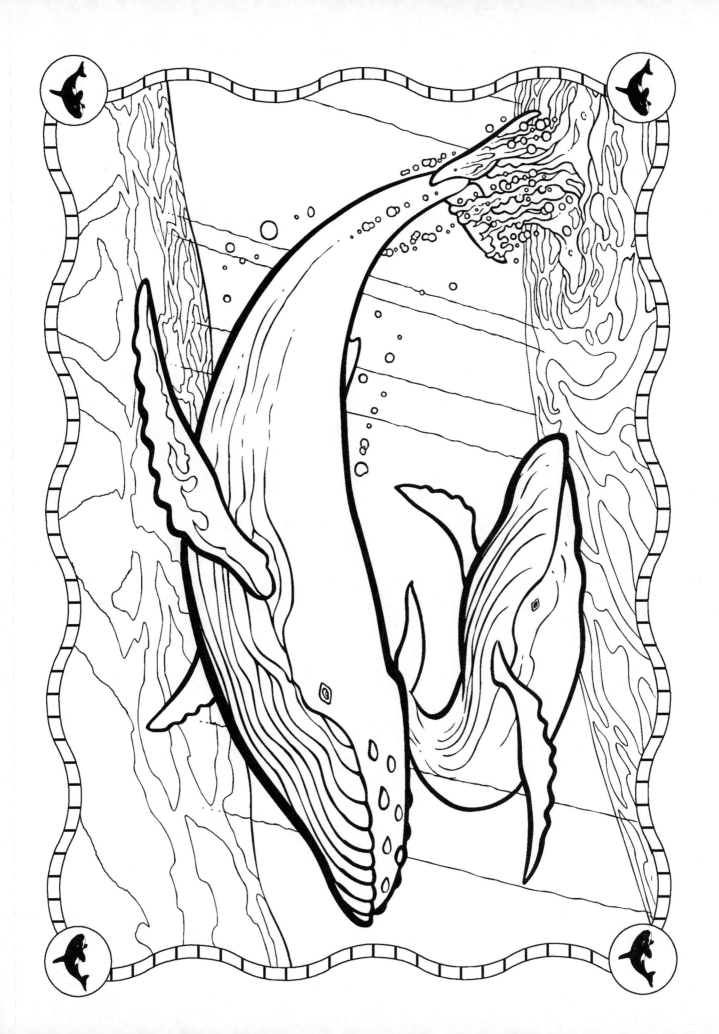

Word Search

Let's go on a whale watch! Maybe you will see the largest animal on Earth, the blue whale. Find the whales and whale words in the puzzle. They are written **across** and **down**.

```
B L U E S B R S T F O G A P M P E B
A H U M P B A C K I R N N Y I S E L
L C P L E A R S E N C D B A N N K U
E U O M R B E L U G A L E U K G R B
E P D O M F B B O W H E A D E A S B
N A R W H A L E K Z B L O W H O L E
M A R E L R A K I L L E R T M E W R
```

blue	baleen	bowhead	humpback
killer	blubber	sperm	blowhole
minke	beluga	narwhal	orca
fin	pod		

Animals That Live in the Water

Hidden Pictures

Find the ocean animals hidden in the picture. Colour the picture.

FARM
ANIMALS

Chicken

Duck

Cow

Horse

Pig

Sheep

Goat

Duck

Ducks are birds that spend part of the time in water. Their webbed feet act as paddles to move them easily through the water. Most ducks get their food from water or from the areas around water. Some ducks eat fish. Others eat water plants and small water animals. Ducks keep dry by oiling their top feathers with oil from a special gland

near their tail. They have a layer of soft fluffy feathers, called down, under the top feathers. Down keeps the duck warm.

Farmers raise ducks for their feathers, eggs and meat. Duck feathers are used to stuff pillows and make winter coats. Ducks raised on farms do not get their food from water. The farmer feeds them a kind of food made just for ducks.

Think and Learn

1. What helps ducks move through water?_____

2. Most ducks get their food from_____.

3. What is down? _____

_____

4. Farmers raise ducks for feathers, eggs and _____.

Pig

Pigs are farm animals with short legs and a long round body. Their body is covered with short bristles. Pigs cannot sweat to cool their body in hot weather. Instead, they lie in the mud during hot weather to cool off. Pigs have a sharp sense of smell but poor eyesight. The end of their flat snout is very sensitive to touch. Pigs use their snout for finding and digging up food.

Farmers all over the world raise pigs. Pigs are raised for their meat, which is called pork. Many other products, such as leather, glue, soap, fertilizer and medicines, are made from other parts of the pig. Farmers feed pigs corn and other grains. Pigs also eat "pig food" made with meat scraps, milk, peanuts, soybeans and other foods.

Think and Learn

1. How do pigs cool themselves?_____

2. Pigs use their_____ for finding and digging up food.

3. Pigs are raised for their meat, which is called_____.

4. What are some other products made from parts of the pig?

_____

Horse

The horse is a very useful animal. Long ago, people used horses to go places and move things. Now, many people use horses for fun. Some people, however, still use horses to herd cattle and sheep. Horses are built for running. They have long legs and strong feet. Their wide nostrils bring a lot of air into the lungs. They also have sharp senses of sight, hearing and smell.

Horses eat grass and grains. Their back teeth are wide and flat to grind grass into small pieces. These teeth never stop growing. Their front teeth are narrower and sharp. They help the horse bite off grass from the ground.

Think and Learn

1. What do people use horses for today?_____

_____

2. Horses are built for _____.

3. What do horses eat?_____

4. How do horses use their back teeth? _____

_____

HORSES

Pull-Out Storybook

There are more than 150 breeds of horses. These breeds are divided into three main groups, according to size. Light horses, such as quarter horses, are lean and athletic. Most weigh less than 590 kilograms. Heavy horses, such as shires, are the biggest and strongest horses. Some weigh more than 900 kilograms. Ponies, such as Shetland ponies, are the smallest horses. A pony stands less than 1.5 metres tall and usually weighs less than 362 kilograms.

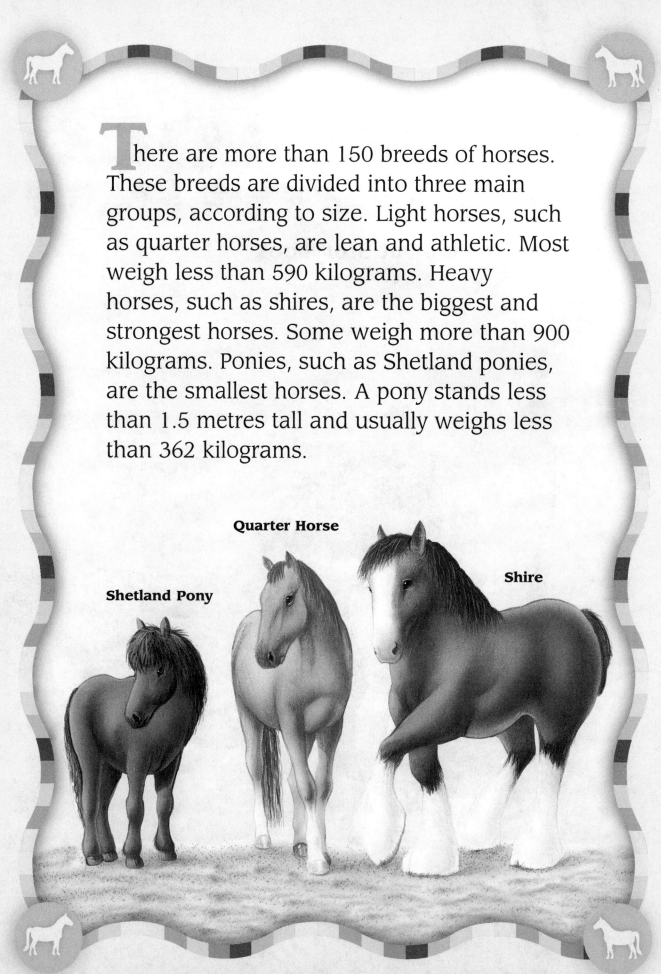

Shetland Pony

Quarter Horse

Shire

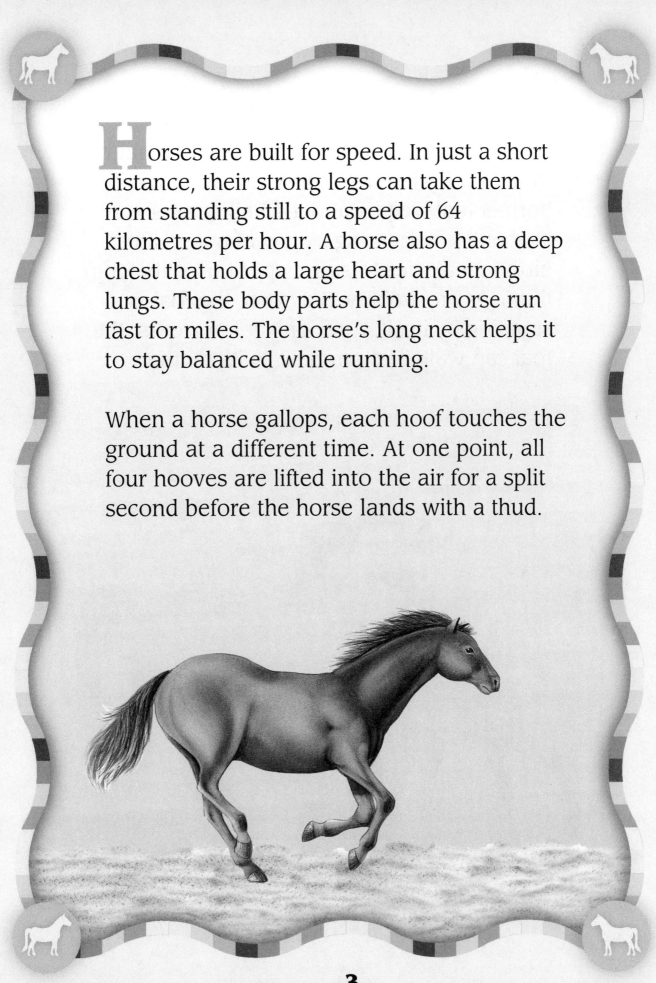

Horses are built for speed. In just a short distance, their strong legs can take them from standing still to a speed of 64 kilometres per hour. A horse also has a deep chest that holds a large heart and strong lungs. These body parts help the horse run fast for miles. The horse's long neck helps it to stay balanced while running.

When a horse gallops, each hoof touches the ground at a different time. At one point, all four hooves are lifted into the air for a split second before the horse lands with a thud.

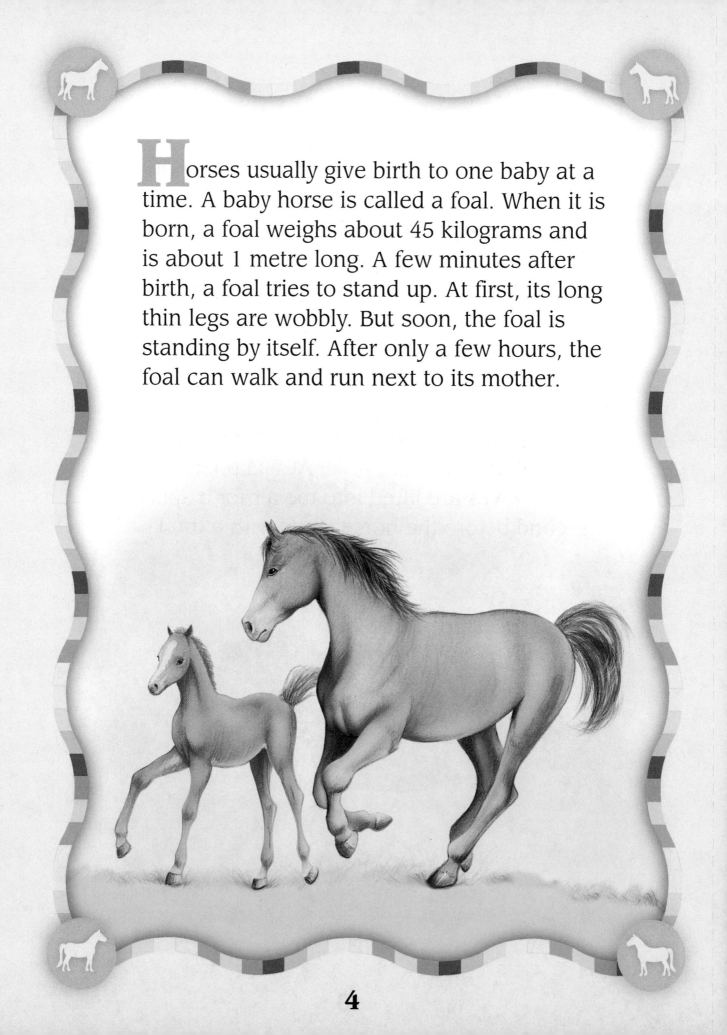

Horses usually give birth to one baby at a time. A baby horse is called a foal. When it is born, a foal weighs about 45 kilograms and is about 1 metre long. A few minutes after birth, a foal tries to stand up. At first, its long thin legs are wobbly. But soon, the foal is standing by itself. After only a few hours, the foal can walk and run next to its mother.

Foals are weaned, or separated, from their mother at about 6 months old. During this time, the young horses often are kept together to help them get used to being away from their mother.

Foals are very lively and playful. They love to jump, kick and run. They enjoy playing games or galloping across a field with other young horses.

Horses "talk" by making sounds and using body movements. Horses whinny or snort when they are excited. The position of a horse's ears tells how the horse is feeling. Ears laid back show fear or anger. Ears pricked up show friendliness. Horses often circle and sniff each other when they first meet.

curious

angry

afraid

friendly

Horses have been helping people for thousands of years. At one time, horses were the fastest way of traveling on land. People have ridden horses to hunt for food, charge into battle and round up livestock. Horses have also been used to haul heavy loads, pull carts and carriages and plow land. Today, people use horses for fun and sport.

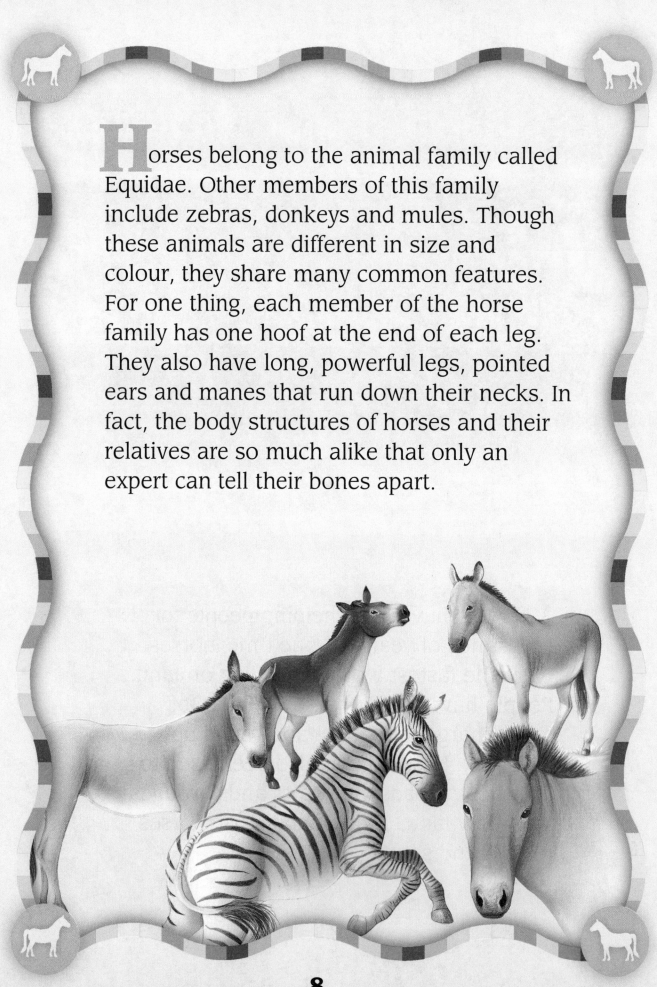

Horses belong to the animal family called Equidae. Other members of this family include zebras, donkeys and mules. Though these animals are different in size and colour, they share many common features. For one thing, each member of the horse family has one hoof at the end of each leg. They also have long, powerful legs, pointed ears and manes that run down their necks. In fact, the body structures of horses and their relatives are so much alike that only an expert can tell their bones apart.

Cow

Cows are large farm animals with split hooves. They have long tails that help swat insects away. Cows eat grass, hay, corn and soybeans. They break down their food in a stomach that has four parts. When breaking down food, cows move it from the stomach back into their mouth to chew it again. The food that moves back into their mouth is called a cud. Cows chew the cud and swallow it again. Then, the food moves through the other parts of the stomach.

Cows are one of the most important farm animals. Farmers raise cows for their milk and their meat, called beef. Cow's milk is used to make cheese, butter, yogourt and ice cream. Other parts of a cow's body are used to make leather, soap and glue.

Think and Learn

1. What do cows eat? _____

2. Cows have a stomach that has _____ parts.

3. Meat from cows is called _____.

4. What foods are made from cow's milk? _____

_____

Chicken

Chickens are ground birds. They have a plump body and rounded wings. Chickens can fly but for only short distances. They fly to get away from danger. Chickens have pointed beaks and strong claws that they use to scratch in the dirt and get food. Different kinds of chickens have feathers of different colours.

Chickens are raised on farms all over the world. Farmers raise chickens for their eggs and their meat, called poultry. Some chickens are raised only for their meat. Other chickens are raised just to lay eggs. Some farmers raise only baby chicks. They sell the chicks to other farmers who raise them for meat or eggs. Farmers feed chickens a mixture of ground corn, wheat and soybeans.

Think and Learn

1. Chickens fly for _____ distances.

2. How do chickens use their strong claws? _____
_____

3. What are chickens raised for?_____

4. What do farmers feed chickens? _____
_____

Sheep

Sheep are related to cows and goats. Like cows, sheep have a stomach that is divided into four parts. Sheep also have split hooves. Sheep do not need a lot of water to live. They like to eat grass and shrubs. When sheep eat, they bite off grass very close to the ground. If sheep are kept in the same pasture for a long time, they can kill all the grass.

Sheep are raised all over the world. However, the most sheep are raised in Australia and New Zealand. Sheep are very important animals because they give wool, milk and meat, called lamb or mutton. Wool is used to make clothing, blankets and rugs. Sheep's milk is used to make cheese.

Think and Learn

1. What other farm animals are sheep related to?

   _____

2. Sheep do not need a lot of _____ to live.

3. Where are the most sheep raised? _____

   _____

4. What are sheep raised for? _____

Goat

Goats are related to sheep and cows. Like sheep and cows, goats have split hooves and a four-part stomach. Goats have long shaggy hair. Most goats, both male and female, have a beard. Goats are known for eating almost anything. Because they have small mouths and flexible lips, goats can easily pick off only the healthful parts of a plant. They find food even in places where few plants can grow.

Farmers raise goats for their wool, milk and meat. People living in rocky, mountainous areas rely on goats for meat. People in the United States use goats mainly for wool and milk. Some people even keep goats as pets. Goat's milk is used for drinking and making cheese. The wool is used to make clothing and blankets.

Think and Learn

1. How are goats like sheep and cows?_____

_____

2. Goats can pick off only the _____ parts of a plant.

3. Goats are raised for_____.

4. Goat's milk is used for drinking and making _____.

FAVOURITE PETS

Cat

Rabbit

Guinea Pig

Toad

Frog

Dog

Dog

Dogs are popular pets throughout the world. Dogs have been bred through the years for certain jobs, such as guarding, hunting and herding. Some dogs have been bred just to be pets. Dogs come in all sizes, colours and personalities. When choosing a dog for a pet, the dog's qualities must fit in with the family's lifestyle.

Taking care of a dog is a big responsibility. Dogs need to be fed every day. They need clean, fresh water all the time and a warm, dry place to sleep. Dogs also need regular exercise, especially if they are big dogs. Dogs must be brushed and bathed regularly. Dogs also need medical check-ups every year. They must have vaccines and medicines to stay healthy.

Think and Learn

1. What jobs have dogs been bred for? _____

_____

2. Dogs should be fed _____.

3. Dogs need regular _____.

4. Every year, dogs need medical _____.

DOGS

Pull-Out Storybook

Irish Wolfhound

Saint Bernard

Chihuahua

Dogs were the first animals to be made into pets. The first pet dogs were wolves. Over the years, dogs have formed different characteristics from wolves. Now, there are more than 400 different breeds of dogs. These dog breeds have been divided into several main groups, such as herding dogs, sporting dogs, hounds, working dogs and toy dogs.

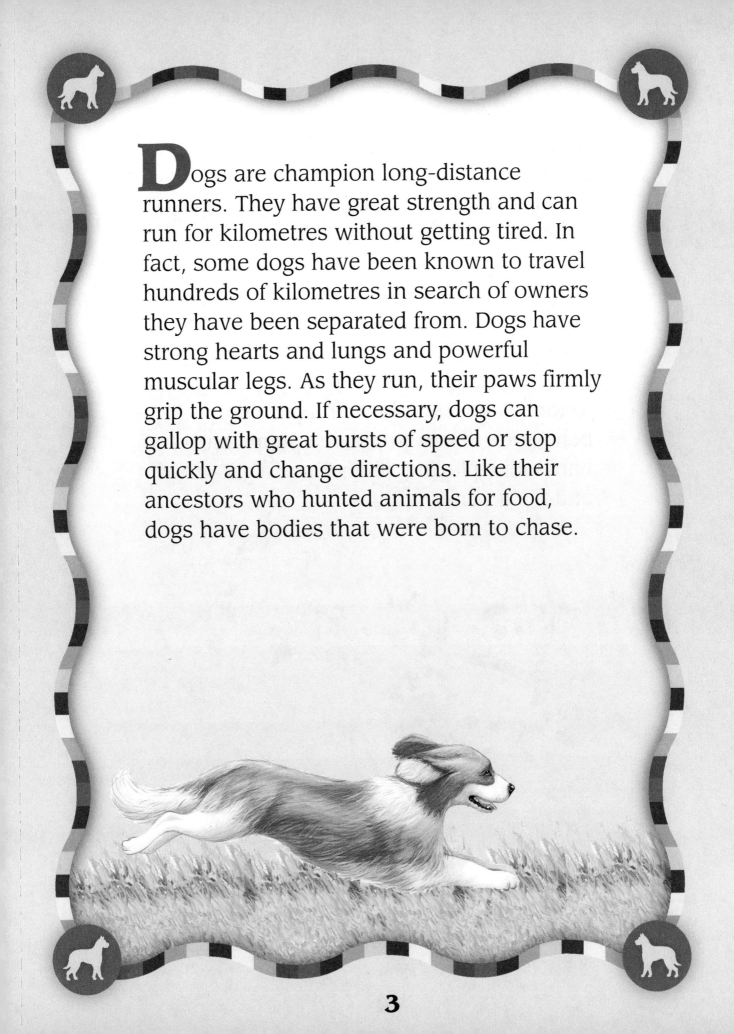

Dogs are champion long-distance runners. They have great strength and can run for kilometres without getting tired. In fact, some dogs have been known to travel hundreds of kilometres in search of owners they have been separated from. Dogs have strong hearts and lungs and powerful muscular legs. As they run, their paws firmly grip the ground. If necessary, dogs can gallop with great bursts of speed or stop quickly and change directions. Like their ancestors who hunted animals for food, dogs have bodies that were born to chase.

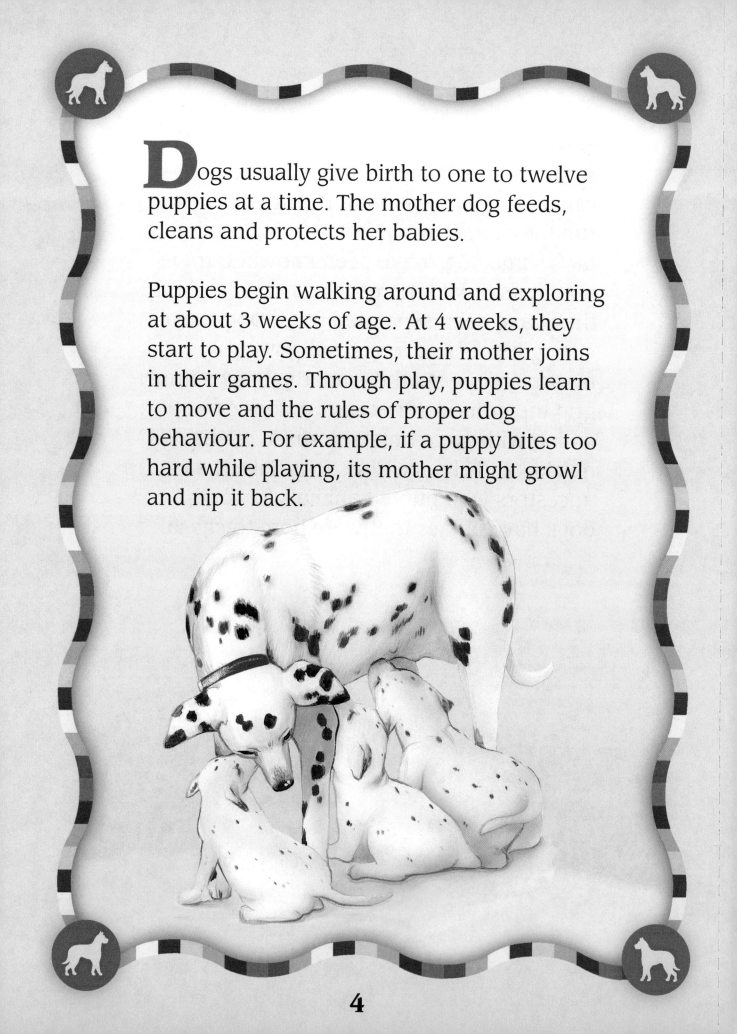

Dogs usually give birth to one to twelve puppies at a time. The mother dog feeds, cleans and protects her babies.

Puppies begin walking around and exploring at about 3 weeks of age. At 4 weeks, they start to play. Sometimes, their mother joins in their games. Through play, puppies learn to move and the rules of proper dog behaviour. For example, if a puppy bites too hard while playing, its mother might growl and nip it back.

Dogs enjoy playing at any age. When they are young, play is an important part of their growth. Puppies who have played with other dogs and with people are more likely to become healthy adult dogs. Adult dogs need daily exercise to stay fit and healthy. Play also strengthens the bond between the dog and its owner.

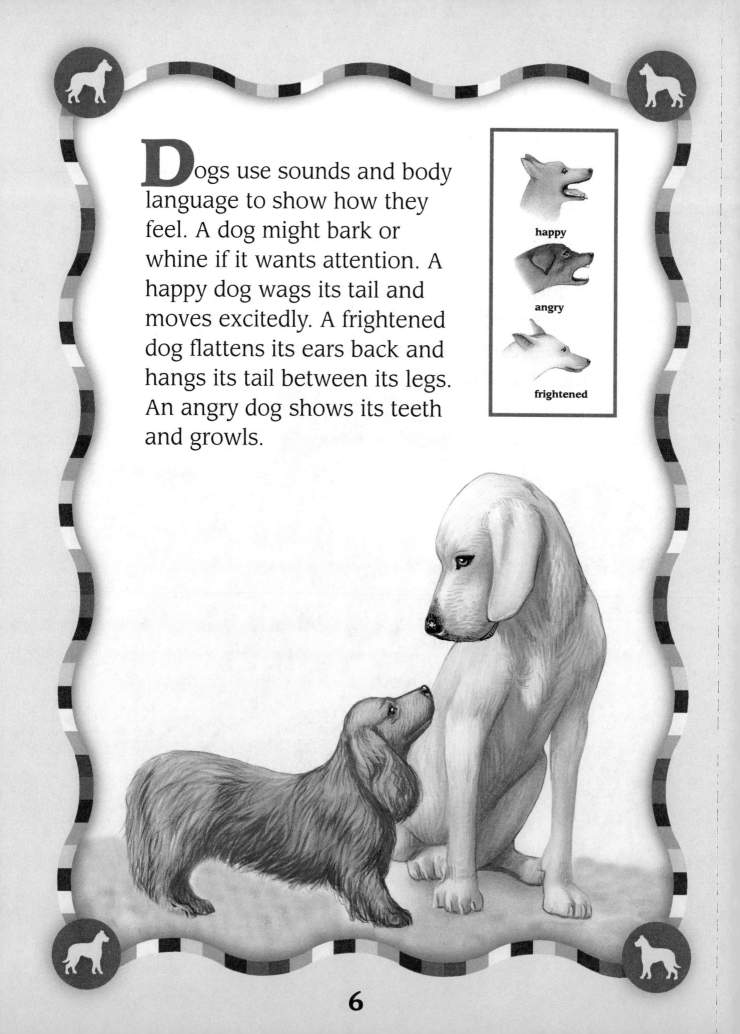

Dogs use sounds and body language to show how they feel. A dog might bark or whine if it wants attention. A happy dog wags its tail and moves excitedly. A frightened dog flattens its ears back and hangs its tail between its legs. An angry dog shows its teeth and growls.

happy

angry

frightened

Dogs have been helping people for thousands of years. Dogs are good helpers because they are smart and easy to train. They are also devoted to their owners if they are treated well. Originally, people used dogs to guard homes or herd livestock. Over time, people used dogs for more jobs. In Arctic regions, people relied on dogs for pulling sleds and hunting. During wars, dogs were used to deliver messages or find injured soldiers. Today, some dogs are trained to help people who are blind or deaf. Others help the police find lost people or criminals and sniff out drugs.

Dogs belong to the animal family called Canidae. This family includes wolves, coyotes, foxes and jackals. Dogs and their wild cousins are found all over the world. They have special features that help them to live in their surroundings.

Coyote

African Wild Dog

Jackal

Fennec Fox

Arctic Fox

Grey Fox

Wolf

Cat

Cats have been favourite pets for thousands of years. At first, people had cats to get rid of pests, such as mice and snakes. Cats are skilled hunters. They have keen senses, sharp claws and the ability to jump and climb. Today, most people have cats to keep them company. Cats are smart but rather independent animals. They make good pets for people who are not home often.

Cats need to be fed every day. They must always have fresh water for drinking. Cats are clean animals and groom themselves often. However, cats should be brushed regularly to remove dead hair, especially if the cat has long hair. Cats must also be taken to the veterinarian for medical check-ups.

Think and Learn

1. Why did people first keep cats as pets?_____

   _____

2. Cats have keen senses and sharp_____ .

3. Cats are clean animals and_____ themselves.

4. Cats must go to the_____ for check-ups.

Animal Friends

Plants, animals and people must share our world. How can you be kind to our animal friends? Under each picture, write one way that you can be kind to that animal.

Be Kind to Our Animal Friends

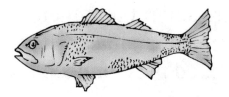

_____   _____

_____   _____

_____   _____

_____

_____

_____

CATS

Pull-Out Storybook

There are many different breeds of cats. Cats are divided into two main groups, depending on the length of their hair. Long-haired cats have long silky coats. These cats probably came from cold areas, where thick coats protected them from harsh winters. Short-haired cats have short sleek coats. These breeds are easier to care for because their coats need less grooming.

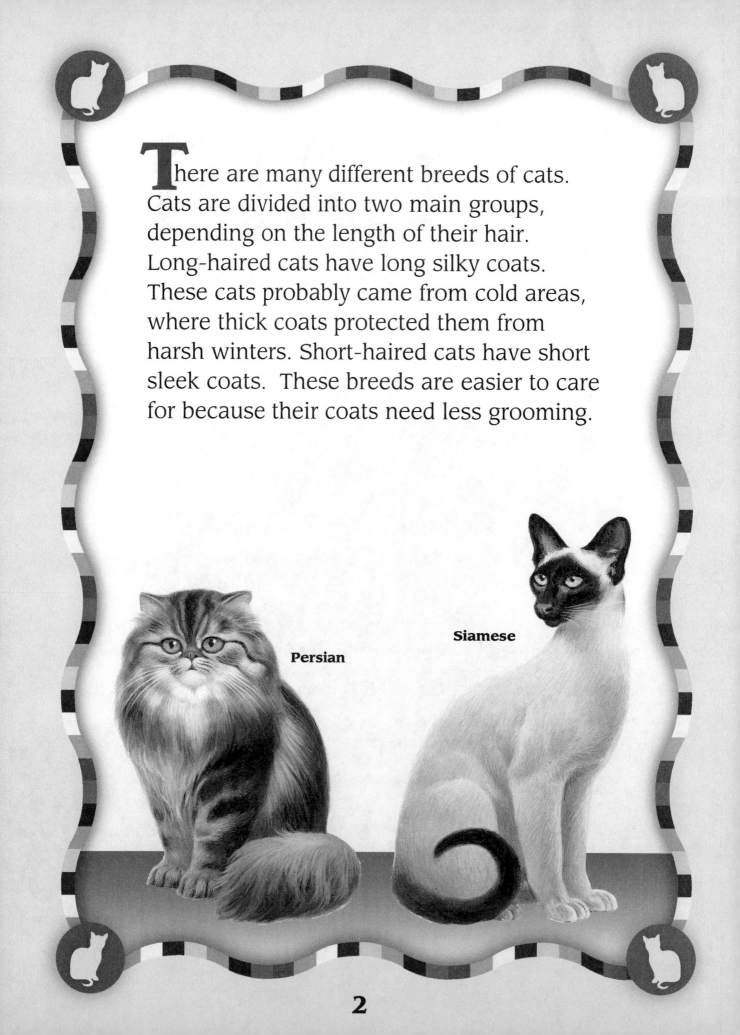

Persian

Siamese

Cats are natural athletes. With their flexible body, they can run, leap and climb. When they fall, they flip and twist their body to land on their feet. Cats have good balance and can walk easily along thin ledges.

Daytime

Nighttime

Cats are excellent hunters. Cats have a keen sense of hearing that helps them to hear even the slightest movement of another animal. Cats also have sharp eyesight. During the day, a cat's pupils are narrow. The pupil is the dark part in the middle of the eye that opens and closes to let in light. At night, a cat's pupils widen to let more light enter. Cats have a mirror-like layer of skin at the back of each eye. This helps them to see even small objects in very dim light.

Cats usually have three to five kittens at a time. The kittens depend entirely on their mother to feed, clean and protect them. At first, the mother cat spends almost all of her time caring for her babies, leaving them only to eat or to use the litter box. As the kittens grow older and more independent, the mother leaves them for longer periods of time. Once the kittens are 6 to 10 weeks of age, they can be separated from their mother. By this time, the mother has taught her kittens how to live on their own.

Kittens love to play! When kittens play, they exercise their body to help it grow strong. Kittens learn to hunt when they stalk and pounce on objects. When they play-fight, they learn to defend themselves. All these play activities teach kittens how to live on their own.

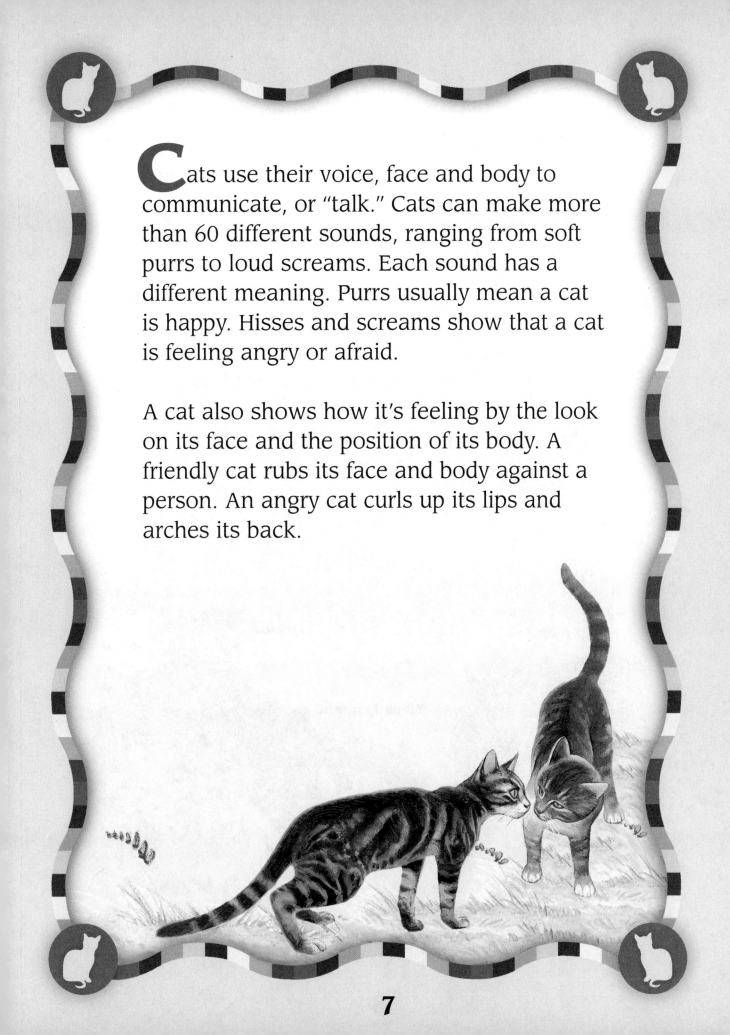

Cats use their voice, face and body to communicate, or "talk." Cats can make more than 60 different sounds, ranging from soft purrs to loud screams. Each sound has a different meaning. Purrs usually mean a cat is happy. Hisses and screams show that a cat is feeling angry or afraid.

A cat also shows how it's feeling by the look on its face and the position of its body. A friendly cat rubs its face and body against a person. An angry cat curls up its lips and arches its back.

Cats belong to a family of animals called Felidae. There are more than 30 different kinds of cats. They include lions, tigers, ocelots and pumas as well as house cats. Most wild cats live alone. The lion is the only wild cat that lives in a group. The tiger is the largest member of the cat family. Ocelots are skillful climbers. The black leopard has a coat so dark that its black spots are invisible. The jaguar is very strong. It can drag an animal much heavier than itself.

Lion

Ocelot

Jaguar

Black Leopard

Cheetah

House Cat

Puma

Tiger

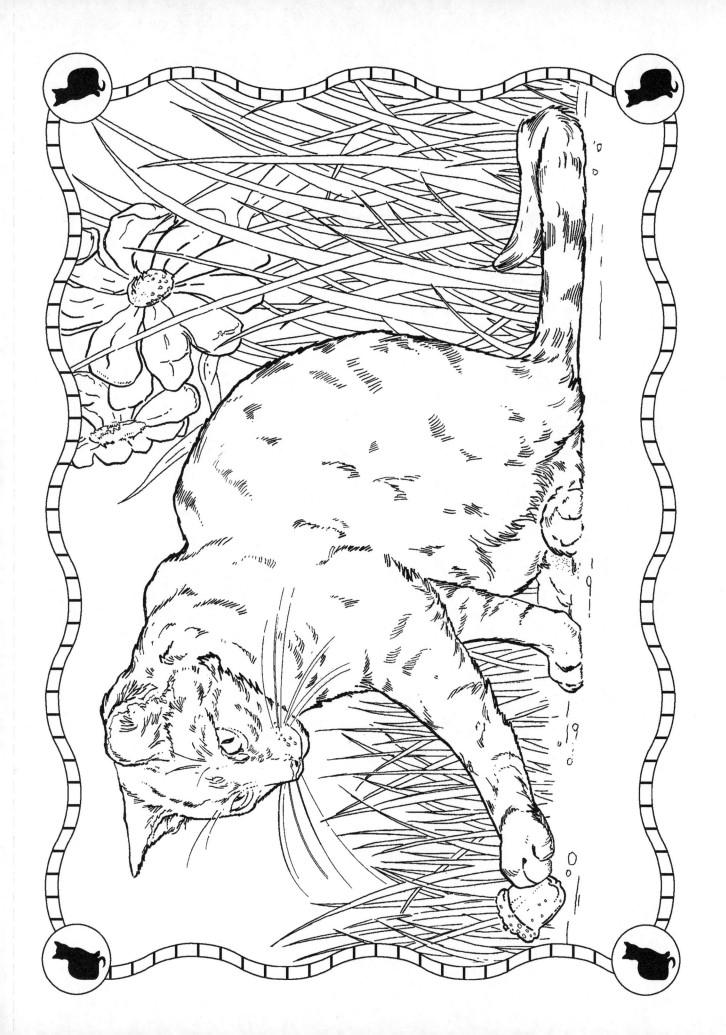

Rabbit

Rabbits are rodents with long ears and fluffy tails. Rodents are animals with front teeth that grow all the time. Pet rabbits must always have something to chew on. If not, their front teeth will grow too long for them to chew food normally.

Pet rabbits need a hutch, or a cage, to live in. They can be kept outside in a shady place during the summer. In winter, they must be kept in a heated garage or a cool basement. Rabbits eat pellets made just for them. They need fresh hay to eat every day. They also like fresh vegetables, clover and grass. A water bottle filled with clean water should always be kept in the cage. Most rabbits do not like to be held for a long time. Never pick up a rabbit by its ears.

Think and Learn

1. A rodent has front _____ that grow all the time.

2. What do pet rabbits live in? _____

3. What do rabbits eat? _____

_____

4. Never pick up a rabbit by its _____.

Guinea Pig

A guinea pig is a small animal with a large head, short legs and small ears. They grow to 35 centimetres long and weigh about 0.5 kilograms. Guinea pigs are not really pigs. They are rodents. Rodents have front teeth that never stop growing. For this reason, guinea pigs must always have a piece of wood to gnaw on.

Guinea pigs make good classroom pets. They are easy to care for, and they don't often bite. Guinea pigs need a cage through which air can easily move. They should have food and fresh water in their cage at all times. Guinea pigs eat grain, fresh vegetables and hay. Guinea pigs are most active at night. They are quiet during the day and sleep in a burrow they make in their cage.

Think and Learn

1. Guinea pigs are not pigs; they are _____.

2. What is the length of a guinea pig? _____

3. Why do guinea pigs make good classroom pets? _____

_____

4. Guinea pigs are most active_____.

Frog

Frogs are animals that spend part of their life in water. Some frogs live mostly in water. Other frogs live mostly on land. Almost all frogs lay their eggs in or near water. Tadpoles hatch from the eggs. Tadpoles swim and grow in water. As they grow, they change from a fishlike animal to an adult frog.

Pet frogs need a lot of care. Frogs are kept in aquariums. The kind of pet frog determines the environment in the aquarium. Some kinds of frogs live in half water and half land environments. Others live in all water environments. Still others live in all land environments. Frogs must be fed regularly. Many frogs eat live insects, such as crickets. Others eat frozen worms.

Think and Learn

1. Frogs spend part of their life in_____.

2. _____ hatch from frog eggs.

3. Where are pet frogs kept? _____

4. What do pet frogs eat? _____

_____

Compare and Contrast

Read about frogs and toads in the "Frogs" storybook. Then, use the Venn diagram and the facts you have learned to compare and contrast these two animals.

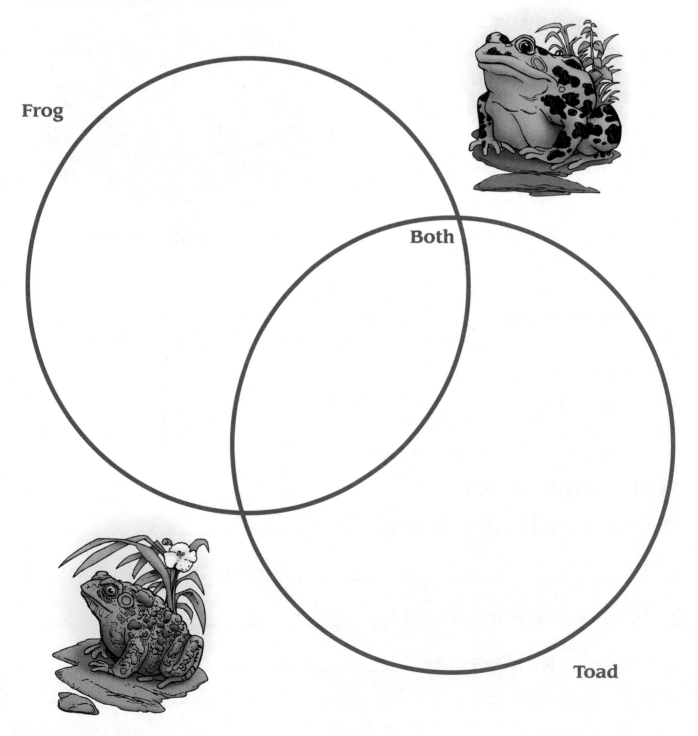

Frog

Both

Toad

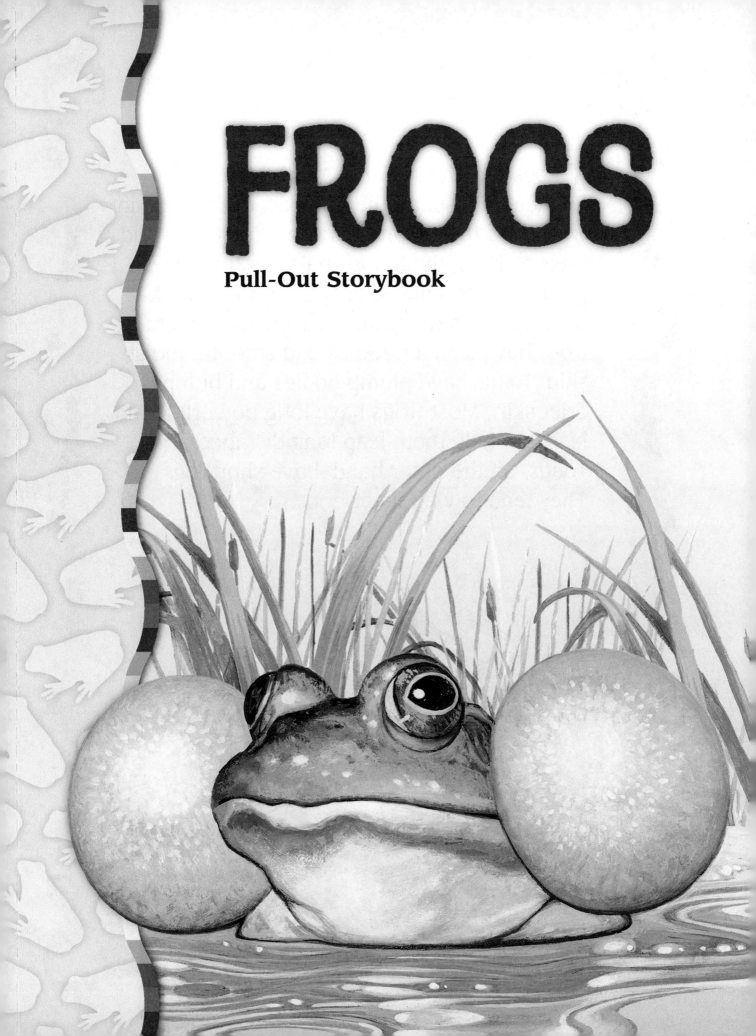

FROGS

Pull-Out Storybook

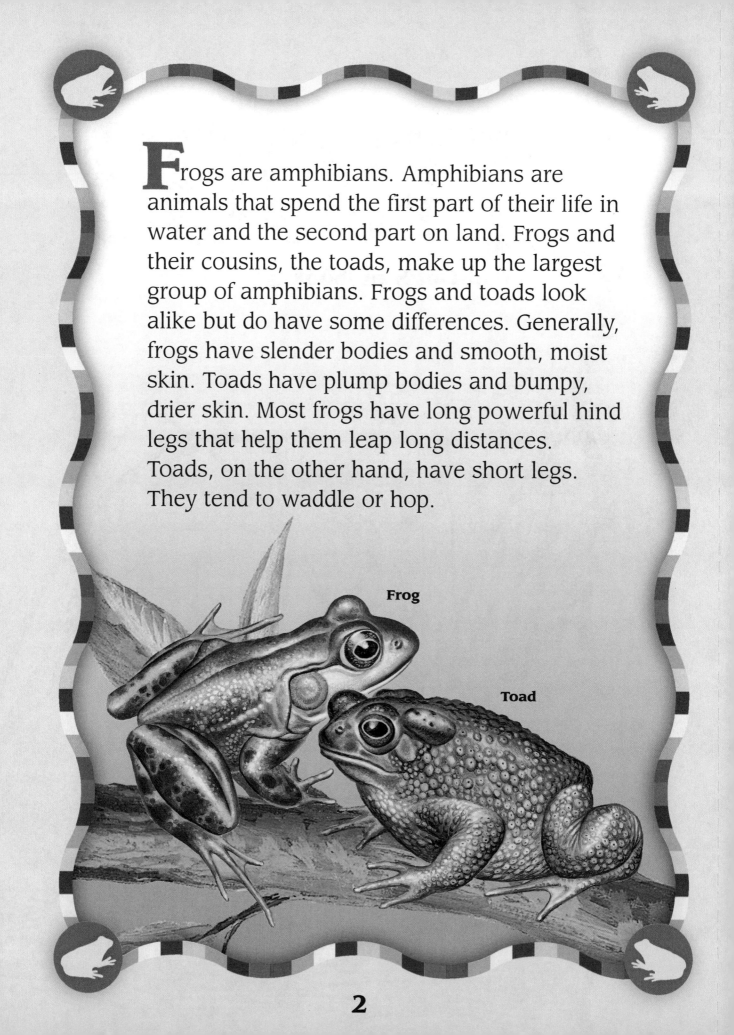

Frogs are amphibians. Amphibians are animals that spend the first part of their life in water and the second part on land. Frogs and their cousins, the toads, make up the largest group of amphibians. Frogs and toads look alike but do have some differences. Generally, frogs have slender bodies and smooth, moist skin. Toads have plump bodies and bumpy, drier skin. Most frogs have long powerful hind legs that help them leap long distances. Toads, on the other hand, have short legs. They tend to waddle or hop.

Frog

Toad

Like all amphibians, frogs are cold-blooded. This means that their body temperature changes to match the temperature of their surroundings.

The smooth, moist skin of frogs does more than protect the body. Although frogs breathe with lungs, they also take in air through their skin. Frogs take in water through their skin, too. Instead of drinking with their mouths, they simply sit in water and soak it up like a sponge.

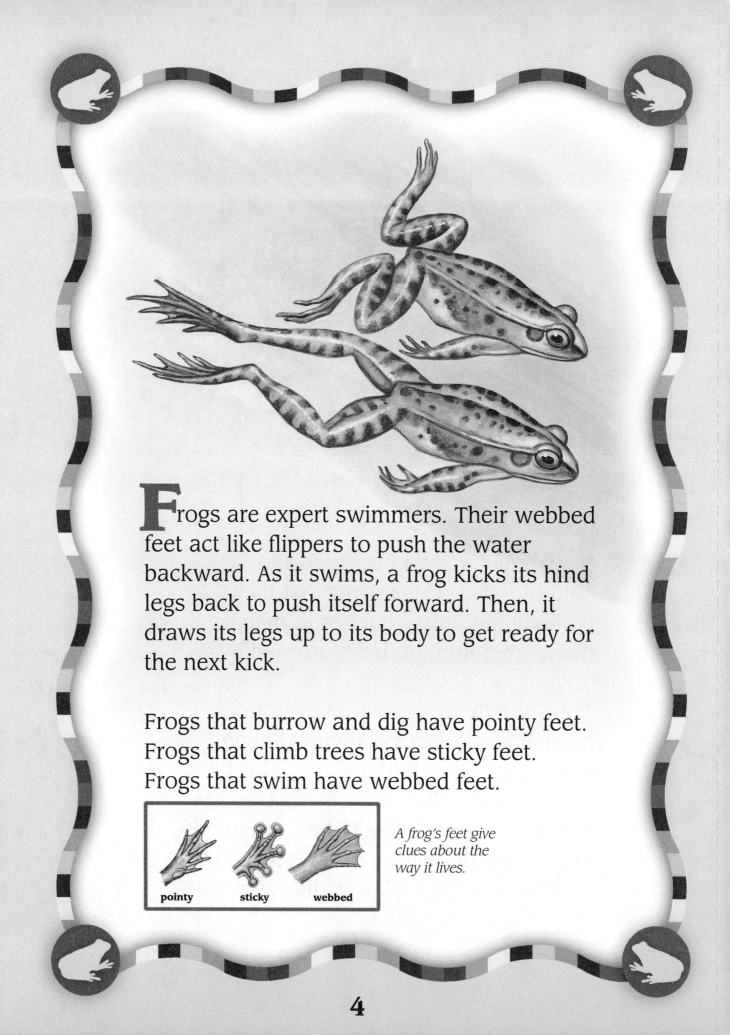

Frogs are expert swimmers. Their webbed feet act like flippers to push the water backward. As it swims, a frog kicks its hind legs back to push itself forward. Then, it draws its legs up to its body to get ready for the next kick.

Frogs that burrow and dig have pointy feet. Frogs that climb trees have sticky feet. Frogs that swim have webbed feet.

pointy   sticky   webbed

A frog's feet give clues about the way it lives.

Most frogs eat insects. Large frogs even eat mice, rats and lizards. Frogs hunt mainly by sight. Their large bulging eyes can see the tiniest movements of their prey. When ready to attack, a frog flicks out its weapon—a long tongue with a sticky tip. The frog traps its prey on the end of its tongue, then whips the prey into its mouth. If the prey is too far for their tongue to reach, frogs jump up and grab the prey in their mouth.

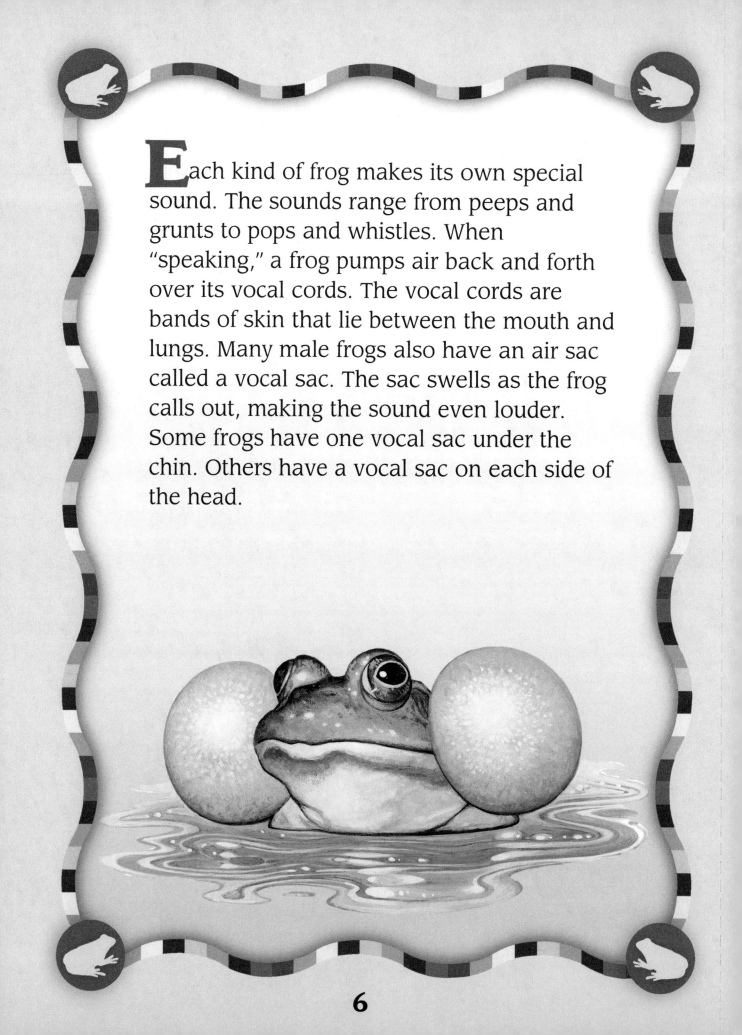

Each kind of frog makes its own special sound. The sounds range from peeps and grunts to pops and whistles. When "speaking," a frog pumps air back and forth over its vocal cords. The vocal cords are bands of skin that lie between the mouth and lungs. Many male frogs also have an air sac called a vocal sac. The sac swells as the frog calls out, making the sound even louder. Some frogs have one vocal sac under the chin. Others have a vocal sac on each side of the head.

Life Cycle of a Frog

Frogs lay their eggs in water. They may lay hundreds, or even thousands, of eggs at a time. But only a few of these eggs develop into adult frogs.

The babies that hatch from the eggs are called tadpoles. With their round head, legless body and long tail, they look more like fish than frogs. Unlike adult frogs, tadpoles breathe with gills. As tadpoles grow, their lungs start to form, their legs appear and their gills and tail begin shrinking. Eventually, they lose their gills and tail altogether.

Flying Frog

Red-Eyed Tree Frog

Frogs and toads belong to a group of animals called Anura, meaning "tailless." There are more than 3,000 different kinds of frogs and toads around the world. Though many of these animals are easy to recognize as "froglike" or "toadlike," some have unusual features. Most of these features help the animals survive in their environments.

Hairy Frog

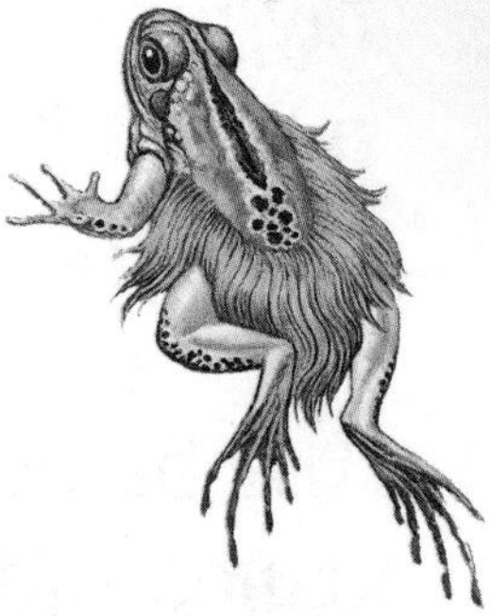

Bony-Headed Tree Frog

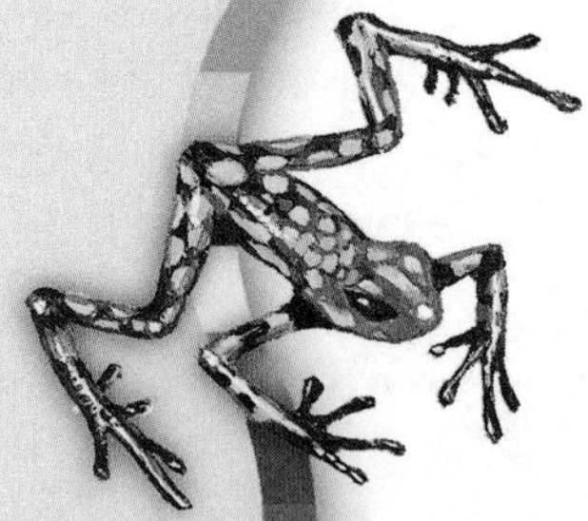

Goliath Frog

Poison Dart Frogs

SCIENCE
and ANIMALS

Vertebrates

Life Cycles

Reptiles

Food Chains

Amphibians

Invertebrates

Birds

Animal Adaptations

Fish

Mammals

Classification Systems

Scientists divide all living things into major groups. Then they divide these major groups into smaller groups. And they divide the smaller groups into still smaller groups. This is called a classification system.

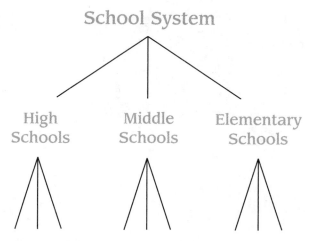

School System

High Schools   Middle Schools   Elementary Schools

Class Class Class   Class Class Class   Class Class Class

Your school uses a classification system, too. The whole school system includes all the schools in your area. High schools, junior high or middle schools and elementary schools make up the school system. You go to school in a certain elementary school. You are in a certain class within your school.

Think and Learn

1. Scientists use a classification system to divide _____ _____ into major groups and smaller groups.

2. What are the different kinds of schools that make up your school system? _____

_____

3. What are elementary schools divided into? _____

Classifying Animals

Just as your school system includes the several different kinds of schools, all of Earth's living things make up several major groups. Scientists call these major groups kingdoms. Two of the kingdoms of living things are the Plant Kingdom and the Animal Kingdom. The Animal Kingdom contains all the animals in the world.

Scientists divide each kingdom into large groups called phyla (FIH luh). Each phylum (FIH luhm) is divided into smaller groups called classes. Each class contains smaller groups called orders. In this way, scientists classify all living things on Earth.

Living Things

Kingdom Kingdom Animal Kingdom Plant Kingdom Kingdom

Phylum Phylum Phylum Phylum

Class Class Class Class

Order Order Order

Think and Learn

1. What do scientists call the major groups of living things?

   _____

2. What are two kingdoms of living things? _____

   _____

3. Kingdoms are divided into large groups called _____.

4. Scientists divide phyla into_____.

Science and Animals

Classifying Vertebrates

Animals that have backbones are called vertebrates (VER tuh bruhts). Scientists classify vertebrates into five main groups called classes. The five main classes of vertebrates are shown below. Write the correct class name under the picture. Then, colour each of the vertebrates.

Birds have feathers and wings. Baby birds hatch from eggs.

Fish live in water and breathe through gills. Scales cover their body.

Amphibians live some of their life in water and some on land. Adults breathe with lungs.

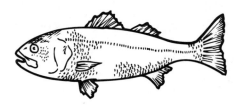

_____

_____

Mammals have hair on their bodies. They feed milk to their young.

_____

Reptiles live on land. They have dry scaly skin and breathe with lungs.

_____

_____

reptile   fish   amphibian
bird   mammal

Backbones

Animals with backbones are called vertebrates. Each skeleton below shows a different class of vertebrates. Colour the backbone in each skeleton. Then, write the class below each animal.

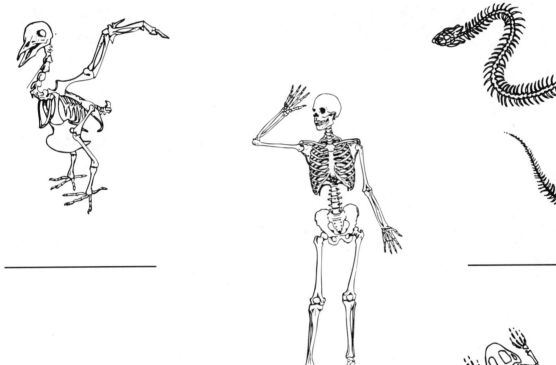

_____   _____

_____

_____   _____

---

reptile   fish   amphibian
bird   mammal

Classy Vertebrates

Scientists group the vertebrates into five main classes. Write the name of the vertebrate class for each picture.

_____ _____ _____ _____

_____ _____ _____ _____

_____ _____ _____ _____

reptile   fish   amphibian
bird   mammal

Animals With Backbones

Vertebrates are animals that have backbones. There are five main classes of vertebrates. Read the characteristics listed in the second column. Then, write the name of the class in the first column. Write an example of each class in the third column.

class	characteristics	example
	• live in water • breathe with gills	
	• live partly in water and partly on land • breathe with lungs as adults	
	• have dry, scaly skin • breathe with lungs	
	• have feathers and wings • breathe with lungs	
	• body covered with hair • feed young with milk	

reptiles   fish   trout   amphibians

birds   mammals   bear   hawk

toad   turtle

Parts of a Fish

Fish make up one class of vertebrates. There are many different kinds of fish. They vary greatly in size and shape. Most fish have certain features in common, however.

Fish eat plants and other animals with a mouth. They see where they're going with their eyes. Fish breathe under water through structures called gills on the sides of their heads.

The bodies of fish are covered with tiny scales. Scales make fish smooth on the outside and help them swim easily through the water. Fish move through the water by using their fins. They have several body fins. The tail fin helps them move fast and in the direction they want to go.

Think and Learn

1. _____ allow fish to see underwater.

2. Fish use _____ to breathe underwater.

3. What do fish use their fins for? _____
_____

4. Do all fish look alike? _____

Parts of a Fish

Label the parts of the fish.

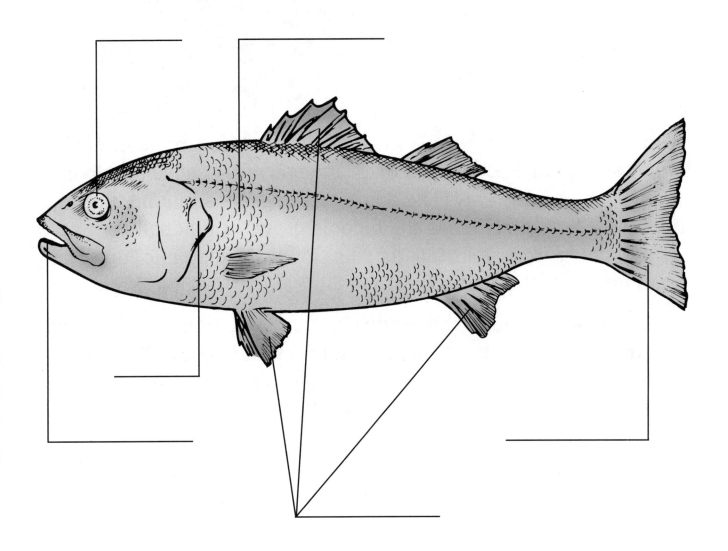

mouth	gill	body fins
eye	scales	tail fin

Science and Animals

Life Cycle of a Frog

Frogs are amphibians. They begin their lives as though they were fish but are more like land animals as adults. Frogs pass through stages during their lives. The series of stages in the life of an animal is called its life cycle.

A frog's life cycle begins when an adult frog lays a mass of eggs in a pond or stream. Each egg hatches one baby frog called a tadpole. A tadpole is in many ways like a fish. It has a tail, and it breathes underwater through gills. As the tadpole grows, it gradually grows legs and begins to lose its tail. Its gills slowly develop into lungs for breathing air. At this stage, the animal is called a tadpole frog.

A tadpole frog gradually develops into a young frog. A young frog lives in water and on land. It has legs, lungs and no tail. The young frog grows to become an adult frog. The life cycle begins again when a mother adult frog lays a mass of eggs in water.

Think and Learn

1. A frog is called a _____ when it has a tail and breathes through gills.

2. When a tadpole becomes a frog, it grows legs and develops lungs. What does it lose? _____

3. The series of stages in the life of an animal is called its _____ .

Life Cycle of a Frog

Label the steps in the life cycle of the frog.

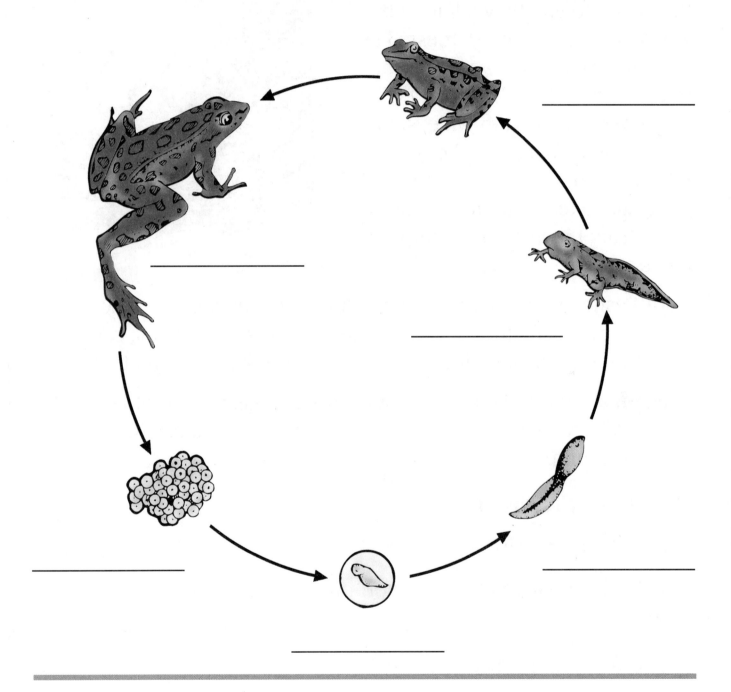

_____

_____

_____

_____

_____

_____

tadpole   egg   tadpole frog
adult frog   young frog   egg mass

Parts of a Rattlesnake

Rattlesnakes are poisonous snakes. When they bite an animal they want to eat, they kill it with a poison called venom. Rattlesnakes store their venom in a venom sac in the back of their head. When they open their mouth wide, sharp teeth called fangs extend down from the top of the mouth. When the snake bites an animal, venom flows from the venom sac into the fangs and into the animal.

Rattlesnakes can see and smell. But they mainly sense other animals by feeling their warmth. These snakes have holes, called pits, on the sides of their head that can sense heat around them.

When a rattlesnake is afraid, it makes a noise with a rattle at its tail. When the snake shakes its tail, the rattle makes a loud buzzing sound.

Think and Learn

1. A rattlesnake stores its poison in a _____.

2. A rattlesnake sends its poison into an animal through its _____.

3. A rattlesnake senses heat with its _____.

4. When a rattlesnake is afraid, it makes a noise with a _____ at the end of its tail.

Parts of a Rattlesnake

Label the parts of a rattlesnake.

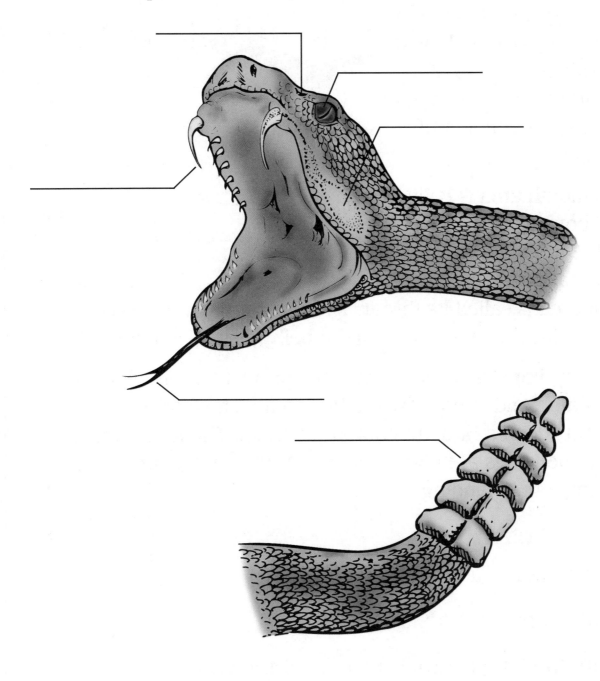

---

fang	pit	venom sac
rattle	eye	tongue

Science and Animals

Parts of a Bird

Scientists and bird watchers use special terms to describe a bird. These terms can help you notice the different parts of a bird. In that way, you can begin to tell birds apart and identify different ones.

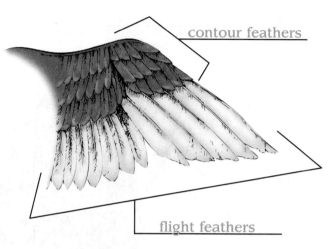

contour feathers

flight feathers

A bird's mouth area is called its beak. Above the beak are its eyes. The area on the top of the head is called the crown. The bird's neck area is called its throat. The chest area of a bird is called its breast. A bird also has a back and a belly, just as you do.

Feathers are important for a bird. They protect the bird from sun, wind and water, and they allow the bird to fly. The feathers that cover the outside of a bird are contour feathers. The long contour feathers on the wings are flight feathers. A bird's tail feathers help both in flying and in landing.

Think and Learn

1. The chest area of a bird is called its _____.

2. The top of a bird's head is called the _____.

3. What are the long contour feathers at the end of the wing called? _____

Parts of a Bird

Label the parts of a bird.

crown   throat   contour feathers
eye   breast   flight feathers
beak   back   tail feathers
belly

Bird Beaks

Bird beaks vary greatly in both shape and size. By looking closely at a bird's beak, you can often tell what kind of food that bird eats. Some birds feed on small animals, while other birds eat seeds. Their beaks are different, because they are used differently. Hawks, for example, have a beak made for tearing the meat of small animals, such as mice. The tiny hummingbird has a beak made for sucking liquid from flowers.

Cardinals have a strong beak good for cracking seeds. Fast-flying swallows have small beaks made for catching insects. Robins have pointed beaks for stabbing worms. Woodpeckers have strong beaks just right for pounding holes in wood as they look for insects.

Many water birds also have different kinds of beaks. A pelican has a large beak made for scooping up fishes. An anhinga has a sharp beak good for stabbing fish that swim by.

Write how each bird uses its beak.

Hawk _____

Cardinal_____

_____

_____

Bird Beaks

Write how each bird uses its beak.

Pelican _____

_____

Hummingbird _____

_____

Swallow_____

_____

Robin _____

_____

Anhinga _____

_____

Woodpecker_____

_____

Feathered Friends' Feet

Just as a bird's beak can tell you what it eats, a bird's feet can tell you many things about its habits or home. Think about what you already know about the birds listed below. How do each of these birds use their feet in a special way?

Sparrow _____

Woodpecker _____

_____

_____

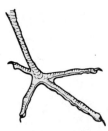

Duck _____

Hawk _____

_____

_____

Heron _____

_____

---

for perching on branches
for wading in mud
for climbing

for catching small animals
for swimming

Strangers in the Night

It's much easier to identify a bird when you can see its colour, size and shape. At night, however, it is difficult to see. Identify these birds just by their shapes, or silhouettes.

heron	duck	hummingbird
robin	hawk	cardinal
crow	owl	blue jay
gull		

What's a Mammal?

When you think of an animal, you probably think about a mammal. Mammals live in every part of the world. They range from tiny mice to the largest animals on Earth, the whales. Mammals include dogs, cats, cows, bears, kangaroos, raccoons, rabbits, elephants, dolphins, and many others. Human beings are also mammals.

Mammals are the only animals with hair. Any animal with hair is a mammal. Even whales have a few hairs on their body. Most mammals are covered with hair. The hair keeps the body warm and dry. When mammals give birth, the mother feeds her young with milk from her body. No other animals feed their young with milk.

Mammals have large well-developed brains compared with other animals. These large brains make mammals very intelligent animals.

Think and Learn

1. Mammals have large well-developed_____.

2. The largest mammal on Earth is the_____.

3. How does hair protect a mammal?_____

_____

4. Baby mammals get _____ from their mother's body.

What's a Mammal?

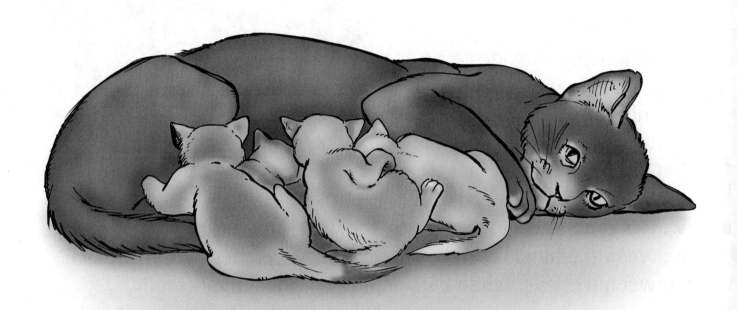

Think and Learn

1. Look at the picture above. How do you know the mother is a mammal? _____

_____

2. In the picture above, what are the babies doing that only young mammals do? _____

_____

_____

The Mammal With Wings

Bats are the only mammals that can fly. Some squirrels can glide, but bats really fly like birds. They can fly because they have wings.

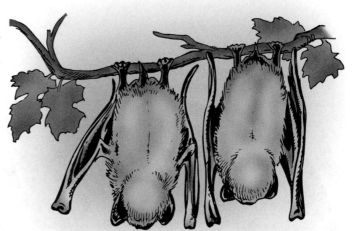

A bat wing is made of a thin layer of skin called a wing membrane. This skin stretches between the long fingers on a bat's hands. The thumb is the only finger not attached to the wing membrane. On most bats, the wing membrane also stretches between the hands and the legs. It even stretches across the tail between the legs. When bats flap their wings, they can fly.

Bats fly mainly at night, when they hunt flying insects. They can find insects in the dark by using their large sensitive ears. During the day, most bats sleep by hanging upside down.

Think and Learn

1. Bats are the only mammals that can _____.

2. A _____ stretches between a bat's fingers.

3. When do bats hunt for food?_____

4. Bats sense where insects are flying with their _____.

The Mammal With Wings

Label the parts of a bat.

---

foot

thumb

ear

fingers

wing membrane

tail

Animals Without Backbones

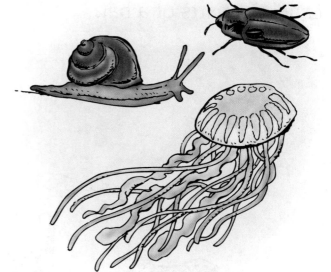

Animals that have a backbone are called vertebrates. Animals without a backbone are called invertebrates. There are many more invertebrates than vertebrates. More than nine out of ten animals on Earth are invertebrates.

The many different kinds of invertebrates vary greatly in shape and structure. They have only one thing in common. None have a backbone. Some, such as insects and lobsters, have a hard covering on the outside called an exoskeleton. Clams and snails have shells around their soft bodies. Other invertebrates, such as sponges and jellyfish, have no hard covering or shell.

What are some invertebrates you have seen? Sponges, jellyfish, earthworms, clams, snails, octopuses, starfishes, spiders, lobsters and insects are all invertebrates.

Think and Learn

1. Animals without a backbone are called _____.

2. Insects have an _____ on the outside of their body.

3. What are two invertebrates that have no outer covering or shell? _____

Animals Without Backbones

Write whether each animal is a vertebrate or an invertebrate.

_____

_____

_____

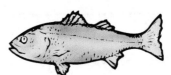

_____

_____

_____

_____

_____

_____

Science and Animals

Kinds of Insects

There are many kinds of insects. This table shows some common insects that represent different insect groups.

Insect	Characteristics
Stag beetle	large rounded insect with large mouth that looks like a deer's antlers
Dragonfly	large insect with huge front and back wings
Dog flea	tiny wingless insect that sucks blood from dogs
Moth	insect with feathery antennae and broad wings
Housefly	small two-winged insect found almost everywhere
Praying mantis	large insect with front legs that look like they are folded in prayer
Water bug	large rounded insect with wings folded back and pierce-sucking mouths
Wasp	large thin insect with narrow wings and a stinger at the rear

Kinds of Insects

Write the name of each insect on the line.

_____   _____   _____

_____   _____

_____   _____   _____

moth   wasp   stag beetle
praying mantis   housefly   dragonfly
dog flea   water bug

297

Spiders and Insects

Both spiders and insects are invertebrates. But spiders are not insects, though many people think so. If you look closely at a spider and an insect, you can see how different they are.

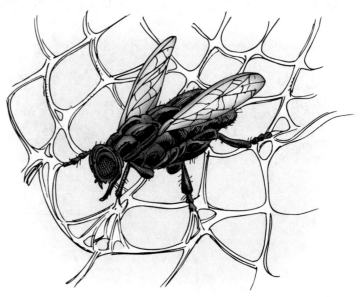

An insect has three main body parts. The head is in front. The chest is the next part. The abdomen is behind the chest. Most insects have wings attached to the chest. Insects also have six legs attached to the chest, three on each side.

A spider has two main body parts. The head and chest together make up one part. The abdomen is behind. A spider has eight legs attached to the head-and-chest part, four on each side. Spiders do not have wings.

Think and Learn

1. Insects and spiders are both _____.

2. An insect has _____ main body parts.

3. A spider has _____ main body parts.

4. How many legs does an insect have? _____

5. How many legs does a spider have? _____

Spiders and Insects

Label the parts of the insect and the spider.

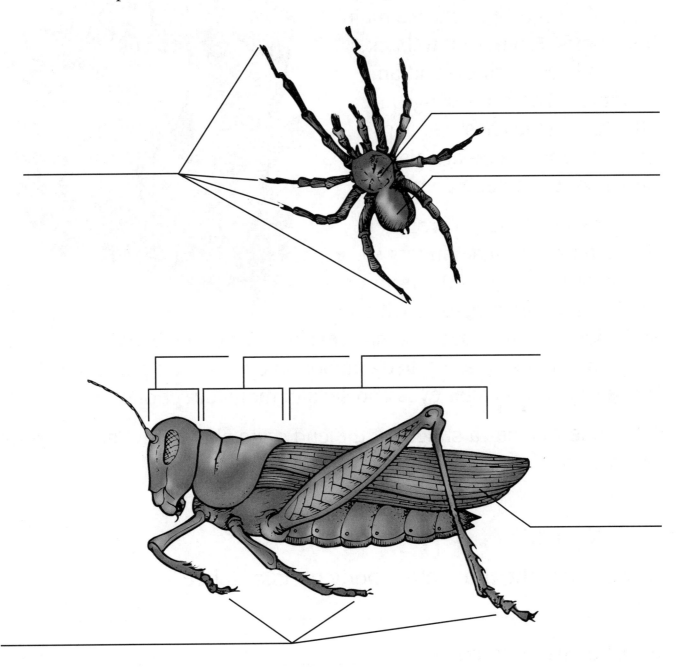

eight legs   wings   head and chest

abdomen   head   six legs

chest

Parts of a Honeybee

A honeybee is a flying insect. Like all insects, it has three main body parts. From front to back, it has a head, a chest, and an abdomen. The bee's wings are attached to the chest. Six legs—three on each side—are also attached to the bee's chest.

A bee senses its environment through its antennae and its eyes. The antennae are on the front of the head. A bee senses touch and smell with them. A bee also has several eyes on its head. The large eyes on either side are called compound eyes. A compound eye is made of many smaller eyes and sees in many directions.

A honeybee has a stinger at the end of its abdomen. The stinger is one way a bee protects itself.

Think and Learn

1. What are the three main body parts of a bee? _____
_____

2. A bee has two large _____ eyes.

3. A bee defends itself with its _____.

4. A bee senses smell and touch with its _____.

Parts of a Honeybee

Label the parts of a honeybee.

stinger

wings

head

chest

antenna

compound eye

abdomen

Life Cycle of a Monarch

Monarch butterflies are beautiful insects. The monarchs you see flying from flower to flower are all adults. During a monarch's life cycle, its body changes shape from a wormlike animal to a lovely winged insect. This change is called metamorphosis (meht uh MOR fuh sis).

The life cycle of a monarch begins when an adult lays eggs on a leaf. A caterpillar, which looks like a worm, hatches from each egg. The caterpillar grows as it eats leaves and other food. When it grows large enough, the caterpillar begins wrapping itself in a silk covering called a cocoon. When it's inside the cocoon, the monarch is called a pupa. Great changes then take place. After a time, an adult monarch butterfly finally comes out of the cocoon. Metamorphosis is complete.

Think and Learn

1. The great change in body shape that happens during a monarch's life cycle is called _____.

2. A monarch egg hatches a _____.

3. The pupa is wrapped inside a _____ made of silk.

4. What comes out of a cocoon? _____

Life Cycle of a Monarch

Label the steps in the life cycle of a monarch.

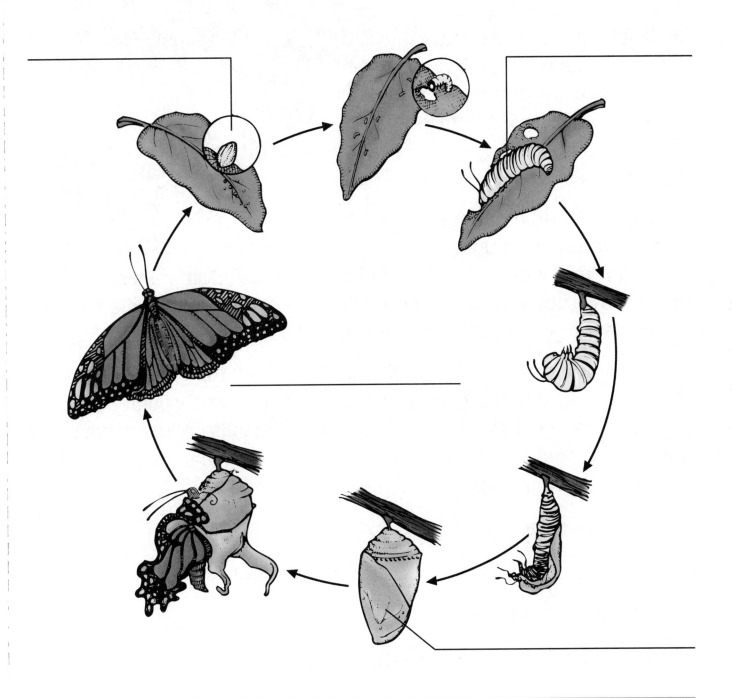

egg
caterpillar

adult butterfly

pupa in a cocoon

Parts of a Clam

Clams are invertebrates that live in water. A hard shell surrounds the animal's soft body. Clams can move around by using a muscle called a foot. They stick the foot out of the shell and push against a lake or ocean floor.

Clams eat and breathe by pulling water inside their shells through a tube called a siphon (SIH fuhn). Sometimes, clams bury themselves in sand for protection. To eat, they extend a siphon up to the top of the sand and suck in water.

Most of the soft body inside the shell is called the mantle. The shell is attached to the mantle. When water comes through one siphon, it passes through the clam's gills. The gills collect oxygen and bits of food from the water. The water then leaves the animal through the second siphon.

Think and Learn

1. A _____ surrounds and protects a clam.

2. A clam moves by using its _____.

3. How does water flow into the clam? _____

   _____

4. The clam's _____ collect oxygen and food from water.

Parts of a Clam

Label the parts of a clam.

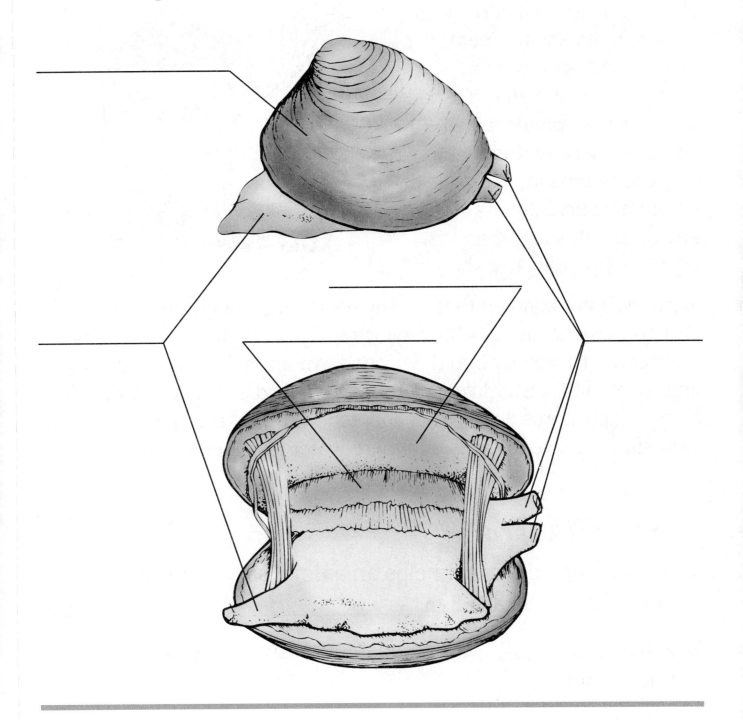

gills   siphons   mantle
shell   foot

Animal Adaptations

Each kind of animal has characteristics that allow it to survive in its environment. For example, a fish has gills for breathing underwater. If it had lungs like mammals, a fish could not survive underwater. Any characteristic that helps an animal survive in its environment is called an adaptation (a dap TAY shun).

Animals are adapted to their environment through their body structure. Some animals have wings to fly through the air. Others have claws to burrow into the ground. An animal's body must fit its environment if it is to live and survive. A good example is a camel's body, which stores water. This adaptation makes the camel well-suited to live in a desert, where water is scarce.

Think and Learn

1. Any characteristic that helps an animal survive in its environment is called an _____.

2. A fish's _____ are an adaptation that allow it to breathe underwater.

3. A bird's _____ are an adaptation for flying.

Animal Adaptations

Describe an adaptation of each animal that helps it live in its environment.

Clam _____

_____

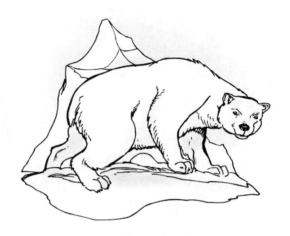

Polar Bear _____

_____

Spider _____

_____

Duck _____

_____

Animal Defences

Each of these animals has an adaptation that helps it defend itself from enemies. For each animal, describe its adaptation.

clam

_____

_____

skunk

_____

_____

honeybee

_____

_____

porcupine

_____

_____

walking stick

_____

_____

pigeon

_____

_____

hard shell
stinger
pointed quills

fast flyer
bad smell

blends in with
environment

Animal Locomotion

One important animal adaptation is the way in which an animal moves around in its environment. The way in which an animal moves is called locomotion.

Complete the table by writing a one-word description of each animal's main method of locomotion. Then, name the body part used to make this movement.

Animal	Method of Locomotion	Body Part Used for Movement
rabbit		
fish		
clam		
dragonfly		

Science and Animals

Food Chains

Animals need energy to stay alive. They get this energy by eating food. Some animals eat plants. Some eat other animals. And some eat both plants and other animals. Think of all the living things that feed on one another in an environment. This is called a food chain. Each living thing in a food chain is a "link" in the "chain." The energy of food passes from one living thing to another through the food chain.

The food chain shown on this page begins with underwater plants in a pond. The plants make up the first link in the food chain. A fish eats the plants. The fish is the second link in the food chain. Finally, an eagle swoops down and catches the fish. The eagle becomes the last link in this food chain.

Think and Learn

1. What are all the living things that feed on one another in an environment called?_____

2. Each plant or animal in a food chain is one _____ in the chain.

3. What kind of living thing almost always begins a food chain? _____

Food Chains

The living things in one food chain are shown below. Write the name of each on the lines.

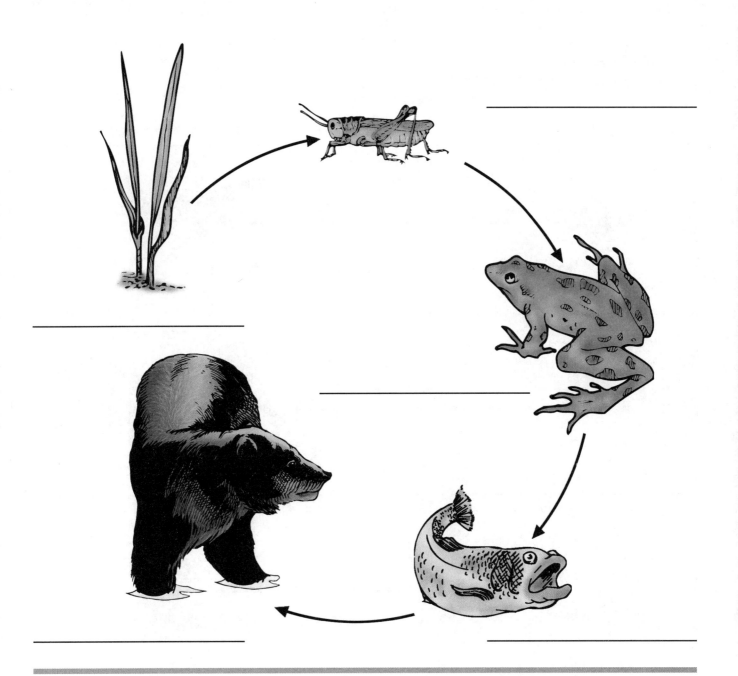

_____

_____

_____

_____

_____

---

bear   grass   grasshopper
fish   frog

Find the Missing Link

Write the name of the missing link in each food chain. Then draw the missing link above the word.

carrots   rabbit   _____

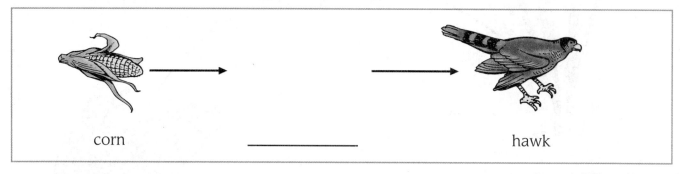

corn   _____   hawk

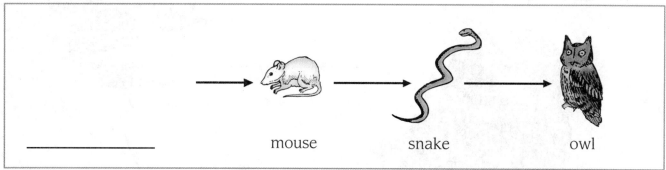

_____   mouse   snake   owl

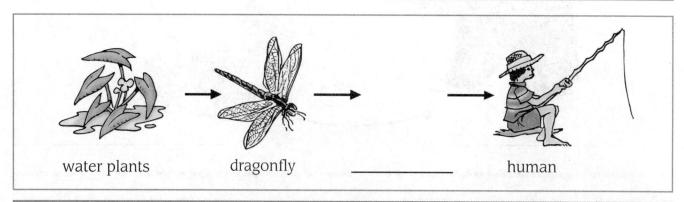

water plants   dragonfly   _____   human

mouse   plants   wolf   fish

ANIMAL FACTS and FUN

What's Its Name?

How Long Does It Live?

Animal Safari

What's Its Name?

What do you call a mother duck or a baby goat? This table gives you some answers to those and other questions about animal names.

Animal	Male	Female	Young
Bear	boar	sow	cub
Cat	tom	queen	kitten
Cattle	bull	cow	calf
Chicken	rooster	hen	chick
Deer	buck	doe	fawn
Duck	drake	duck	duckling
Elephant	bull	cow	calf
Fox	renard	vixen	kit
Goat	buck	doe	kid
Hog	boar	sow	piglet
Kangaroo	buck	doe	joey
Lion	lion	lioness	cub
Sheep	buck	ewe	lamb
Swan	cob	pen	cygnet
Tiger	tiger	tigress	cub
Turkey	tom	hen	poult
Whale	bull	cow	calf

What's Its Name?

For each family group, label the members with the correct names.

_____
_____
_____

_____
_____
_____

_____
_____
_____

_____
_____
_____

How Long Does It Live?

Animal	Years of Life	Animal	Years of Life
Mammals		**Birds**	
Cat	14	Blue jay	6–9
Chimpanzee	30–40	Cardinal	13
Deer	20	Ostrich	40
Dog	12–20	Pigeon	6
Elephant	50–70	Robin	17
Grizzly bear	25	Snowy owl	10
Hippopotamus	41	**Reptiles**	
Horse	20–30	Crocodile	25–50
Lion	13	Garter snake	3–4
Mouse	1	Rattlesnake	14–15
Sheep	10–20	Box turtle	80
Tiger	20	**Fishes**	
Wolf	12–16	Goldfish	10
Amphibians		Salmon	4–5
Bullfrog	5	Trout	11
Salamander	20	Sturgeon	50

How Long Does It Live?

Write how long each of these animals lives.

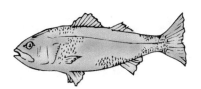

trout _____

bullfrog _____

mouse _____

_____

_____

_____

ostrich _____

horse_____

box turtle _____

_____

_____

_____

Think and Learn

1. Which lives longer, a tiger or a crocodile? _____

2. Which lives longer, a mouse or a goldfish? _____

3. Suppose you had two pets, a dog and a box turtle. Which
pet could have a longer life? _____

Write About It

Choose an interesting animal that you have read about. Draw a picture of the animal. Then, write a paragraph that tells some fascinating facts about the animal you chose.

_____

_____

_____

_____

_____

_____

_____

_____

Animal Safari

An Alphabet of Animals

Prepare

● Tear out the gameboard. Cut a piece of cardboard the same size. Glue the gameboard onto the cardboard.

● Cut out the cards below. Cut squares of construction paper the same size. Glue the cards onto the construction paper squares.

● Use your own small plastic animals as game pieces.

Rules

1. Give each player the same number of cards.
2. Have each player turn over the top card. Count the letters in the animal name.
3. The player who has the animal name that comes first in ABC order goes first. Move ahead the number of spaces that equals the number of letters in the word.
4. When you land on a space, follow any directions on that space.
5. Players take turns moving until someone reaches FINISH.

ape	bird	walrus	deer	elephant
frog	bear	cheetah	owl	octopus
goat	giraffe	monkey	snake	moose
zebra	lion	penguin	tiger	whale

Animal Safari

START

FINISH

Heavy rain
Wait 1 turn.

Slipped on ice
Slide ahead 2 spaces.

Vines
Swing ahead 3 spaces.

Boa
Go back 3 spaces.

Bear hug
Go back 1 space.

Overnight safari camp
Wait 1 turn.

Beaver dam
Wait 1 turn.

Kangaroo crossing
Hop ahead 1 space.

Rhino stampede
Go back 2 spaces.

Dolphin ride
Go back 3 spaces.

Jellyfish sting
Go back 1.

Shark attack
Go back 5 spaces.

Answer Key

Caribou

Caribou (CAIR ah boo) are sometimes called "reindeer." They are large animals weighing 136 to 272 kilograms. Both male and female caribou have very large antlers. In fact, the female caribou is the only female member of the deer family able to grow antlers. Caribou have long hair and woolly fur. They are great long-distance runners and can easily outrun a pack of wolves. Their wide hooves help them walk easily through snow. Caribou can also swim.

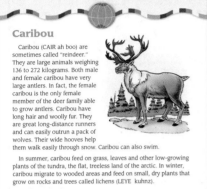

In summer, caribou feed on grass, leaves and other low-growing plants of the tundra, the flat, treeless land of the arctic. In winter, caribou migrate to wooded areas and feed on small, dry plants that grow on rocks and trees called lichens (LEYE kuhnz).

Think and Learn

1. How much do caribou weigh? __136-272 kilograms__

2. Caribou are members of the __deer__ family.

3. Where do caribou migrate in winter? __wooded areas__

4. What do caribou eat during summer? __grass, leaves and low-growing plants of the tundra__

Arctic Region and Antarctica   6

6

Ermine

Ermine (ER mehn) are members of the weasel family. They are tiny animals, weighing less than a kilogram. Ermine have huge dark eyes and long whiskers. They have smooth, silky fur. During the spring and summer, their fur is brown. When autumn approaches, ermine grow a new coat of thick, snow-white fur. This white fur helps ermine blend in with their snowy environment.

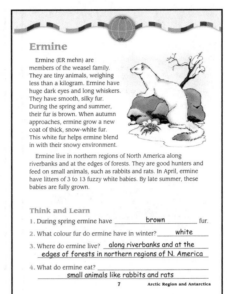

Ermine live in northern regions of North America along riverbanks and at the edges of forests. They are good hunters and feed on small animals, such as rabbits and rats. In April, ermine have litters of 3 to 13 fuzzy white babies. By late summer, these babies are fully grown.

Think and Learn

1. During spring ermine have __brown__ fur.

2. What colour fur do ermine have in winter? __white__

3. Where do ermine live? __along riverbanks and at the edges of forests in northern regions of N. America__

4. What do ermine eat? __small animals like rabbits and rats__

7   Arctic Region and Antarctica

7

Lemming

Lemmings are chubby little animals belonging to the rodent family. They look very much like hamsters and guinea pigs. Lemmings dig in the soil to build their nests, which they line with grass. They eat plants and live in areas where food is often scarce.

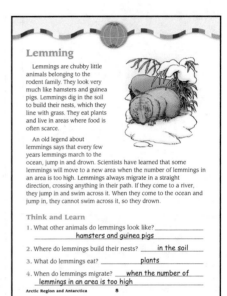

An old legend about lemmings says that every few years lemmings march to the ocean, jump in and drown. Scientists have learned that some lemmings will move to a new area when the number of lemmings in an area is too high. Lemmings always migrate in a straight direction, crossing anything in their path. If they come to a river, they jump in and swim across it. When they come to the ocean and jump in, they cannot swim across it, so they drown.

Think and Learn

1. What other animals do lemmings look like? __hamsters and guinea pigs__

2. Where do lemmings build their nests? __in the soil__

3. What do lemmings eat? __plants__

4. When do lemmings migrate? __when the number of lemmings in an area is too high__

Arctic Region and Antarctica   8

8

Musk Ox

Musk oxen are huge animals with large heads and short legs. They grow to 1.5 metres tall at the shoulders and weigh up to 400 kilograms. Musk oxen have long dark brown hair that almost touches the ground. Thick woolly fur under the hair keeps them warm and dry. They use their hooves to scratch through the snow to find grass, willows and other plants to eat.

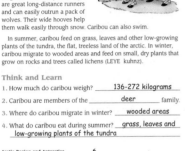

Musk oxen live together on the tundra in herds of 20 to 100. When danger is near, the adult musk oxen gather in a circle, facing outward. The calves stay in the centre of the circle for protection. When the adult oxen lower their heads, showing their enormous horns, even a pack of wolves will not come near.

Think and Learn

1. Musk oxen have __short__ legs.

2. Musk ox hair almost touches the __ground__.

3. How do musk oxen find food? __by scratching through the snow with their hoofs__

4. How big are herds of musk oxen? __20-100__

9   Arctic Region and Antarctica

9

Orca (Killer Whale)

The black and white orca (OR kuh) is a large dolphin that is often called a "killer whale." It grows up to 9 metres long and weighs 3,000 to 9,000 kilograms. The orca has 40 to 48 large pointed teeth that it uses to catch and hold its prey. It eats over 45 kilograms of food every day.

Orcas live and travel in family groups called pods. They are affectionate animals and are often seen touching each other. Female orcas give birth to one baby every 3 to 10 years. The baby will stay with its mother for 10 years. Orcas are very intelligent animals. They communicate with each other by making sounds.

Think and Learn

1. Is an orca a dolphin or a whale? __a dolphin__

2. What colour is an orca? __black and white__

3. How much food does an orca eat each day? __45 kilograms__

4. Orcas travel in family groups called __pods__.

5. Orcas communicate by making __sounds__.

Arctic Region and Antarctica   10

10

Polar Bear

Polar bears are the world's largest four-legged meat-eating animals—2.7 metres tall and 725 kilograms! They have special features to help them live in the arctic. Their thick fur and a layer of fat keep them warm. Their small ears lose less body heat. Pads on the bottom of their feet keep them from slipping on ice. Polar bears are excellent swimmers. Webbing between their clawed toes helps them swim. Polar bears hunt seals, walruses, small whales and fish. In the summer months, they eat berries and plants.

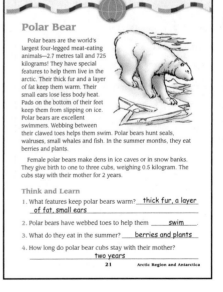

Female polar bears make dens in ice caves or in snow banks. They give birth to one to three cubs, weighing 0.5 kilogram. The cubs stay with their mother for 2 years.

Think and Learn

1. What features keep polar bears warm? __thick fur, a layer of fat, small ears__

2. Polar bears have webbed toes to help them __swim__.

3. What do they eat in the summer? __berries and plants__

4. How long do polar bear cubs stay with their mother? __two years__

21   Arctic Region and Antarctica

21

Answer Key

Seal

Seals are animals with special features to live in water. Their flippers move them quickly and gracefully through water. Their bodies are covered with oily fur and a layer of blubber, or fat, to keep them warm. There are two kinds of seals—sea lions and true seals. Sea lions have ears outside their heads, but true seals have no outer ears. While sea lions can move easily on land, true seals must use their chest muscles to move on land. True seals never have to leave the water.

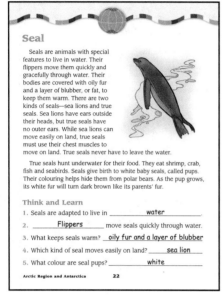

True seals hunt underwater for their food. They eat shrimp, crab, fish and seabirds. Seals give birth to white baby seals, called pups. Their colouring helps hide them from polar bears. As the pup grows, its white fur will turn dark brown like its parents' fur.

Think and Learn

1. Seals are adapted to live in _____water_____ .
2. _____Flippers_____ move seals quickly through water.
3. What keeps seals warm? _oily fur and a layer of blubber_
4. Which kind of seal moves easily on land? ___sea lion___
5. What colour are seal pups? _____white_____

22

Predator and Prey

Polar bears live along frozen shores and on ice floating in arctic waters. The polar bear is a predator (PRED uh tur) because it hunts other animals for food. The animals hunted by predators are called prey. When hunting for seals, polar bears like to wait by a seal's breathing hole in the ice. The seal may not see the polar bear waiting by the breathing hole. The polar bear's white fur helps it blend in with its snowy environment. When the seal comes up to breathe, the polar bear catches it. Seals are dark brown to help them blend in with their environment. When a polar bear looks down into the water, the water reflects the colour of the ocean bottom, which is dark brown or black. Sometimes the polar bear does not see the seal.

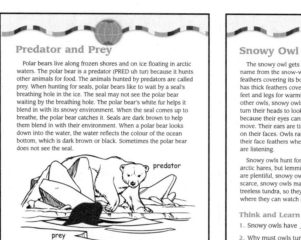

predator

prey

1. Colour the picture to show how the animals blend into the environment.
2. Label the predator and the prey in the picture.

23

Snowy Owl

The snowy owl gets its name from the snow-white feathers covering its body. It has thick feathers covering its feet and legs for warmth. Like other owls, snowy owls must turn their heads to look around because their eyes cannot move. Their ears are tiny slits on their faces. Owls raise their face feathers when they are listening.

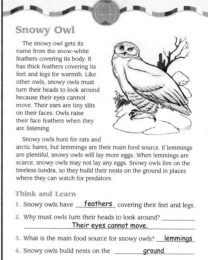

Snowy owls hunt for rats and arctic hares, but lemmings are their main food source. If lemmings are plentiful, snowy owls will lay more eggs. When lemmings are scarce, snowy owls may not lay any eggs. Snowy owls live on the treeless tundra, so they build their nests on the ground in places where they can watch for predators.

Think and Learn

1. Snowy owls have ___feathers___ covering their feet and legs.
2. Why must owls turn their heads to look around? _____ Their eyes cannot move.
3. What is the main food source for snowy owls? ___lemmings___
4. Snowy owls build nests on the _____ground_____ .

24

Walrus

The walrus is a huge animal, weighing between 1,800 and 2,700 kilograms. Its thick skin and layer of blubber protect it from the cold. Both male and female walruses have ivory tusks. They use their tusks to pull themselves across ice and for protection against polar bears.

Walruses are excellent swimmers. They can stay out at sea for days. They feed on the ocean floor by using their "moustache" bristles to feel for clams. Then, they use their snouts to dig the clams out. Walruses live together in herds containing thousands of walruses. One of their favorite things to do is sleep. When one walrus is awakened, it slaps another walrus. This goes on until the whole herd is awake. In time, they will fall back to sleep.

Think and Learn

1. How much does a walrus weigh? _1,800–2,700 kilograms_
2. Why are the tusks of a walrus important? __ They help the walrus to move on ice and are used for protection.
3. What do walruses eat? _____clams_____
4. Walruses live together in _____herds_____

25

Wolverine

The wolverine is the largest member of the weasel family. It reaches a height of 0.3 metre at the shoulder and weighs 13 to 23 kilograms. Wolverines are covered with long, shaggy, dark brown hair. Water does not freeze to their fur.

For their size, wolverines are probably the strongest and fiercest animals of the North. Often, wolverines chase away a bear or a mountain lion from its food so they can eat the food. After a wolverine eats a large meal, it will not eat again for a few days. Female wolverines give birth to two or three cubs in a litter. They are born in early summer already covered in woolly fur coats. By winter, the cubs can live on their own.

Think and Learn

1. The wolverine is the largest member of the ___weasel___ family.
2. What is special about wolverine fur? __It never freezes.__
3. Why are wolverines thought of as fierce animals? __They will chase away a bear or mountain lion from its food.__
4. When are wolverine cubs born? __in early summer__

26

Bald Eagle

The bald eagle is a bird of prey, or a bird that catches and eats other animals. It is a large bird, with a wingspan reaching 2.5 metres. The bald eagle is well known for its white head and neck. Most bald eagles live near water because they love to eat fish. Their hooked bills and long, curved claws help them to catch fish.

Of all the eagles, bald eagles build the largest nests. Some nests have been measured at 2.5 metres across! Eagles lay two ivory-white eggs. The eaglets are born brown. They do not look like adults until they are three years old. The bald eagle has been the national bird of the United States since 1782.

Think and Learn

1. The bald eagle has a wingspan of _____ 2.5 metres
2. What colour is the bald eagle's head? _____white_____
3. What helps bald eagles catch fish? __their hooked bills and long, curved claws__
4. The bald eagle is the national bird of _the United States_

28

Answer Key

Beaver

The beaver is a member of the rodent family. It grows to a length of 0.6 metre and usually weighs 15 to 18 kilograms. The beaver has dark brown fur that keeps the animal warm and dry. Its strong jaws have two cutting teeth, called incisors. The incisors keep growing all through a beaver's life so that these teeth are never worn down. Beavers use their incisors to cut down trees. Beavers eat twigs and bark from trees that grow near water.

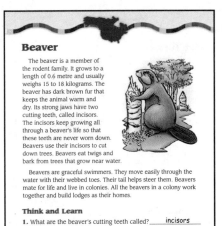

Beavers are graceful swimmers. They move easily through the water with their webbed toes. Their tail helps steer them. Beavers mate for life and live in colonies. All the beavers in a colony work together and build lodges as their homes.

Think and Learn

1. What are the beaver's cutting teeth called? __incisors__
2. What do beavers eat? __twigs and bark from trees__
3. How does a beaver use its tail? __for steering in water__
4. What is a beaver home called? __a lodge__

29   North America

29

Beaver Lodges

Beavers in a colony work together to build their lodges. Lodges are made of tree branches and grass. Beavers use mud to keep the branches in place. A lodge can be 1 to 2 metres high and 2 metres across. It has two rooms. The living room is above the water. It is where the beavers sleep and keep warm. The underwater storage room is where they keep their food. If the water level drops, beavers build dams. Dams raise the water level around the lodge so the storage room stays under water.

1. In the beaver lodge above, label the entrance, the living room and the storage room.
2. Is the entrance above water or below water? __below water__

North America   30

30

Grey Wolf

The grey wolf is the largest member of the wild dog family. This animal can reach a length of 1.2 metres and can weigh 45 kilograms. Grey wolves live in northern forests. They hunt for deer, elk and moose in packs of 3 to 24. Wolves, like other members of the dog family, can go for several days without food.

The leader for the wolf pack is the strongest male. Other wolves show respect by lowering their ears and putting their tails between their legs. Wolves mate for life. A female gives birth to a litter of 3 to 13 young, called pups. The pups are helpless at first. Other members of the pack help the parents care for the cubs.

Think and Learn

1. The grey wolf is a member of the __wild dog__ family.
2. Where do grey wolves live? __in northern forests__
3. Grey wolves hunt in __packs__
4. How do wolves show respect to the leader? __by lowering their ears and putting their tails between their legs__

31   North America

31

Word Search

Find the names of North American animals in the puzzle. They are written **across** and **down**.

caribou	beaver	eagle	armadillo
fox	skunk	bear	pronghorn
wolf	deer	rabbit	porcupine
bat	weasel	antelope	

North America   32   © 2000 Tribune Education. All Rights Reserved.

32

Grizzly Bear

Grizzly bears once lived in large numbers from Canada to Mexico. Now, most grizzly bears live in national parks. Male grizzly bears stand 2.5 metres tall and weigh 360 to 450 kilograms. Grizzly bears have very good senses of smell and hearing. These senses make up for their poor eyesight.

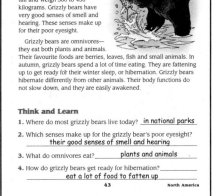

Grizzly bears are omnivores—they eat both plants and animals. Their favourite foods are berries, leaves, fish and small animals. In autumn, grizzly bears spend a lot of time eating. They are fattening up to get ready for their winter sleep, or hibernation. Grizzly bears hibernate differently from other animals. Their body functions do not slow down, and they are easily awakened.

Think and Learn

1. Where do most grizzly bears live today? __in national parks__
2. Which senses make up for the grizzly bear's poor eyesight? __their good senses of smell and hearing__
3. What do omnivores eat? __plants and animals__
4. How do grizzly bears get ready for hibernation? __eat a lot of food to fatten up__

43   North America

43

Dot-to-Dot

Connect the dots. Colour the picture.

North America   44

44

Everything About Animals

Answer Key

Moose

The largest member of the deer family is the moose. These huge animals are 3 metres long and weigh about 816 kilograms. Male moose have very large, flattened antlers. Every year they shed their antlers and grow a new pair in spring. Moose enjoy water and are excellent swimmers. They usually live near marshes, lakes or in moist forests.

During the summer months, moose eat water plants, roots, leaves and grass. In winter, moose walk easily through the deep snow. They find tree shoots and twigs to eat. Moose live alone in the summer. When winter arrives, it is common for small bands of moose to stay together in the woods for warmth and protection.

Think and Learn

1. The moose is a member of the ____deer____ family.

2. Each year moose shed their __antlers__, then grow a new pair.

3. Where do moose usually live?
____near marshes, lakes, or in moist forests____

4. Why do moose stay together in small bands in winter?
____for warmth and protection____

55

Otter

Otters are members of the weasel family. Their long bodies have special features, or adaptations, that allow them to live most of the time in water. Otters have flat tails and webbed feet that help them swim. Their coarse, outer fur is waterproof. They also close their nostrils and ears when underwater.

Otters make their homes by digging burrows or finding caves near water. They mainly eat fish that they catch while swimming. But they also eat crayfish, frogs, snails and insects. Otters are fun to watch because they are so playful. They love to slide on their bellies down banks of mud or snow and splash into the water. They communicate with each other by barking, chirping and growling.

Think and Learn

1. Where do otters spend most of their time? ____in water____

2. Otters have ____webbed____ feet.

3. What do otters eat?
____fish, crayfish, frogs, snails and insects____

4. How do otters communicate with each other?
____by barking, chirping and growling____

56

Wild Turkey

Wild turkeys are large birds that live mainly on the ground. Males, or toms, may weigh as much as 10 kilograms. Females, or hens, weigh only 5 kilograms. Tom turkeys look different from hens. They have a flap of skin, called a snood, that falls over the beak. They also have a wattle, a flap of skin that grows from the throat. Both toms and hens have short rounded wings and heavy bodies. They fly for only short distances. They also have strong feet with four toes. This makes them very fast runners.

Wild turkeys live in woods near water. They eat seeds and insects but sometimes eat frogs or lizards. When threatened, they usually run away and hide. Wild turkeys sleep in tree branches at night.

Think and Learn

1. Where do wild turkeys live? ____in woods near water____

2. What features do toms have that hens do not? ____
____snoods and wattles____

3. What makes turkeys fast runners?
____strong feet with four toes____

4. Where do wild turkeys sleep? ____in tree branches____

57

Porcupine

The porcupine (POR kyoo pighn) is a gnawing animal that is best known for its strong, sharp quills. Quills are bunches of hair that have grown together. The quills are white with black tips. They cover a porcupine's tail, sides and back. Porcupines are rather small, weighing between 6 and 9 kilograms. They are also peaceful and never attack other animals.

Porcupines are nocturnal. This means they sleep during the day and are active at night. They spend most of the night in trees looking for food. They might climb 18 to 21 metres up a tree to reach young leaves. In summer, they eat seeds, fruits and leaves. In winter, they eat twigs, leaves, bark and pine needles.

Think and Learn

1. What are quills? bunches of hair that have grown together

2. Why don't porcupines attack other animals? ____
____because they are peaceful____

3. Porcupines are ____nocturnal____, they sleep during the day.

4. What do porcupines eat during the summer? ____
____seeds, fruit, and leaves____

58

Colour Me

I am a ____porcupine____.

59

Striped Skunk

The skunk is known for its black and white fur and its horrible odour. The striped skunk is the most common kind of skunk. It gets its name from the white stripes running down its back. Skunks are about the size of a small cat, measuring 38 centimetres long. They weigh 2 to 3 kilograms. Skunks have short legs, an arched back, a long bushy tail and a patch of white fur on the forehead.

Skunks make their dens in burrows, hollow trees and under buildings. They are found in forests, grasslands and in towns. Even though skunks annoy people with their odour, skunks are very helpful animals. Skunks eat harmful insects, rats, mice and other small animals that damage crops and fields.

Think and Learn

1. What two things are skunks known for? ____
____their black and white fur and horrible odour____

2. A skunk is about the same size as a small ____cat____.

3. Where are skunks found? in forests, grasslands and towns

4. How are skunks helpful to people? ____
____They eat harmful insects, rats and mice.____

60

Answer Key

Animal Defences

Skunks and porcupines have adaptations that help them defend themselves. Because of their colouring, skunks do not blend in with their environment. If an animal threatens a skunk, the skunk warns the animal by stomping its feet. If the animal does not leave, the skunk sprays the animal with a bad-smelling liquid.

Porcupines ignore most animals. However, if a porcupine feels threatened, it raises the quills on its sides and back. Then, it swings its quill-covered tail at the animal. The quills are barbed. They get stuck in the skin of the animal and are very painful.

Think and Learn

1. How does a skunk warn an animal to go away?
   by stomping its feet

2. What does a porcupine do when it feels threatened?
   It raises the quills on its sides and back.
   Then, it swings its quill-covered tail at the animal.

61   North America

61

White-Tailed Deer

The white-tailed deer is easy to recognize by its snow-white tail. White-tailed deer are found throughout North America, but they are most common in southern Canada and northern United States. Only the males, called bucks, grow antlers. These antlers are shed each winter. White-tailed deer eat nuts and berries, as well as the buds and twigs from trees.

White-tailed deer are fast runners and great jumpers. Bucks frequently fight during mating season. They use their antlers and hooves as weapons. Female deer, called does, give birth to one to three fawns in the spring. The fawns are covered with white spots that disappear in six months.

Think and Learn

1. What are white-tailed deer recognized by? _snow-white tail_

2. Only bucks grow _antlers_

3. What do deer eat? _nuts, berries, tree buds and twigs_

4. How is a fawn's colouring different from an adult deer?
   Fawns are covered with white spots.

North America   62

62

Pronghorn

The pronghorn is North America's fastest animal. It can run about 64 kilometres per hour and jump very high. The pronghorn is mostly covered with reddish-brown fur and has white fur on the lower parts of its body, including the tail. The pronghorn lifts its fur straight up to cool its body in hot weather. In cold weather, it holds its fur flat against its body for warmth. The pronghorn has long horns that it never sheds.

Pronghorn live in the grasslands of western United States and Canada. They eat shrubs, sagebrush, grass and twigs. In summer, they live in small groups. As winter comes, they form large herds of 100 or more.

Think and Learn

1. The pronghorn is North America's _fastest_ animal.

2. How does a pronghorn keep cool in hot weather?
   It lifts its fur straight up.

3. Where do pronghorn live?
   in grasslands of western U.S. and Canada

4. What do pronghorn eat? _shrubs, sagebush, grass and twigs_

63   North America

63

Compare and Contrast

Read about the white-tailed deer and the pronghorn. Then, use the Venn diagram and the facts you have learned to compare and contrast these two animals. Write facts that tell only about the white-tailed deer on the left, facts that tell only about pronghorn on the right and facts that tell about both in the middle.

White-Tailed Deer

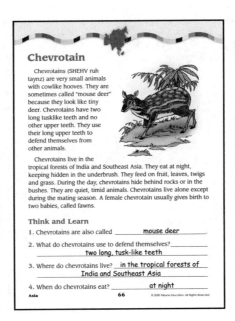

-shed antlers
-eat nuts, berries, tree buds, and twigs
-live in southern Canada and northern United States

Both

-live in N.A.
-fast runners
-good jumpers
-white tail

-horns are never shed
-live in large herds in winter
-lift fur straight up to cool off in summer
-live in grasslands of western United States and Canada
-eat shrubs, sagebush, grass and twigs
-live in small groups in summer

Pronghorn

North America   64   © 2000 Tribune Education. All Rights Reserved.

64

Chevrotain

Chevrotains (SHEHV ruh taynz) are very small animals with cowlike hooves. They are sometimes called "mouse deer" because they look like tiny deer. Chevrotains have two long tusklike teeth and no other upper teeth. They use their long upper teeth to defend themselves from other animals.

Chevrotains live in the tropical forests of India and Southeast Asia. They eat at night, keeping hidden in the underbrush. They feed on fruit, leaves, twigs and grass. During the day, chevrotains hide behind rocks or in the bushes. They are quiet, timid animals. Chevrotains live alone except during the mating season. A female chevrotain usually gives birth to two babies, called fawns.

Think and Learn

1. Chevrotains are also called _mouse deer_

2. What do chevrotains use to defend themselves?
   two long, tusk-like teeth

3. Where do chevrotains live? _in the tropical forests of India and Southeast Asia_

4. When do chevrotains eat? _at night_

Asia   66   © 2000 Tribune Education. All Rights Reserved.

66

Giant Panda

The giant panda is a very large black and white furry animal. Scientists used to classify pandas as part of the raccoon family. Now, they classify pandas as bears. The giant panda is found in bamboo forests in the mountains of west central China.

Pandas reach a height of 1.5 metres and weigh about 90 kilograms. They easily climb trees and spend most of their time eating bamboo plants. They eat every part of the plant. Pandas have a special thumblike toe on their front feet used for holding bamboo stems. Their teeth are large and wide to help them grind up the bamboo.

Think and Learn

1. Scientists now classify the giant panda as a _as bears_

2. Where do giant pandas live? _in bamboo forests in China_

3. Pandas eat all parts of the _bamboo_ plant.

4. How do pandas use the thumblike toe on their front feet?
   for holding bamboo

67   Asia

67

Everything About Animals

Answer Key

A Vanishing Act

The panda is one of many endangered animals. Endangered animals may soon disappear from Earth. That's what happened to dinosaurs, dodo birds and passenger pigeons. They disappeared, or became extinct.

Write the letter that comes before each letter in the alphabet to decode the names of some endangered animals.

A B C D E F G H I J K L M N O P Q R S T U V W X Y Z

M O U N T A I N   G O R I L L A
N P V O U B J O   H P S J M M B

A F R I C A N   E L E P H A N T
B G S J D B O   F M F Q I B O U

W H O O P I N G   C R A N E
X I J P Q J O H   D S B O F

B L A C K   R H I N O
C M B D L   S I J O P

G I A N T   P A N D A
H J B O U   Q B O E B

S E A   L I O N
T F B   M J P O

G R E Y   W O L F
H F B Z   X P M G

C H E E T A H
D I F F U B I

Asia   68

68

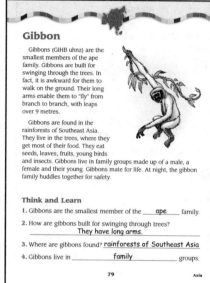

Gibbon

Gibbons (GIHB uhnz) are the smallest members of the ape family. Gibbons are built for swinging through the trees. In fact, it is awkward for them to walk on the ground. Their long arms enable them to "fly" from branch to branch, with leaps over 9 metres.

Gibbons are found in the rainforests of Southeast Asia. They live in the trees, where they get most of their food. They eat seeds, leaves, fruits, young birds and insects. Gibbons live in family groups made up of a male, a female and their young. Gibbons mate for life. At night, the gibbon family huddles together for safety.

Think and Learn

1. Gibbons are the smallest member of the _____ape_____ family.
2. How are gibbons built for swinging through trees?
   _____They have long arms._____
3. Where are gibbons found? _____rainforests of Southeast Asia_____
4. Gibbons live in _____family_____ groups.

79   Asia

79

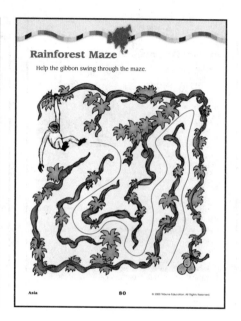

Rainforest Maze

Help the gibbon swing through the maze.

Asia   80   © 2000 Tribune Education. All Rights Reserved.

80

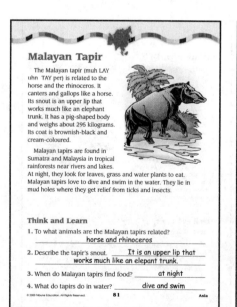

Malayan Tapir

The Malayan tapir (muh LAY uhn TAY per) is related to the horse and the rhinoceros. It canters and gallops like a horse. Its snout is an upper lip that works much like an elephant trunk. It has a pig-shaped body and weighs about 295 kilograms. Its coat is brownish-black and cream-coloured.

Malayan tapirs are found in Sumatra and Malaysia in tropical rainforests near rivers and lakes. At night, they look for leaves, grass and water plants to eat. Malayan tapirs love to dive and swim in the water. They lie in mud holes where they get relief from ticks and insects.

Think and Learn

1. To what animals are the Malayan tapirs related?
   _____horse and rhinoceros_____
2. Describe the tapir's snout. _____It is an upper lip that works much like an elephant trunk._____
3. When do Malayan tapirs find food? _____at night_____
4. What do tapirs do in water? _____dive and swim_____

© 2000 Tribune Education. All Rights Reserved.   81   Asia

81

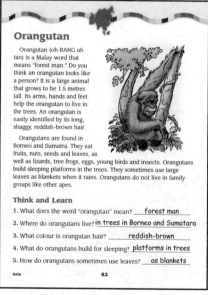

Orangutan

Orangutan (oh RANG uh tan) is a Malay word that means "forest man." Do you think an orangutan looks like a person? It is a large animal that grows to be 1.5 metres tall. Its arms, hands and feet help the orangutan to live in the trees. An orangutan is easily identified by its long, shaggy, reddish-brown hair.

Orangutans are found in Borneo and Sumatra. They eat fruits, nuts, seeds and leaves, as well as lizards, tree frogs, eggs, young birds and insects. Orangutans build sleeping platforms in the trees. They sometimes use large leaves as blankets when it rains. Orangutans do not live in family groups like other apes.

Think and Learn

1. What does the word "orangutan" mean? _____forest man_____
2. Where do orangutans live? _____in trees in Borneo and Sumatara_____
3. What colour is orangutan hair? _____reddish-brown_____
4. What do orangutans build for sleeping? _____platforms in trees_____
5. How do orangutans sometimes use leaves? _____as blankets_____

Asia   82

82

Sloth Bear

The sloth bear is a huge, shaggy bear. It has a mane of fur around its neck. Sloth bears have very long snouts. They live in the rocky canyons and hills of India and Sri Lanka. They hunt for termites and bee nests at night. A sloth bear can climb any tree to find food. It uses its long claws to rip open a termite or bee nest. The sloth bear is so noisy when it eats that people can hear it 182 metres away!

Sloth bears sleep in caves during the day. They are also very noisy sleepers. They snore as loud as they eat! Sloth bears live in family units. Both parents care for the cubs. The cubs stay with their parents for 3 years.

Think and Learn

1. Sloth bears have very long _____snouts_____
2. Where do sloth bears live? _____in rocky canyons and hills of India and Sri Lanka_____
3. What do sloth bears eat? _____termites and bees_____
4. What do sloth bears do during the day? _____sleep_____

83   Asia

83

Everything About Animals

Answer Key

Snow Leopard

The snow leopard (snoh LEHP erd) is large cat that lives in the mountains of central Asia. It is 1.5 metres long and weighs about 40 kilograms. The snow leopard is known for its beautiful fur. Its dense undercoat is covered with long grey and cream-coloured hair and speckled with black spots. The snow leopard's large paws are padded for warmth.

The fierce snow leopard does not roar like a lion but purrs like a house cat. Like most cats, snow leopards hunt animals for food. The snow leopard is endangered. It has been overhunted for its fur. It has also lost its natural prey due to the clearing of land for farming.

Think and Learn
1. Where do snow leopards live? <u>mountains of central Asia</u>
2. The snow leopard's paws are padded for <u>warmth</u>.
3. What sound do snow leopards make? <u>They purr.</u>
4. Why are snow leopards endangered? <u>overhunting and loss of prey</u>

Asia   84

84

Tiger

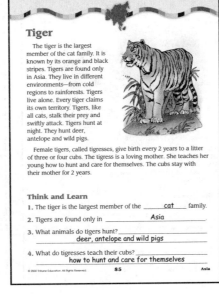

The tiger is the largest member of the cat family. It is known by its orange and black stripes. Tigers are found only in Asia. They live in different environments—from cold regions to rainforests. Tigers live alone. Every tiger claims its own territory. Tigers, like all cats, stalk their prey and swiftly attack. Tigers hunt at night. They hunt deer, antelope and wild pigs.

Female tigers, called tigresses, give birth every 2 years to a litter of three or four cubs. The tigress is a loving mother. She teaches her young how to hunt and care for themselves. The cubs stay with their mother for 2 years.

Think and Learn
1. The tiger is the largest member of the <u>cat</u> family.
2. Tigers are found only in <u>Asia</u>
3. What animals do tigers hunt? <u>deer, antelope and wild pigs</u>
4. What do tigresses teach their cubs? <u>how to hunt and care for themselves</u>

   85   Asia

85

Hidden Pictures

The tiger's stripes help keep it well hidden in the jungle. Find the tigers hidden in the picture. Colour the picture.

Asia   86

86

Water Buffalo

The water buffalo is a gigantic animal that is 3 metres long and 1.8 metres tall. It has thick, greyish-black skin. Water buffalo have large horns. The horns grow out of each side of the head and curve upward. Water buffalo love water. They are often found resting in water up to their noses. Water buffalo also roll in mud until they are covered with it. This helps protect them from insects.

Water buffalo are wild cattle. Some have been tamed and help with rice farming. Rice is grown in flooded fields. Water buffalo can easily pull a plow through water that is knee deep. Although they look like gentle animals, water buffalo can become very fierce. However, they are friendly to people they know.

Think and Learn
1. Large <u>horns</u> grow out of a water buffalo's head.
2. What do water buffalo like to rest in? <u>water</u>
3. Why do water buffalo roll in mud? <u>to help protect themselves from insects</u>
4. How do water buffalo help with rice farming? <u>They pull a plow through water.</u>

87   Asia

87

Wild Boar

The wild boar is a wild hog found in forests throughout Asia. It can reach a length of 1.2 to 1.5 metres and weighs an average of 136 kilograms. Its long piglike snout is used for lifting, pushing and digging. The wild boar has two long tusks that grow out of its lower jaw. These tusks are 30 centimetres long. Wild boars use their tusks to protect themselves.

Wild boars like to eat almost anything. They use their snout to search for leaves, fruit, roots, worms and insects. Wild boars can see and hear well. However, they rely mainly on their sense of smell. Male and female boars travel in separate herds. The female boars raise their young alone.

Think and Learn
1. Where are wild boars found? <u>in forests throughout Asia</u>
2. How do wild boars use their snouts? <u>for lifting, pushing and digging</u>
3. Wild boars use their <u>tusks</u> for protection.
4. Which sense do wild boars rely on most? <u>smell</u>

Asia   88

88

Chinchilla

Chinchillas (chihn CHIHL uhz) look like large mice, but they are actually related to squirrels. They have thick, soft fur. Their blue-grey colour is beautiful. In the 1500s, Spanish explorers brought chinchillas back to Europe. The demand for chinchilla fur nearly caused this animal to be killed off. Today, a small chinchilla population lives in the Andes Mountains.

Chinchillas eat roots and grass. Water is scarce high in the Andes. However, chinchillas get enough water from the plants they eat. Chinchillas are nocturnal, or active at night. They sleep during the day. At sundown, they begin looking for food.

Think and Learn
1. Chinchillas are related to <u>squirrels</u>
2. Describe chinchilla fur. <u>thick, soft, beautiful blue-grey color</u>
3. Where do chinchillas live? <u>in the Andes Mountains</u>
4. How do chinchillas get water? <u>from the plants they eat</u>

Central and South America   90

90

     Everything About Animals

Answer Key

Giant Anteater

The giant anteater is an animal that eats ants and termites. Giant anteaters have three large claws on each paw. They use their claws to rip open ant nests. Giant anteaters have a sticky tongue that is 0.6 metre long. They push their tongue into an anthill to get the ants. Giant anteaters cannot see well. Instead, they find ants with their sharp sense of smell.

Giant anteaters are found only in Central and South America. They never dig burrows or make homes. Instead, they wander alone looking for food until they tire. Then, they lie down in a hidden place, cover their heads with their long bushy tails and fall asleep.

Think and Learn
1. What do giant anteaters eat? __ants and termites__
2. How do giant anteaters use their claws? __to rip open ant nests__
3. Giant anteaters have __sticky__ tongues.
4. Where do giant anteaters sleep? __in a hidden place with their heads covered by their tails__

91   **Central and South America**

91

Giant Armadillo

The giant armadillo (ahr muh DIHL oh) is the largest of all armadillos. It can reach a length of 1.5 metres and weigh as much as 59 kilograms. Giant armadillos are found only near rivers in the eastern part of South America. Early Spanish explorers named the armadillo. The name means "little armored one." Armadillos are covered with hard bony plates called scutes.

Giant armadillos use their long curved claws for digging burrows and for finding food. They eat termites, worms, snakes and insects. Armadillos are quiet animals that prefer to live alone. When threatened, they either run away or crouch low. Their scutes protect their soft undersides.

Think and Learn
1. Where are giant armadillos found? __near rivers in eastern South America__
2. What does the word "armadillo" mean? __little armored one__
3. What are scutes? __hard body plates__
4. What do armadillos use their claws for? __digging burrows and finding food__

Central and South America   92

92

Jaguar

The jaguar (JAG wahr) is a member of the cat family. It is 1.8 metres long and weighs about 136 kilograms. This beautiful animal has yellowish-tan with black dots encircled by black rings. Some jaguars are almost entirely black. The jaguar is found throughout Central and South America in many different habitats. It can live in shrub country, rainforests, mountains and woods.

Jaguars like to hunt almost any kind of animal, including fish, turtles, deer and wild pigs. They often lie on tree branches and wait until they can pounce down on their prey. Not only are jaguars skilled climbers, they are also great swimmers. They will often hunt in the water, especially when the rivers have flooded.

Think and Learn
1. The jaguar is a member of the __cat__ family.
2. In what habitats do jaguars live? __shrub country, rainforests, mountains and woods__
3. Where do jaguars often wait for prey? __in tree branches__
4. Jaguars are skilled __climbers__ and great __swimmers__.

93   **Central and South America**

93

Llama

Llamas (LAH muhz) belong to the camel family. They are 1.2 to 1.5 metres tall and weigh over 90 kilograms. Llamas come in many colours—white, tan, brown and black. Llamas live in the semi-desert region near the Andes Mountains. They eat shrubs and other plants. Like the camel, a llama can live for weeks without water. The llama gets the water it needs from the plants it eats.

Llamas have been tamed for centuries. Their wool is used for making clothing, ropes and blankets. Llamas are useful pack animals. They travel easily through mountains carrying heavy loads. However, if a llama thinks it has worked long enough for one day, it sits down and refuses to move.

Think and Learn
1. Llamas belong to the __camel__ family.
2. What do llamas eat? __shrubs and other plants__
3. Llamas can live for weeks without __water__.
4. Why are llamas useful pack animals? __They travel easily through mountains carrying heavy loads.__

Central and South America   94

94

Macaw

Macaws (muh KAWZ) are the largest members of the parrot family. They come in many bright colors. All macaws have powerful hooked bills. They use their bills to help them climb and to break open nuts and seeds. Macaws have four toes on each foot. Their feet are well suited for perching, climbing and holding objects. Macaws are only found in rainforests. They live in holes that they make in tree trunks.

Macaws are in danger of extinction, or dying out. They are losing their homes as the rainforest is destroyed. Laws protect these birds, but people still capture them to sell as pets. Macaws are not good pets because they like to scream and bite.

Think and Learn
1. Macaws are members of the __parrot__ family.
2. All macaws have powerful, hooked __bills__.
3. What do macaws use their feet for? __perching, climbing and holding objects__
4. Why are macaws in danger of extinction? __They are losing their homes and are captured to sell as pets.__

© 2000 Tribune Education. All Rights Reserved.   95   **Central and South America**

95

Spider Monkey

Spider monkeys are small monkeys well suited for living in trees. In fact, they rarely come down to the ground. These monkeys move quickly through trees by swinging and jumping from branch to branch. Spider monkeys have tails that are longer than their bodies. These tails can easily grab and pick up things.

Spider monkeys are found in rainforests from southern Mexico to the northern part of South America. They eat nuts and fruit and sometimes eggs. Spider monkeys live in groups, or bands, of 10 to 40 monkeys. Every band of monkeys lives in its own area, or territory. One band of monkeys will not go into the territory of another band.

Think and Learn
1. How do spider monkeys move quickly through trees? __by swinging and jumping from branch to branch__
2. Their __tails__ can grab and pick up things.
3. What do spider monkeys eat? __nuts, fruit and eggs__
4. Spider monkeys live in groups called __bands__.

Central and South America   96   © 2000 Tribune Education. All Rights Reserved.

96

Answer Key

Dot-to-Dot

Spider monkeys live in rainforests. They usually run away and hide if another animal scares them. Connect the dots to find the hidden monkey. Then, colour the picture.

97   **Central and South America**

97

Toucan

Toucans (TOO kanz) are birds with large colourful bills. Although a toucan bill looks heavy, it is really very light. The bill is hollow. It is made from a hornlike material. Toucans live in the rainforests of Central and South America. Toucans eat fruit, large insects, lizards and young birds. A toucan sits on a branch and reaches for fruit with its long bill. The curved end of the bill helps the toucan pick the fruit and hold on to it.

Toucans make their nests in the holes of trees. Both the male and female take turns sitting on the eggs. Newly hatched toucans are blind and have no feathers. After 6 to 7 weeks, the young toucans are ready to live on their own.

Think and Learn

1. Toucans have large colourful _____ bills _____

2. Where do toucans live? _____
   _____ rainforests of Central and South America _____

3. What do they eat? _____
   _____ fruit, large insects, lizards, young birds _____

4. Where do toucans make nests? _____ in the holes of trees _____

Central and South America   98

98

Two-Toed Sloth

A sloth (slawth) is an animal that lives in trees. Sloths rarely go down to the ground. In fact, they cannot walk at all. The two-toed sloth has two long, curved claws on its front legs. Sloths use their claws to hold onto tree trunks and branches. They often hang upside down. Sloths move very slowly along tree branches, paw over paw, while hanging upside down.

Two-toed sloths are found from the southern part of Central America to central Brazil and Peru. They eat leaves, twigs and buds. Sloths are nocturnal, or active at night. It is hard to see sloths sleeping in the trees during the day. Green algae often grow on the sloths' fur, so the sloths blend in with the leaves.

Think and Learn

1. Sloths cannot _____ walk _____ at all.

2. What do sloths use to hold onto branches? _____ their claws _____

3. When are sloths active? _____ at night _____

4. How do sloths blend in with tree leaves? _____
   _____ They have green algae growing on their fur. _____

© 2000 Tribune Education. All Rights Reserved.   99   **Central and South America**

99

Woolly Monkey

Woolly monkeys are named for their beautiful thick, woolly coats. They are found in forests along the Amazon River in Columbia, Ecuador, Peru and Brazil. They eat fruit, flowers and leaves. Unlike other tree-living monkeys, woolly monkeys are often found on the ground. While on the ground, they stand straight up, using their tails for support.

Woolly monkeys live in groups, or bands, of 10 to 30 monkeys. They move more slowly than other monkeys. When frightened, they swing through tree branches and hide. Woolly monkeys are friendly. They are often seen in the company of other kinds of monkeys.

Think and Learn

1. Woolly monkeys are named for their _____ their woolly coats _____

2. How do woolly monkeys stand while on the ground? _____
   _____ straight up, using their tails for support _____

3. Woolly monkeys live in groups called _____ bands _____

4. Woolly monkeys move more _____ slowly _____ than other monkeys.

Central and South America   100   © 2000 Tribune Education. All Rights Reserved.

100

Dingo

The dingo (DIHNG goh) is the only wild member of the dog family found in Australia. Dingoes are about the same size as medium-sized dogs. Their ears stand up, and they have bushy tails. Dingoes cannot bark but can yelp and howl. Dingoes are excellent hunters. They hunt alone or in family groups for small animals to eat. Scientists think Aborigines, native Australians, brought dingoes to Australia thousands of years ago.

Dingoes give birth only once a year to three to six puppies. Both parents care for the puppies and keep them hidden. The Aborigines search for the puppies to train them for hunting. Adult dingoes cannot be trained.

Think and Learn

1. The dingo is a member of the _____ dog _____ family.

2. Dingoes cannot _____ bark _____, but they can yelp and howl.

3. What do dingoes hunt for? _____ small animals _____

4. Why do Aborigines look for dingo puppies? _____
   _____ to train them for hunting _____

Australia   102   © 2000 Tribune Education. All Rights Reserved.

102

Dugong

The dugong (DOO gahng) is related to the manatee. Dugongs are mammals, or animals that feed their young with their mothers' milk. Even though dugongs breathe air, they spend their entire life in water. They surface only to breathe about every 1 to 10 minutes. They have an unusual snout. It is rounded, with a large whiskered upper lip. Only male dugongs grow tusks.

Dugongs are found in the Indian Ocean, the Red Sea and off the northern coast of Australia. Dugongs eat only sea grass. They are often called sea cows because they graze on sea grass just as cows graze on field grass.

Think and Learn

1. What are dugongs related to? _____ manatees _____

2. Only male dugongs grow _____ tusks _____

3. Where are dugongs found? _____ in the Indian Ocean, _____
   _____ the Red Sea and off the northern coast of Australia _____

4. Dugongs are often called _____ sea cows _____

© 2000 Tribune Education. All Rights Reserved.   103   **Australia**

103

Answer Key

Echidna

The echidna (ih KIHD nuh) is sometimes called a spiny anteater. It is found throughout Australia in open forests. The echidna's body is covered with coarse hair and pointed spines. Echidnas sleep in hollow logs during the day. At night, they use their sharp claws to scratch up insects. They eat the insects by licking them up with their long sticky tongues. Echidnas do not have teeth.

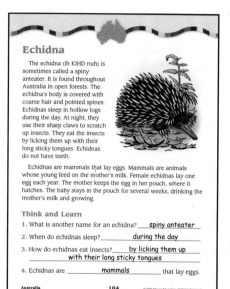

Echidnas are mammals that lay eggs. Mammals are animals whose young feed on the mother's milk. Female echidnas lay one egg each year. The mother keeps the egg in her pouch, where it hatches. The baby stays in the pouch for several weeks, drinking the mother's milk and growing.

Think and Learn

1. What is another name for an echidna? __spiny anteater__
2. When do echidnas sleep? __during the day__
3. How do echidnas eat insects? __by licking them up with their long sticky tongues__
4. Echidnas are __mammals__ that lay eggs.

Australia 104 © 2000 Tribune Education. All Rights Reserved.

104

Giant Grey Kangaroo

The giant grey kangaroo is the largest of all kangaroos. It grows to 2 metres tall. Kangaroos have huge feet and long, powerful tails. When kangaroos stand, they lean on their tails for balance. Kangaroos are found in the open forest and bush country of Australia. They eat fruit, leaves and roots. Kangaroos travel in groups called mobs.

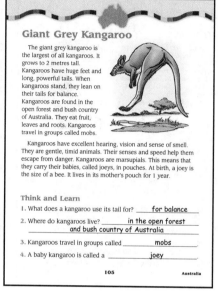

Kangaroos have excellent hearing, vision and sense of smell. They are gentle, timid animals. Their senses and speed help them escape from danger. Kangaroos are marsupials. This means that they carry their babies, called joeys, in pouches. At birth, a joey is the size of a bee. It lives in its mother's pouch for 1 year.

Think and Learn

1. What does a kangaroo use its tail for? __for balance__
2. Where do kangaroos live? __in the open forest and bush country of Australia__
3. Kangaroos travel in groups called __mobs__.
4. A baby kangaroo is called a __joey__.

105 Australia

105

Australian Animal Scramble

Unscramble the words below to find the names of Australian animals. The words below will help you.

1. R A O K A O R B U K __kookaburra__   2. A L K O A __koala__
3. L A B W Y A L __wallaby__
4. D I H A C E N __echidna__
5. G O U D G N __dugong__
6. O G N I D __dingo__
7. B W O T A M __wombat__
8. M A S T A N N A I V L I E D __Tasmanian__ __devil__
9. G N A K A O O R __kangaroo__   10. S Y P A L T P U __platypus__

dingo
wombat
dugong
echidna
platypus
Tasmanian devil
kangaroo
kookaburra
wallaby
koala

Australia 106 © 2000 Tribune Education. All Rights Reserved.

106

Koala

Although many people call the koala (koh AW luh) a koala bear, it is not a bear. The koala is a marsupial—a mammal with a pouch for carrying its young. The koala has beautiful gray, woolly fur. If threatened, koalas defend themselves with their sharp claws.

Koalas eat the leaves of eucalyptus trees. Koalas are found in the eucalyptus forests on the east coast of Australia. The only time a koala climbs down from a tree is to move to another tree. They get the water they need from the leaves they eat. Koalas are nocturnal and sleep 18 hours during the day. Female koalas have one baby at a time. The baby crawls into the mother's pouch, where it stays for 6 months. Then, the mother carries the baby on her back for 4 or 5 months.

Think and Learn

1. What is a marsupial? __a mammal with a pouch for its young__
2. What do koalas eat? __eucalyptus leaves__
3. When do koalas climb down a tree? __to move to another tree__
4. How long does a baby koala stay in its mother's pouch? __for six months__

© 2000 Tribune Education. All Rights Reserved. 107 Australia

107

Kookaburra

The kookaburra (KOOK uh ber uh) is a bird that lives in forests in the southern parts of Australia. It is best known for its loud screaming laughter. The kookaburra screams its laughing sounds at dawn and at dusk. Kookaburras make their homes in holes in trees. They eat a wide variety of foods, such as caterpillars, fish, small mammals, frogs and worms. Insects, however, are their favorite food.

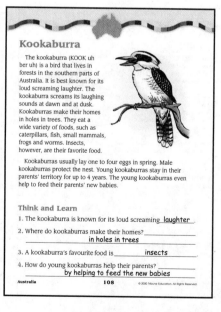

Kookaburras usually lay one to four eggs in spring. Male kookaburras protect the nest. Young kookaburras stay in their parents' territory for up to 4 years. The young kookaburras even help to feed their parents' new babies.

Think and Learn

1. The kookaburra is known for its loud screaming __laughter__.
2. Where do kookaburras make their homes? __in holes in trees__
3. A kookaburra's favourite food is __insects__.
4. How do young kookaburras help their parents? __by helping to feed the new babies__

Australia 108 © 2000 Tribune Education. All Rights Reserved.

108

Platypus

The platypus (PLAT ih pus) is a mammal that has a bill like a duck and a flat, beaverlike tail. It is found near rivers and streams in eastern Australia and Tasmania. The platypus is awkward on land but swims gracefully. It has claws under its webbed toes. It uses its claws for digging burrows and getting food. The platypus eats large amounts of snails, worms, shrimp and small fish.

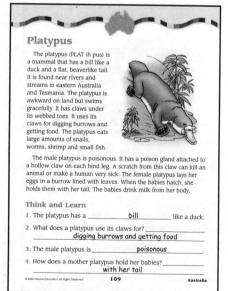

The male platypus is poisonous. It has a poison gland attached to a hollow claw on each hind leg. A scratch from this claw can kill an animal or make a human very sick. The female platypus lays her eggs in a burrow lined with leaves. When the babies hatch, she holds them with her tail. The babies drink milk from her body.

Think and Learn

1. The platypus has a __bill__ like a duck.
2. What does a platypus use its claws for? __digging burrows and getting food__
3. The male platypus is __poisonous__.
4. How does a mother platypus hold her babies? __with her tail__

© 2000 Tribune Education. All Rights Reserved. 109 Australia

109

Everything About Animals

Answer Key

Tasmanian Devil

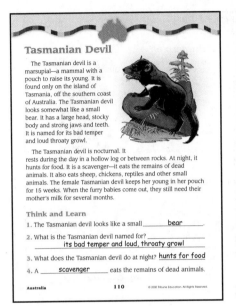

The Tasmanian devil is a marsupial—a mammal with a pouch to raise its young. It is found only on the island of Tasmania, off the southern coast of Australia. The Tasmanian devil looks somewhat like a small bear. It has a large head, stocky body and strong jaws and teeth. It is named for its bad temper and loud throaty growl.

The Tasmanian devil is nocturnal. It rests during the day in a hollow log or between rocks. At night, it hunts for food. It is a scavenger—it eats the remains of dead animals. It also eats sheep, chickens, reptiles and other small animals. The female Tasmanian devil keeps her young in her pouch for 15 weeks. When the furry babies come out, they still need their mother's milk for several months.

Think and Learn

1. The Tasmanian devil looks like a small ___bear___.

2. What is the Tasmanian devil named for? ___its bad temper and loud, throaty growl___

3. What does the Tasmanian devil do at night? ___hunts for food___

4. A ___scavenger___ eats the remains of dead animals.

110

Wallaby

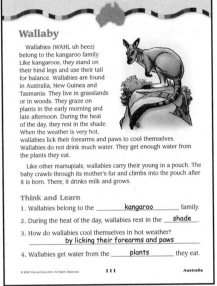

Wallabies (WAHL uh beez) belong to the kangaroo family. Like kangaroos, they stand on their hind legs and use their tail for balance. Wallabies are found in Australia, New Guinea and Tasmania. They live in grasslands or in woods. They graze on plants in the early morning and late afternoon. During the heat of the day, they rest in the shade. When the weather is very hot, wallabies lick their forearms and paws to cool themselves. Wallabies do not drink much water. They get enough water from the plants they eat.

Like other marsupials, wallabies carry their young in a pouch. The baby crawls through its mother's fur and climbs into the pouch after it is born. There, it drinks milk and grows.

Think and Learn

1. Wallabies belong to the ___kangaroo___ family.

2. During the heat of the day, wallabies rest in the ___shade___.

3. How do wallabies cool themselves in hot weather? ___by licking their forearms and paws___

4. Wallabies get water from the ___plants___ they eat.

111

Wombat

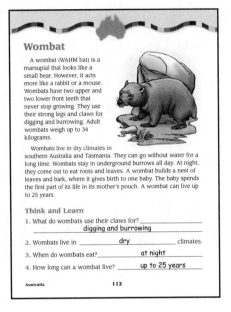

A wombat (WAHM bat) is a marsupial that looks like a small bear. However, it acts more like a rabbit or a mouse. Wombats have two upper and two lower front teeth that never stop growing. They use their strong legs and claws for digging and burrowing. Adult wombats weigh up to 34 kilograms.

Wombats live in dry climates in southern Australia and Tasmania. They can go without water for a long time. Wombats stay in underground burrows all day. At night, they come out to eat roots and leaves. A wombat builds a nest of leaves and bark, where it gives birth to one baby. The baby spends the first part of its life in its mother's pouch. A wombat can live up to 25 years.

Think and Learn

1. What do wombats use their claws for? ___digging and burrowing___

2. Wombats live in ___dry___ climates.

3. When do wombats eat? ___at night___

4. How long can a wombat live? ___up to 25 years___

112

African Elephant

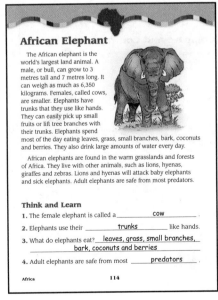

The African elephant is the world's largest land animal. A male, or bull, can grow to 3 metres tall and 7 metres long. It can weigh as much as 6,350 kilograms. Females, called cows, are smaller. Elephants have trunks that they use like hands. They can easily pick up small fruits or lift tree branches with their trunks. Elephants spend most of the day eating leaves, grass, small branches, bark, coconuts and berries. They also drink large amounts of water every day.

African elephants are found in the warm grasslands and forests of Africa. They live with other animals, such as lions, hyenas, giraffes and zebras. Lions and hyenas will attack baby elephants and sick elephants. Adult elephants are safe from most predators.

Think and Learn

1. The female elephant is called a ___cow___.

2. Elephants use their ___trunks___ like hands.

3. What do elephants eat? ___leaves, grass, small branches, bark, coconuts and berries___

4. Adult elephants are safe from most ___predators___.

114

Elephant Adaptations

Adaptations (ad ap TAY shuhnz) are special body parts or behaviors that animals have to survive in their environment. Some elephant adaptations help them live in hot places. They flap their large ears to cool off. They also do not have a thick layer of fat, like arctic animals have.

The most unusual elephant adaptation is its trunk. Elephants use their trunks to get food and water, cool off, breathe, touch things, smell, make sounds and "talk" to other elephants. Small "fingers" at the end of the trunk can pick up very small objects.

Think and Learn

1. Label the elephant adaptations in the picture.

2. How do elephants use their trunks? ___to get food and water, cool off, breathe, touch things, smell, make sounds, "talk" to other elephants and pick things up and carry them___

115

Elephant Facts

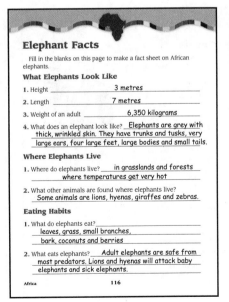

Fill in the blanks on this page to make a fact sheet on African elephants.

What Elephants Look Like

1. Height ___3 metres___

2. Length ___7 metres___

3. Weight of an adult ___6,350 kilograms___

4. What does an elephant look like? ___Elephants are grey with thick, wrinkled skin. They have trunks and tusks, very large ears, four large feet, large bodies and small tails.___

Where Elephants Live

1. Where do elephants live? ___in grasslands and forests where temperatures get very hot___

2. What other animals are found where elephants live? ___Some animals are lions, hyenas, giraffes and zebras.___

Eating Habits

1. What do elephants eat? ___leaves, grass, small branches, bark, coconuts and berries___

2. What eats elephants? ___Adult elephants are safe from most predators. Lions and hyenas will attack baby elephants and sick elephants.___

116

Answer Key

Giraffe

Giraffes are the tallest of all animals. They stand over 5.4 metres tall and weigh over 1,800 kilograms. Even though their necks are so long, they have the same number of neck bones as other animals. Giraffes have sharp eyesight. They can see in all directions without moving their heads. Every giraffe has a different pattern of patches, just as every human has different fingerprints.

Giraffes live in herds on the dry grasslands in Africa. They mainly eat leaves from acacia (uh KAY shuh) trees, which are the most common trees in the area. Giraffes can go weeks without water. When they drink, giraffes spread apart their front legs and lower their long necks to reach the water.

Think and Learn

1. Giraffes are the _____tallest_____ of all animals.

2. Compare the number of neck bones in giraffes to other animals. __same number of neck bones as other animals__

3. What do giraffes eat? ____mainly acacia tree leaves____

4. How do giraffes bend down to get a drink? _____
   ____They must spread apart their front legs.____

127   Africa

127

Dot-to-Dot

Connect the dots. Colour the picture.

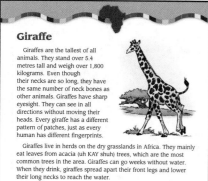

Africa   128

128

Chimpanzee

Chimpanzees (chihm pan ZEEZ) belong to the ape family. They are found in rainforests in Africa. Like apes, they can walk on two feet. However, they prefer to move about on all four legs like monkeys do. Chimpanzees have hands that look like human hands, but their thumbs are shorter. Chimpanzees eat fruit, leaves and insects.

Chimpanzees are one of the few animals that make and use tools. To get termites, chimpanzees trim sticks and put them inside termite hills. Then, they eat the termites that cling to the stick. Chimpanzees also build platforms in trees for sleeping. To communicate, or "talk," to each other, chimpanzees use different sounds.

Think and Learn

1. Is a chimpanzee a monkey or an ape? ____an ape____

2. Where are chimpanzees found? _____
   ____in rainforests in Africa____

3. What do chimpanzees eat? ____fruit, leaves and insects____

4. What can chimpanzees do that most other animals cannot do? ____make and use tools____

© 2000 Tribune Education. All Rights Reserved.   129   Africa

129

Gorilla

The gorilla is the largest member of the ape family. Adult males grow to 1.8 metres in height and weigh 181 kilograms. Females are smaller. Gorillas have broad chests, wide shoulders, long arms and short legs. Their entire body, except for the face, is covered with dark fur. Gorillas are peaceful animals that live in family groups. An adult male always leads the group. Females and their babies make up the rest of the group.

Gorillas are found in different parts of central Africa. Some live in mountain forests. Others live in forests on low ground. Gorillas spend most of the day eating leaves and fruit. At night, gorillas build sleeping platforms on the ground or in trees.

Think and Learn

1. Gorillas belong to the _____ape_____ family.

2. What makes up a gorilla family group? _____
   ____an adult male leader and females and their babies____

3. Where are gorillas found? ____in forests in central Africa____

4. Where do gorillas sleep? _____
   ____on sleeping platforms on the ground or in trees____

Africa   130

130

Apes and Monkeys

Apes and monkeys are the animals most closely related to humans. Apes and monkeys are different. Monkeys have tails. Apes do not. Apes have larger brains than monkeys. Larger brains allow for more difficult actions.

Even though they are different, apes and monkeys are alike in some ways. Both monkeys and apes can stand up on two legs. This keeps their hands free to do some kind of task. They both have hands and feet that look like human hands. Their hands and feet have "thumbs" that move in opposite directions to their fingers. This action lets apes and monkeys use their hands and feet to pick up things and hold them.

ape

monkey

Think and Learn

1. Label the monkey and the ape in the picture.

2. In what ways are monkeys and apes different? __Monkeys have tails. Apes do not. Apes have larger brains.__

3. How are monkeys and apes similar? __Both can stand up on two legs. Both have hands and feet that look like human hands.__

© 2000 Tribune Education. All Rights Reserved.   131   Africa

131

Compare and Contrast

Read about the chimpanzee and the gorilla. Then, use the Venn diagram and the facts you have learned to compare and contrast these two animals.

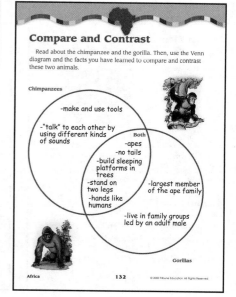

Chimpanzees
- make and use tools
- "talk" to each other by using different kinds of sounds

Both
- apes
- no tails
- build sleeping platforms in trees
- stand on two legs
- hands like humans

- largest member of the ape family
- live in family groups led by an adult male

Gorillas

Africa   132   © 2000 Tribune Education. All Rights Reserved.

132

Answer Key

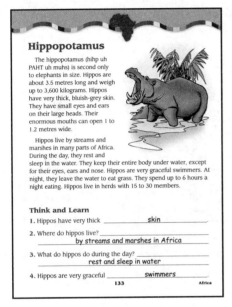

Hippopotamus

The hippopotamus (hihp uh PAHT uh muhs) is second only to elephants in size. Hippos are about 3.5 metres long and weigh up to 3,600 kilograms. Hippos have very thick, bluish-grey skin. They have small eyes and ears on their large heads. Their enormous mouths can open 1 to 1.2 metres wide.

Hippos live by streams and marshes in many parts of Africa. During the day, they rest and sleep in the water. They keep their entire body under water, except for their eyes, ears and nose. Hippos are very graceful swimmers. At night, they leave the water to eat grass. They spend up to 6 hours a night eating. Hippos live in herds with 15 to 30 members.

Think and Learn

1. Hippos have very thick _____skin_____.

2. Where do hippos live? _____by streams and marshes in Africa_____

3. What do hippos do during the day? _____rest and sleep in water_____

4. Hippos are very graceful _____swimmers_____.

133   **Africa**

133

Lion

The lion is one of the largest and fiercest members of the cat family. Lions range in size from 120 to 225 kilograms. Only male lions have a mane, the thick fur around the head. The mane protects lions when they fight to defend their territory, or area in which they live.

Lions sleep during the day and hunt at night. They hunt for antelope, zebras, young elephants and other smaller animals. Lions are social animals. They live in groups called prides. A pride is usually made up of one to six males and four to twelve females with their cubs. Each pride has its own territory. The members of a pride hunt only in their territory.

Think and Learn

1. Why do male lions have manes? _____to protect them when they fight to defend their territory_____

2. When do lions hunt? _____at night_____

3. Lions live in groups called _____prides_____.

4. Each pride hunts in its own _____territory_____.

Africa   134

134

Lion Maze

Complete the maze to help the lion cub find its way back to its pride.

© 2000 Nature Education. All Rights Reserved.   135   **Africa**

135

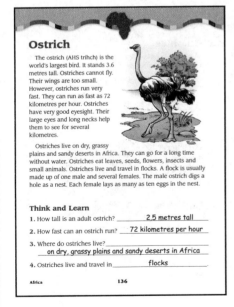

Ostrich

The ostrich (AHS trihch) is the world's largest bird. It stands 3.6 metres tall. Ostriches cannot fly. Their wings are too small. However, ostriches run very fast. They can run as fast as 72 kilometres per hour. Ostriches have very good eyesight. Their large eyes and long necks help them to see for several kilometres.

Ostriches live on dry, grassy plains and sandy deserts in Africa. They can go for a long time without water. Ostriches eat leaves, seeds, flowers, insects and small animals. Ostriches live and travel in flocks. A flock is usually made up of one male and several females. The male ostrich digs a hole as a nest. Each female lays as many as ten eggs in the nest.

Think and Learn

1. How tall is an adult ostrich? _____2.5 metres tall_____

2. How fast can an ostrich run? _____72 kilometres per hour_____

3. Where do ostriches live? _____on dry, grassy plains and sandy deserts in Africa_____

4. Ostriches live and travel in _____flocks_____.

Africa   136

136

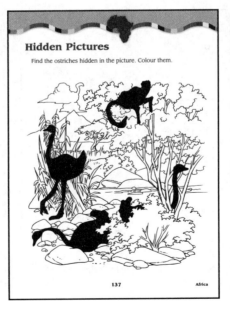

Hidden Pictures

Find the ostriches hidden in the picture. Colour them.

137   **Africa**

137

Black Rhinoceros

The black rhinoceros (righ NAHS er uhs) has tough, wrinkled skin and a two-horned snout. A rhinoceros grows to 3.6 metres long and weighs about 2.8 metric tonnes. It is a relative of the horse. Surprisingly, it can run as fast as a horse for short distances. Rhinoceros horns grow from the same material as hair and claws. Rhinos use the longer front horn to dig and to defend themselves. They use the smaller back horn to dig up bushes and small trees to eat.

The black rhino stays hidden during the day. It comes out at night to search for food and water. Rhinos have very poor eyesight. They rely mostly on their sense of smell. A new odour or sound can cause a rhinoceros to charge.

Think and Learn

1. The black rhinoceros is related to the _____horse_____.

2. How does a rhinoceros use its front horn? _____to dig and to defend itself_____

3. What do rhinoceroses eat? _____bushes and small trees_____

4. What sense do rhinoceroses rely on most? _____smell_____

Africa   138

138

Everything About Animals

Answer Key

Vulture

Vultures (VUL cherz) are large birds of prey, or birds that eat animals. Their wingspan can reach 1.8 to 2.7 metres. Vultures have bare, wrinkled skin on their heads and necks. Their bills are slightly hooked. Vultures live in mountains, grasslands and deserts. They generally do not live in forests or in areas that receive a lot of rain.

Vultures are scavengers. Scavengers feed on the remains of dead animals. Vultures use their sharp eyesight and keen sense of smell to find dead animals. When one vulture finds food, other vultures are quick to follow. Vultures are strong fliers. They come from miles away when food is found.

Think and Learn

1. Vultures are large birds of _____ prey
2. Where do vultures live? _____ mountains, grasslands and deserts
3. What do vultures eat? _____ the remains of dead animals
4. How do vultures find food? _____ with their sharp eyesight and keen sense of smell

139

Africa

139

Zebra

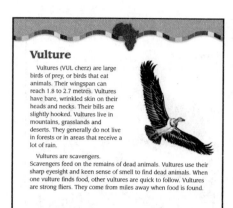

The zebra is a striped animal related to the horse. The zebra's stripes help the animal blend in with its surroundings. A zebra standing in tall grass is very hard to see. Each zebra has its own stripe pattern, like each human has his or her own fingerprints.

Zebras are found in the deserts and grasslands of eastern and southern Africa. They mainly eat grass, and they spend most of their time eating. Zebras live in herds made up of a male, several females and their babies. Zebras protect themselves by staying together in a herd. If they are in danger, they try to run away. Zebras can run as fast as 72 kilometres per hour.

Think and Learn

1. A zebra's _____ stripes _____ help it blend in with its surroundings.
2. Where are zebras found? _____ in deserts and grasslands of eastern and southern Africa
3. Zebras live in _____ herds
4. What do zebras do when they are in danger? _____ run away

Africa

140

© 2000 Tribune Education. All Rights Reserved.

140

Word Search

Find the names of African animals hidden in the puzzle. The animal names are written **across** and **down**.

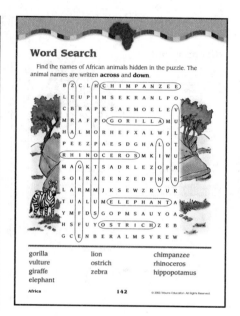

gorilla	lion	chimpanzee
vulture	ostrich	rhinoceros
giraffe	zebra	hippopotamus
elephant		

Africa

142

© 2000 Tribune Education. All Rights Reserved.

142

What Is an Insect?

All insects have three main body parts—head, chest and abdomen. An insect has eyes, a mouth and antennae on its head. Its legs and wings are joined to the chest. The abdomen holds all of the insect's organs, such as the heart and stomach. An insect's body does not have a skeleton, or bones, on the inside. It has a hard covering on the outside called the exoskeleton.

All adult insects have six legs. Different kinds of insects have different legs. For example, some insects have long legs for jumping. Others have legs for digging. Most adult insects have wings. Some, like flies, have one pair of wings. Others, like butterflies and bees, have two pairs.

Think and Learn

1. What are the three main body parts of insects? _____ head, chest and abdomen
2. Legs and wings are joined to the insect's _____ chest
3. What is the hard covering on the outside of an insect's body? _____ the exoskeleton
4. How many legs do insects have? _____ six legs

Insects

144

© 2000 Tribune Education. All Rights Reserved.

144

Ant

Ants are social insects that live and work together in large groups. Ants have two bent antennae on top of their heads. The antennae are used to taste, touch and smell. An ant is helpless if its antennae are damaged. Ants have very strong jaws that are used for digging and for getting food.

Ants are found all over the world, except for the North and South poles. Ants build different kinds of homes. Some ants live in trees. Some build nests in wood or under leaves. Others burrow under rocks. It is common for ants to dig homes in the dirt. Some dig underground tunnels and rooms in the dirt. Others build large anthills that look like tall mounds of dirt.

Think and Learn

1. Why are ants called social insects? _____ They live and work together in large groups.
2. Ants have two bent _____ antennae _____ on top of their heads.
3. Ants use their jaws for _____ digging _____ and for getting food.
4. Where do ants NOT live? _____ at the North and South poles

© 2000 Tribune Education. All Rights Reserved.

145

Insects

145

Ant Colonies

Ants live in groups called colonies. There are three different groups of ants in a colony—the queen ants, the workers and the males. Each ant in the colony has a special job. The queen ants are the largest females. Their only job is to lay eggs. The worker ants are usually females that do not lay eggs. The workers have many jobs. Some workers are nursery ants who care for the eggs. Other worker ants find food and bring it back to the colony. The largest workers are soldier ants who guard the nest. Male ants live in the nest only at certain times. Their job is to mate with the queen ants. After mating, the male ants soon die.

1. Label the ant in the colony that is a nursery ant. Label the soldier ant.
2. What are the three different groups of ants living in an ant colony? _____ queen ants, worker ants and the males

Insects

146

© 2000 Tribune Education. All Rights Reserved.

146

Everything About Animals

336

Answer Key

Bee

Bees are the only insects that make a food that people eat. Bees have a special stomach, called a honey stomach, where they store nectar, the sugar from flowers. Their long, hollow tongues work like straws to suck up nectar. Female bees have a stinger that they use for defence.

Bees live all over the world, except for the North and South poles. Bees build their homes in hollow trees or in beehives. Some bees live in social groups like ants. The queen bee lays eggs. The worker bees build the hive, care for the eggs, find nectar and pollen and defend the hive. The drones are male bees that mate with the queen.

Think and Learn

1. What is a honey stomach? __a special stomach where bees store nectar__

2. Female bees have a __stinger__ they use for defence.

3. Where do bees build their homes? __in hollow trees or in beehives__

4. What are drones? __male bees that mate with the queen__

147

Honeybees

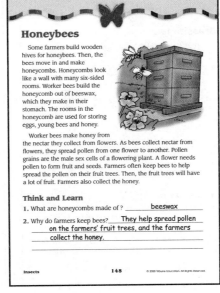

Some farmers build wooden hives for honeybees. Then, the bees move in and make honeycombs. Honeycombs look like a wall with many six-sided rooms. Worker bees build the honeycomb out of beeswax, which they make in their stomach. The rooms in the honeycomb are used for storing eggs, young bees and honey.

Worker bees make honey from the nectar they collect from flowers. As bees collect nectar from flowers, they spread pollen from one flower to another. Pollen grains are the male sex cells of a flowering plant. A flower needs pollen to form fruit and seeds. Farmers often keep bees to help spread the pollen on their fruit trees. Then, the fruit trees will have a lot of fruit. Farmers also collect the honey.

Think and Learn

1. What are honeycombs made of ? __beeswax__

2. Why do farmers keep bees? __They help spread pollen on the farmers' fruit trees, and the farmers collect the honey.__

148

Bzzz, Bzzz, Bzzz

Complete the sentences below by filling in the missing words. Then, write each word in a cell of the honeycomb with the matching number.

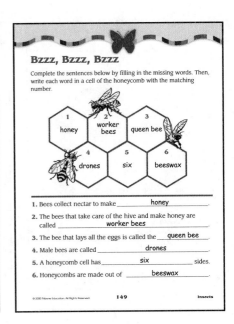

| 1 honey | 2 worker bees | 3 queen bee |
| 4 drones | 5 six | 6 beeswax |

1. Bees collect nectar to make __honey__

2. The bees that take care of the hive and make honey are called __worker bees__.

3. The bee that lays all the eggs is called the __queen bee__.

4. Male bees are called __drones__.

5. A honeycomb cell has __six__ sides.

6. Honeycombs are made out of __beeswax__.

149

Beetle

Beetles are the largest group of insects and come in every colour of the rainbow. All beetles have two pairs of wings. The outer wings are hard. They protect the inner, or flight, wings. The flight wings are thin and clear. They stay folded under the outer wings until needed for flight. Beetles have very strong jaws to grab and chew food.

Beetles are found all over the world. Beetles make their homes in many different places, from in water to under the ground. Beetles can be harmful or helpful to people, depending on what they eat. Some beetles damage the plants in gardens and farmers' fields. Other beetles eat harmful insects.

Think and Learn

1. Beetles are the __largest__ group of insects.

2. Which wings do beetles use for flight? __the thin, clear inner wings__

3. Beetles have strong __jaws__ to grab and chew food.

4. How are beetles helpful to people? __by eating harmful insects__

150

Butterfly

Butterflies are beautiful insects. The body of a butterfly is long and slender. They have knobs at the ends of their antennae, which are used for smelling. Their wings are covered with tiny scales that give the wings their colour. All butterflies hatch as caterpillars, which look like worms. The caterpillars change to adult butterflies in a cocoon, or paperlike case.

Butterflies are found everywhere. They live on mountains and in deserts. As caterpillars, they eat leaves and fruit, often damaging crops. As butterflies, they cannot bite or chew. For food, they drink nectar, the sugary liquid, from flowers. Butterflies fly only during the day. When resting, they fold their wings straight up.

Think and Learn

1. What do butterflies use their antennae for? __smelling__

2. Tiny __scales__ give butterfly wings their colour.

3. What do caterpillars eat? __leaves and fruit__

4. When do butterflies fly? __only during the day__

151

Cricket

Crickets are jumping insects. Most crickets are either black or brown in colour and are about 2.5 centimetres long. Crickets have two pairs of wings. Both pairs of wings lie flat over the cricket's back. Only male crickets make the chirping sound that crickets are known for. They make the sound by rubbing their wings together. They make this sound to attract female crickets. Crickets hear sounds with a special body part on their front legs.

Crickets are found in many parts of the world. They hide during the day and are active at night. This is when they chirp and search for food. Crickets eat grain and the remains of other insects.

Think and Learn

1. Crickets are __jumping__ insects.

2. How do male crickets chirp? __by rubbing their wings together__

3. How do crickets hear? __with a special body part on their front legs__

4. When do crickets search for food? __at night__

152

Answer Key

Fly

Flies are very common insects. People see and hear them everywhere. There are many different kinds of flies, such as house flies, fruit flies, gnats and deer flies. Flies have only one pair of wings. The buzzing sound you hear when a fly flies by is the sound of its wings beating together. Flies use their antennae to touch and smell things. Flies have tiny, hairy pads on the bottoms of their feet. These help flies cling to walls and walk upside down on ceilings.

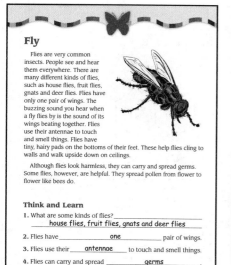

Although flies look harmless, they can carry and spread germs. Some flies, however, are helpful. They spread pollen from flower to flower like bees do.

Think and Learn

1. What are some kinds of flies? __house flies, fruit flies, gnats and deer flies__
2. Flies have __one__ pair of wings.
3. Flies use their __antennae__ to touch and smell things.
4. Flies can carry and spread __germs__.

153 Insects

153

Grasshopper

Grasshoppers are built for jumping. Grasshoppers have long thin legs with powerful muscles. Most grasshoppers have large fragile wings that are protected by a second pair of wings. Like crickets, male grasshoppers make sounds by rubbing their wings together. Although grasshoppers can fly, they fly for only short distances. They move mainly by leaping and jumping.

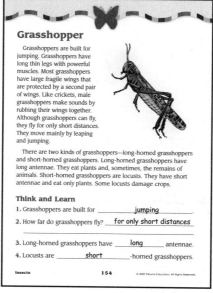

There are two kinds of grasshoppers—long-horned grasshoppers and short-horned grasshoppers. Long-horned grasshoppers have long antennae. They eat plants and, sometimes, the remains of animals. Short-horned grasshoppers are locusts. They have short antennae and eat only plants. Some locusts damage crops.

Think and Learn

1. Grasshoppers are built for __jumping__.
2. How far do grasshoppers fly? __for only short distances__
3. Long-horned grasshoppers have __long__ antennae.
4. Locusts are __short__-horned grasshoppers.

Insects **154**

154

Mosquito

The mosquito is a kind of fly. Like all flies, mosquitoes have only one pair of wings. Mosquito wings can beat 1,000 times each second. The mosquito's head is almost entirely covered by its two large eyes. The antennae, used for hearing and smelling, are located between the eyes. Female mosquitoes have thin antennae. Male mosquitoes have feathery antennae.

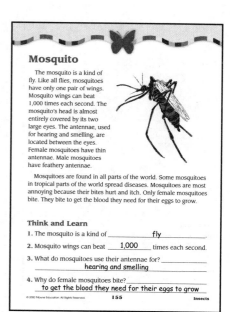

Mosquitoes are found in all parts of the world. Some mosquitoes in tropical parts of the world spread diseases. Mosquitoes are most annoying because their bites hurt and itch. Only female mosquitoes bite. They bite to get the blood they need for their eggs to grow.

Think and Learn

1. The mosquito is a kind of __fly__.
2. Mosquito wings can beat __1,000__ times each second.
3. What do mosquitoes use their antennae for? __hearing and smelling__
4. Why do female mosquitoes bite? __to get the blood they need for their eggs to grow__

155 Insects

155

Moth

Moths are closely related to butterflies. Butterflies and moths are so much alike that it is sometimes hard to tell them apart. Unlike butterflies, moths have chubby bodies and usually fly only at night. Moth antennae look feathery. The antennae give moths their senses of touch and smell. Moths cannot bite or chew. They have a mouth that looks and works like a drinking straw. Moths eat sap and nectar.

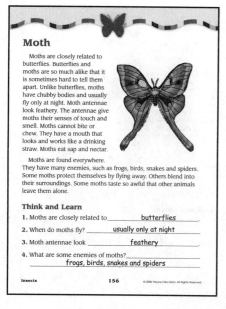

Moths are found everywhere. They have many enemies, such as frogs, birds, snakes and spiders. Some moths protect themselves by flying away. Others blend into their surroundings. Some moths taste so awful that other animals leave them alone.

Think and Learn

1. Moths are closely related to __butterflies__.
2. When do moths fly? __usually only at night__
3. Moth antennae look __feathery__.
4. What are some enemies of moths? __frogs, birds, snakes and spiders__

Insects **156**

156

What Is a Reptile?

Reptiles are cold-blooded animals with scaly skin. Cold-blooded animals cannot control their body temperature. Their body temperature is the same as the temperature of their surroundings. However, many reptiles keep their body temperature even by moving to sunny or shady spots during the day.

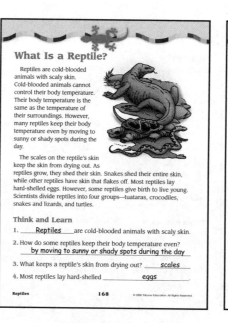

The scales on the reptile's skin keep the skin from drying out. As reptiles grow, they shed their skin. Snakes shed their entire skin, while other reptiles have skin that flakes off. Most reptiles lay hard-shelled eggs. However, some reptiles give birth to live young. Scientists divide reptiles into four groups—tuataras, crocodiles, snakes and lizards, and turtles.

Think and Learn

1. __Reptiles__ are cold-blooded animals with scaly skin.
2. How do some reptiles keep their body temperature even? __by moving to sunny or shady spots during the day__
3. What keeps a reptile's skin from drying out? __scales__
4. Most reptiles lay hard-shelled __eggs__.

Reptiles **168**

168

Tuatara

The tuatara (too uh TAW ruh) looks like a lizard but is actually the last remaining animal in its group. Tuataras lived during the time of the first dinosaurs, about 220 million years ago. They have not changed since that time. Tuataras have a third eye on top of their head. They also have two rows of upper teeth. A row of horny plates runs along their back. These plates rise straight up when tuataras are frightened.

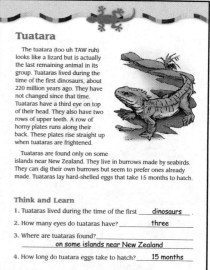

Tuataras are found only on some islands near New Zealand. They live in burrows made by seabirds. They can dig their own burrows but seem to prefer ones already made. Tuataras lay hard-shelled eggs that take 15 months to hatch.

Think and Learn

1. Tuataras lived during the time of the first __dinosaurs__.
2. How many eyes do tuataras have? __three__
3. Where are tuataras found? __on some islands near New Zealand__
4. How long do tuatara eggs take to hatch? __15 months__

169 Reptiles

169

Answer Key

Crocodile

Crocodiles (KRAHK uh dighlz) are the largest reptiles. They can reach 7.5 metres in length. Of all the animals belonging to the crocodile group, crocodiles are the most dangerous. Crocodiles have long narrow snouts. When their mouths are closed, their lower teeth show.

Crocodiles are found in the tropical parts of the world. They catch fish and small land animals for food. Like alligators, crocodiles are most active at night. During the day, they rest in the sun. Often a crocodile lies with its mouth open to help cool its body. When its mouth is open, the crocodile lets birds go in it and peck out leftover pieces of food.

Think and Learn

1. Crocodiles are the _____largest_____ reptiles.

2. Describe the shape of a crocodile's snout. _____
   long and narrow

3. What do crocodiles eat? __fish and small land animals__

4. How does a crocodile cool its body? _____
   by lying with its mouth open

Reptiles   170

170

Alligator

Alligators (AL ih gay terz) belong to the crocodile group of reptiles. Although they are members of this group, alligators and crocodiles are two different animals. Alligators have wide rounded snouts. When their mouths are closed, their lower teeth are inside. Alligators are smaller than crocodiles. They grow up to 3.5 metres long.

Alligators are found in southeastern United States and in parts of China. They eat frogs, fish, snakes, turtles and small mammals. Like crocodiles, alligators are good swimmers. Alligators move through the water by moving their tails from side to side. Female alligators lay as many as 50 eggs and guard the eggs until they hatch. Mother alligators care for their young for up to a year.

Think and Learn

1. Alligators belong to the ____crocodile____ group of reptiles.

2. Describe the shape of an alligator's snout. _____
   wide and rounded

3. How do alligators move through water? _____
   by moving their tails from side to side

4. Mother alligators care for their young for up to a __year__.

171   Reptiles

171

Compare and Contrast

Read about crocodiles and alligators. Then, use the Venn diagram and the facts you have learned to compare and contrast these two animals.

Crocodile

- largest reptile
- long, narrow snout
- lower teeth show outside snout
- most dangerous
- grow to 7.5 metres long

Both
- rest in sun during day
- active at night
- good swimmer
- crocodile group of reptiles

- grow to 3.5 metres long
- lower teeth are inside the snout when mouth is closed
- wide rounded snout

Alligator

Reptiles   172

172

Lizard

Lizards and snakes make up the largest group of reptiles. Most lizards have four legs with five clawed toes on each leg. Some lizards do not have legs. Lizards have movable eyelids and good eyesight. They do not have ears, but they have ear openings on the sides of their head. Lizards use their tongue for smelling.

Lizards are found in all parts of the world, except the North and South poles. Most lizards eat insects and small mammals. Some lizards eat plants. Lizards protect themselves by blending in with their surroundings, making their bodies look bigger, or making hissing sounds. Some lizards have tails that break off and keep wiggling, while the lizard escapes. Later, it grows a new tail.

Think and Learn

1. Lizards have ____movable____ eyelids.

2. What do lizards use their tongues for? ____smelling____

3. What do most lizards eat? _____
   Most eat insects and small mammals. Some eat plants.

4. Some lizards protect themselves by losing their ____tails__.

173   Reptiles

173

Chameleon

Chameleons (kuh MEEL yuhnz) are lizards that can change their body colour to match their surroundings. They can blend in so well that they actually look invisible! Chameleon bodies are flat on the sides. Their eyes are large and bulging. Each eye works separately from the other. They can look in different directions at the same time.

Chameleons are slow-moving lizards. They do not chase down their food. Instead, a chameleon sits quietly and waits for food to come to it. When a chameleon sees an insect, it shoots out its sticky tongue and catches the insect. Chameleons are found only in Africa and Madagascar.

Think and Learn

1. What changes on chameleons? ____their colour____

2. How can chameleons look in different directions at the same time? _Each eye works separately from the other._

3. Chameleons catch insects with their sticky ____tongue____

4. Where are chameleons found? _in Africa and Madagascar_

Reptiles   174

174

Snake

Snakes are reptiles that have long bodies and no legs. Snakes move by sliding on their belly. Snakes cannot shut their eyes, because they do not have eyelids. Their eyes are covered with clear scales. Snakes do not have ear slits. Instead, they "hear" sounds by feeling the movement of air around them. Snakes have a long forked tongue that helps them smell.

Snakes eat other animals. The size of animal they can eat depends on the size of their mouth. A snake swallows its food whole. Snakes do not eat often. Most snakes eat only a few times a year. Snakes, like all other reptiles, lay eggs or give birth to live young. They do not take care of their young.

Think and Learn

1. How do snakes move? __by sliding on their belly__

2. What covers a snake's eyes? ____clear scales____

3. Snakes use their long, forked __tongue__ to help them smell.

4. How often do most snakes eat? __only a few times a year__

175   Reptiles

175

Answer Key

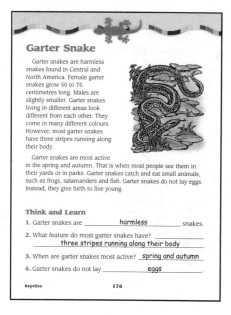

Garter Snake

Garter snakes are harmless snakes found in Central and North America. Female garter snakes grow 50 to 75 centimetres long. Males are slightly smaller. Garter snakes living in different areas look different from each other. They come in many different colours. However, most garter snakes have three stripes running along their body.

Garter snakes are most active in the spring and autumn. That is when most people see them in their yards or in parks. Garter snakes catch and eat small animals, such as frogs, salamanders and fish. Garter snakes do not lay eggs. Instead, they give birth to live young.

Think and Learn

1. Garter snakes are _____harmless_____ snakes.

2. What feature do most garter snakes have? _____
   _____three stripes running along their body_____

3. When are garter snakes most active? _spring and autumn_

4. Garter snakes do not lay _____eggs_____.

Reptiles   176

176

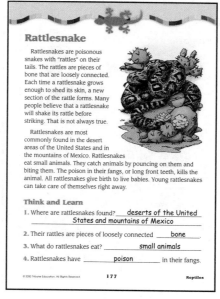

Rattlesnake

Rattlesnakes are poisonous snakes with "rattles" on their tails. The rattles are pieces of bone that are loosely connected. Each time a rattlesnake grows enough to shed its skin, a new section of the rattle forms. Many people believe that a rattlesnake will shake its rattle before striking. That is not always true.

Rattlesnakes are most commonly found in the desert areas of the United States and in the mountains of Mexico. Rattlesnakes eat small animals. They catch animals by pouncing on them and biting them. The poison in their fangs, or long front teeth, kills the animal. All rattlesnakes give birth to live babies. Young rattlesnakes can take care of themselves right away.

Think and Learn

1. Where are rattlesnakes found? _deserts of the United_
   States and mountains of Mexico

2. Their rattles are pieces of loosely connected _bone_.

3. What do rattlesnakes eat? _small animals_

4. Rattlesnakes have _poison_ in their fangs.

© 2000 Tribune Education. All Rights Reserved.   **177**   Reptiles

177

Turtle

Turtles are reptiles with shells. Turtle shells are made of either horny plates or tough leathery skin. The shell protects the turtle's body. Many turtles can pull their legs and head inside their shell. Turtles do not have teeth. They cut their food with their hard sharp beak. They also breathe air with lungs. All turtles lay eggs and bury them in soil. The warmth from the sun helps the eggs hatch.

Turtles are found all over the world. Some turtles spend most of their time in water. Other turtles spend some time both in the water and on land. There are also turtles that live only on land. Turtles eat both plants and animals.

Think and Learn

1. Turtles are reptiles with _shells_.

2. How do turtles cut their food? _____
   with their hard, sharp beaks

3. All turtles lay _eggs_.

4. What do turtles eat? _both plants and animals_

Reptiles   178   © 2000 Tribune Education. All Rights Reserved.

178

Sea Turtle

Sea turtles are turtles that live in the ocean. Sea turtles are very large. They range in size from 0.6 to 2.4 metres and weigh from 45 to 816 kilograms. Instead of claws, sea turtles have flippers to help them swim easily through water. Sea turtles have flat shells instead of rounded shells like land turtles. Flat shells also help them move more easily through water.

Sea turtles are found in warm oceans throughout the world. They eat fish, shrimp, crabs, jellyfish and plants. Sea turtles dig holes and lay their eggs on sandy beaches. The eggs lay buried in the sand for a couple of months before they hatch. When the eggs hatch, the babies dig out of the sand and head for the ocean.

Think and Learn

1. Flippers and _flat_ shells help sea turtles move in the water.

2. Where are sea turtles found? _in warm oceans_

3. Sea turtles eat fish, shrimp, crabs, jellyfish and _plants_.

4. Sea turtles lay their eggs on sandy _beaches_.

179   Reptiles

179

Reptile Puzzle

Fill in the spaces of the puzzle with the correct animal name.

Puzzle answers: SEATURTLE, GARTERSNAKE, TUATARA, RATTLESNAKE, SNAKE, CROCODILE, TURTLE, ALLIGATOR, LIZARD, CHAMELEON

snake	tuatara	chameleon
turtle	alligator	sea turtle
lizard	crocodile	garter snake

Reptiles   180   © 2000 Tribune Education. All Rights Reserved.

180

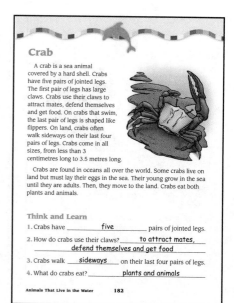

Crab

A crab is a sea animal covered by a hard shell. Crabs have five pairs of jointed legs. The first pair of legs has large claws. Crabs use their claws to attract mates, defend themselves and get food. On crabs that swim, the last pair of legs is shaped like flippers. On land, crabs often walk sideways on their last four pairs of legs. Crabs come in all sizes, from less than 3 centimetres long to 3.5 metres long.

Crabs are found in oceans all over the world. Some crabs live on land but must lay their eggs in the sea. Their young grow in the sea until they are adults. Then, they move to the land. Crabs eat both plants and animals.

Think and Learn

1. Crabs have _five_ pairs of jointed legs.

2. How do crabs use their claws? _to attract mates,_
   defend themselves and get food

3. Crabs walk _sideways_ on their last four pairs of legs.

4. What do crabs eat? _plants and animals_

Animals That Live in the Water   182

182

Complete Book of Animals   **340**

Answer Key

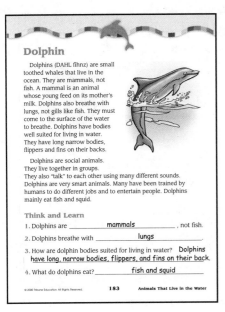

Dolphin

Dolphins (DAHL fihnz) are small toothed whales that live in the ocean. They are mammals, not fish. A mammal is an animal whose young feed on its mother's milk. Dolphins also breathe with lungs, not gills like fish. They must come to the surface of the water to breathe. Dolphins have bodies well suited for living in water. They have long narrow bodies, flippers and fins on their backs.

Dolphins are social animals. They live together in groups. They also "talk" to each other using many different sounds. Dolphins are very smart animals. Many have been trained by humans to do different jobs and to entertain people. Dolphins mainly eat fish and squid.

Think and Learn

1. Dolphins are _____mammals_____ , not fish.

2. Dolphins breathe with _____lungs_____ .

3. How are dolphin bodies suited for living in water? Dolphins have long, narrow bodies, flippers, and fins on their back.

4. What do dolphins eat? _____fish and squid_____

© 2000 Tribune Education. All Rights Reserved.   **183**   Animals That Live in the Water

183

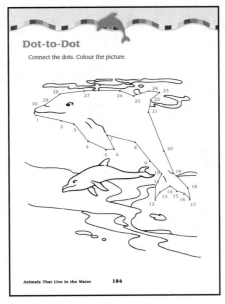

Dot-to-Dot

Connect the dots. Colour the picture.

Animals That Live in the Water   **184**

184

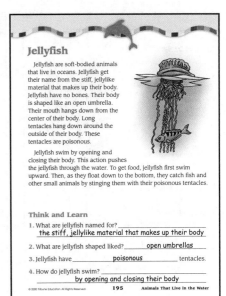

Jellyfish

Jellyfish are soft-bodied animals that live in oceans. Jellyfish get their name from the stiff, jellylike material that makes up their body. Jellyfish have no bones. Their body is shaped like an open umbrella. Their mouth hangs down from the center of their body. Long tentacles hang down around the outside of their body. These tentacles are poisonous.

Jellyfish swim by opening and closing their body. This action pushes the jellyfish through the water. To get food, jellyfish first swim upward. Then, as they float down to the bottom, they catch fish and other small animals by stinging them with their poisonous tentacles.

Think and Learn

1. What are jellyfish named for? _____
the stiff, jellylike material that makes up their body

2. What are jellyfish shaped liked? _____open umbrellas_____

3. Jellyfish have _____poisonous_____ tentacles.

4. How do jellyfish swim? _____
by opening and closing their body

© 2000 Tribune Education. All Rights Reserved.   **195**   Animals That Live in the Water

195

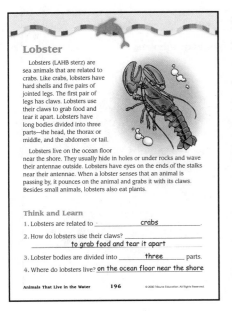

Lobster

Lobsters (LAHB sterz) are sea animals that are related to crabs. Like crabs, lobsters have hard shells and five pairs of jointed legs. The first pair of legs has claws. Lobsters use their claws to grab food and tear it apart. Lobsters have long bodies divided into three parts—the head, the thorax or middle, and the abdomen or tail.

Lobsters live on the ocean floor near the shore. They usually hide in holes or under rocks and wave their antennae outside. Lobsters have eyes on the ends of the stalks near their antennae. When a lobster senses that an animal is passing by, it pounces on the animal and grabs it with its claws. Besides small animals, lobsters also eat plants.

Think and Learn

1. Lobsters are related to _____crabs_____ .

2. How do lobsters use their claws? _____
to grab food and tear it apart

3. Lobster bodies are divided into _____three_____ parts.

4. Where do lobsters live? on the ocean floor near the shore

Animals That Live in the Water   **196**   © 2000 Tribune Education. All Rights Reserved.

196

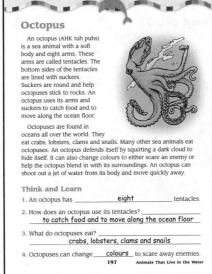

Octopus

An octopus (AHK tuh puhs) is a sea animal with a soft body and eight arms. These arms are called tentacles. The bottom sides of the tentacles are lined with suckers. Suckers are round and help octopuses stick to rocks. An octopus uses its arms and suckers to catch food and to move along the ocean floor.

Octopuses are found in oceans all over the world. They eat crabs, lobsters, clams and snails. Many other sea animals eat octopuses. An octopus defends itself by squirting a dark cloud to hide itself. It can also change colours to either scare an enemy or help the octopus blend in with its surroundings. An octopus can shoot out a jet of water from its body and move quickly away.

Think and Learn

1. An octopus has _____eight_____ tentacles.

2. How does an octopus use its tentacles? _____
to catch food and to move along the ocean floor

3. What do octopuses eat? _____
crabs, lobsters, clams and snails

4. Octopuses can change _____colours_____ to scare away enemies.

197   Animals That Live in the Water

197

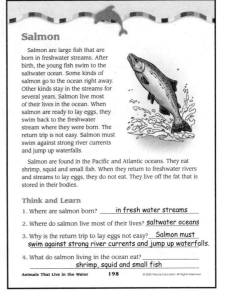

Salmon

Salmon are large fish that are born in freshwater streams. After birth, the young fish swim to the saltwater ocean. Some kinds of salmon go to the ocean right away. Other kinds stay in the streams for several years. Salmon live most of their lives in the ocean. When salmon are ready to lay eggs, they swim back to the freshwater stream where they were born. The return trip is not easy. Salmon must swim against strong river currents and jump up waterfalls.

Salmon are found in the Pacific and Atlantic oceans. They eat shrimp, squid and small fish. When they return to freshwater rivers and streams to lay eggs, they do not eat. They live off the fat that is stored in their bodies.

Think and Learn

1. Where are salmon born? _____in fresh water streams_____

2. Where do salmon live most of their lives? saltwater oceans

3. Why is the return trip to lay eggs not easy? _____Salmon must swim against strong river currents and jump up waterfalls.

4. What do salmon living in the ocean eat? _____
shrimp, squid and small fish

Animals That Live in the Water   **198**   © 2000 Tribune Education. All Rights Reserved.

198

341

Everything About Animals

Answer Key

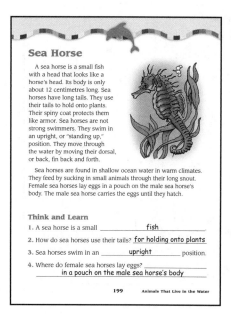

Sea Horse

A sea horse is a small fish with a head that looks like a horse's head. Its body is only about 12 centimetres long. Sea horses have long tails. They use their tails to hold onto plants. Their spiny coat protects them like armor. Sea horses are not strong swimmers. They swim in an upright, or "standing up," position. They move through the water by moving their dorsal, or back, fin back and forth.

Sea horses are found in shallow ocean water in warm climates. They feed by sucking in small animals through their long snout. Female sea horses lay eggs in a pouch on the male sea horse's body. The male sea horse carries the eggs until they hatch.

Think and Learn

1. A sea horse is a small _____fish_____.

2. How do sea horses use their tails? __for holding onto plants__

3. Sea horses swim in an _____upright_____ position.

4. Where do female sea horses lay eggs? _____
   __in a pouch on the male sea horse's body__

199   Animals That Live in the Water

199

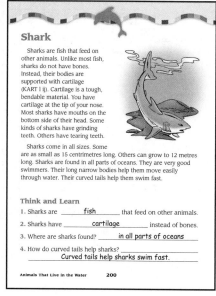

Shark

Sharks are fish that feed on other animals. Unlike most fish, sharks do not have bones. Instead, their bodies are supported with cartilage (KART l ij). Cartilage is a tough, bendable material. You have cartilage at the tip of your nose. Most sharks have mouths on the bottom side of their head. Some kinds of sharks have grinding teeth. Others have tearing teeth.

Sharks come in all sizes. Some are as small as 15 centimetres long. Others can grow to 12 metres long. Sharks are found in all parts of oceans. They are very good swimmers. Their long narrow bodies help them move easily through water. Their curved tails help them swim fast.

Think and Learn

1. Sharks are _____fish_____ that feed on other animals.

2. Sharks have _____cartilage_____ instead of bones.

3. Where are sharks found? __in all parts of oceans__

4. How do curved tails help sharks? _____
   __Curved tails help sharks swim fast.__

Animals That Live in the Water   **200**

200

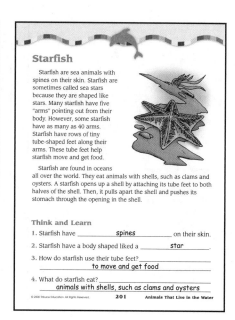

Starfish

Starfish are sea animals with spines on their skin. Starfish are sometimes called sea stars because they are shaped like stars. Many starfish have five "arms" pointing out from their body. However, some starfish have as many as 40 arms. Starfish have rows of tiny tube-shaped feet along their arms. These tube feet help starfish move and get food.

Starfish are found in oceans all over the world. They eat animals with shells, such as clams and oysters. A starfish opens up a shell by attaching its tube feet to both halves of the shell. Then, it pulls apart the shell and pushes its stomach through the opening in the shell.

Think and Learn

1. Starfish have _____spines_____ on their skin.

2. Starfish have a body shaped liked a _____star_____.

3. How do starfish use their tube feet? _____
   __to move and get food__

4. What do starfish eat? _____
   __animals with shells, such as clams and oysters__

© 2000 Tribune Education. All Rights Reserved.   **201**   Animals That Live in the Water

201

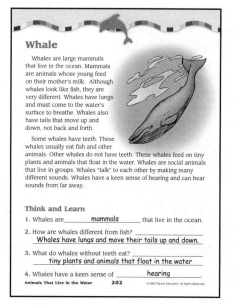

Whale

Whales are large mammals that live in the ocean. Mammals are animals whose young feed on their mother's milk. Although whales look like fish, they are very different. Whales have lungs and must come to the water's surface to breathe. Whales also have tails that move up and down, not back and forth.

Some whales have teeth. These whales usually eat fish and other animals. Other whales do not have teeth. These whales feed on tiny plants and animals that float in the water. Whales are social animals that live in groups. Whales "talk" to each other by making many different sounds. Whales have a keen sense of hearing and can hear sounds from far away.

Think and Learn

1. Whales are _____mammals_____ that live in the ocean.

2. How are whales different from fish? _____
   __Whales have lungs and move their tails up and down.__

3. What do whales without teeth eat? _____
   __tiny plants and animals that float in the water__

4. Whales have a keen sense of _____hearing_____.

Animals That Live in the Water   **202**   © 2000 Tribune Education. All Rights Reserved.

202

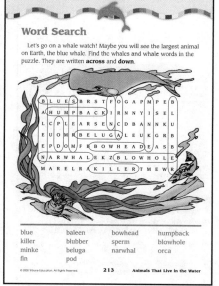

Word Search

Let's go on a whale watch! Maybe you will see the largest animal on Earth, the blue whale. Find the whales and whale words in the puzzle. They are written **across** and **down**.

blue	baleen	bowhead	humpback
killer	blubber	sperm	blowhole
minke	beluga	narwhal	orca
fin	pod		

© 2000 Tribune Education. All Rights Reserved.   **213**   Animals That Live in the Water

213

Hidden Pictures

Find the ocean animals hidden in the picture. Colour the picture.

Animals That Live in the Water   **214**

214

Everything About Animals   **342**

Answer Key

Duck

Ducks are birds that spend part of the time in water. Their webbed feet act as paddles to move them easily through the water. Most ducks get their food from water or from the areas around water. Some ducks eat fish. Others eat water plants and small water animals. Ducks keep dry by oiling their top feathers with oil from a special gland near their tail. They have a layer of soft fluffy feathers, called down, under the top feathers. Down keeps the duck warm.

Farmers raise ducks for their feathers, eggs and meat. Duck feathers are used to stuff pillows and make winter coats. Ducks raised on farms do not get their food from water. The farmer feeds them a kind of food made just for ducks.

Think and Learn

1. What helps ducks move through water? ___webbed feet___

2. Most ducks get their food from ___water___.

3. What is down? ___a layer of soft, fluffy feathers under the top feathers___

4. Farmers raise ducks for feathers, eggs and ___meat___

Farm Animals　216　© 2000 Tribune Education. All Rights Reserved.

216

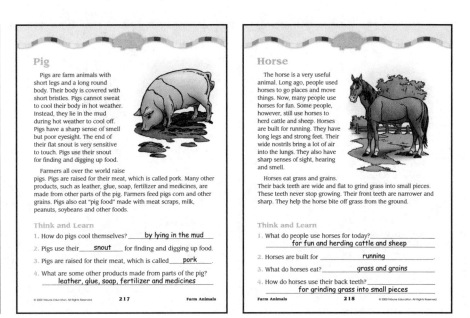

Pig

Pigs are farm animals with short legs and a long round body. Their body is covered with short bristles. Pigs cannot sweat to cool their body in hot weather. Instead, they lie in the mud during hot weather to cool off. Pigs have a sharp sense of smell but poor eyesight. The end of their flat snout is very sensitive to touch. Pigs use their snout for finding and digging up food.

Farmers all over the world raise pigs. Pigs are raised for their meat, which is called pork. Many other products, such as leather, glue, soap, fertilizer and medicines, are made from other parts of the pig. Farmers feed pigs corn and other grains. Pigs also eat "pig food" made with meat scraps, milk, peanuts, soybeans and other foods.

Think and Learn

1. How do pigs cool themselves? ___by lying in the mud___

2. Pigs use their ___snout___ for finding and digging up food.

3. Pigs are raised for their meat, which is called ___pork___

4. What are some other products made from parts of the pig? ___leather, glue, soap, fertilizer and medicines___

© 2000 Tribune Education. All Rights Reserved.　217　**Farm Animals**

217

Horse

The horse is a very useful animal. Long ago, people used horses to go places and move things. Now, many people use horses for fun. Some people, however, still use horses to herd cattle and sheep. Horses are built for running. They have long legs and strong feet. Their wide nostrils bring a lot of air into the lungs. They also have sharp senses of sight, hearing and smell.

Horses eat grass and grains. Their back teeth are wide and flat to grind grass into small pieces. These teeth never stop growing. Their front teeth are narrower and sharp. They help the horse bite off grass from the ground.

Think and Learn

1. What do people use horses for today? ___for fun and herding cattle and sheep___

2. Horses are built for ___running___

3. What do horses eat? ___grass and grains___

4. How do horses use their back teeth? ___for grinding grass into small pieces___

Farm Animals　218　© 2000 Tribune Education. All Rights Reserved.

218

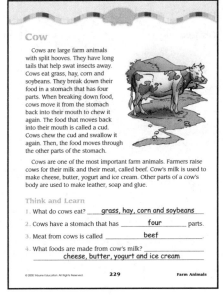

Cow

Cows are large farm animals with split hooves. They have long tails that help swat insects away. Cows eat grass, hay, corn and soybeans. They break down their food in a stomach that has four parts. When breaking down food, cows move it from the stomach back into their mouth to chew it again. The food that moves back into their mouth is called a cud. Cows chew the cud and swallow it again. Then, the food moves through the other parts of the stomach.

Cows are one of the most important farm animals. Farmers raise cows for their milk and their meat, called beef. Cow's milk is used to make cheese, butter, yogurt and ice cream. Other parts of a cow's body are used to make leather, soap and glue.

Think and Learn

1. What do cows eat? ___grass, hay, corn and soybeans___

2. Cows have a stomach that has ___four___ parts.

3. Meat from cows is called ___beef___

4. What foods are made from cow's milk? ___cheese, butter, yogurt and ice cream___

© 2000 Tribune Education. All Rights Reserved.　229　**Farm Animals**

229

Chicken

Chickens are ground birds. They have a plump body and rounded wings. Chickens can fly but for only short distances. They fly to get away from danger. Chickens have pointed beaks and strong claws that they use to scratch in the dirt and get food. Different kinds of chickens have feathers of different colours.

Chickens are raised on farms all over the world. Farmers raise chickens for their eggs and their meat, called poultry. Some chickens are raised only for their meat. Other chickens are raised just to lay eggs. Some farmers raise only baby chicks. They sell the chicks to other farmers who raise them for meat or eggs. Farmers feed chickens a mixture of ground corn, wheat and soybeans.

Think and Learn

1. Chickens fly for ___short___ distances.

2. How do chickens use their strong claws? ___for scratching in the dirt to get food___

3. What are chickens raised for? ___eggs and meat___

4. What do farmers feed chickens? ___corn, wheat and soybeans___

Farm Animals　230

230

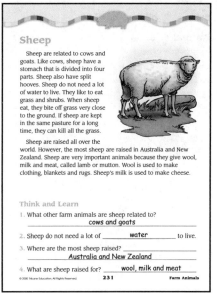

Sheep

Sheep are related to cows and goats. Like cows, sheep have a stomach that is divided into four parts. Sheep also have split hooves. Sheep do not need a lot of water to live. They like to eat grass and shrubs. When sheep eat, they bite off grass very close to the ground. If sheep are kept in the same pasture for a long time, they can kill all the grass.

Sheep are raised all over the world. However, the most sheep are raised in Australia and New Zealand. Sheep are very important animals because they give wool, milk and meat, called lamb or mutton. Wool is used to make clothing, blankets and rugs. Sheep's milk is used to make cheese.

Think and Learn

1. What other farm animals are sheep related to? ___cows and goats___

2. Sheep do not need a lot of ___water___ to live.

3. Where are the most sheep raised? ___Australia and New Zealand___

4. What are sheep raised for? ___wool, milk and meat___

© 2000 Tribune Education. All Rights Reserved.　231　**Farm Animals**

231

Answer Key

Goat

Goats are related to sheep and cows. Like sheep and cows, goats have split hooves and a four-part stomach. Goats have long shaggy hair. Most goats, both male and female, have a beard. Goats are known for eating almost anything. Because they have small mouths and flexible lips, goats can easily pick off only the healthful parts of a plant. They find food even in places where few plants can grow.

Farmers raise goats for their wool, milk and meat. People living in rocky, mountainous areas rely on goats for meat. People in the United States use goats mainly for wool and milk. Some people even keep goats as pets. Goat's milk is used for drinking and making cheese. The wool is used to make clothing and blankets.

Think and Learn

1. How are goats like sheep and cows? _____
   They have split hooves and a four-part stomach.
2. Goats can pick off only the __healthful__ parts of a plant.
3. Goats are raised for __wool, milk and meat__
4. Goat's milk is used for drinking and making __cheese__

232

Dog

Dogs are popular pets throughout the world. Dogs have been bred through the years for certain jobs, such as guarding, hunting and herding. Some dogs have been bred just to be pets. Dogs come in all sizes, colors and personalities. When choosing a dog for a pet, the dog's qualities must fit in with the family's lifestyle.

Taking care of a dog is a big responsibility. Dogs need to be fed every day. They need clean, fresh water all the time and a warm, dry place to sleep. Dogs also need regular exercise, especially if they are big dogs. Dogs must be brushed and bathed regularly. Dogs also need medical check-ups every year. They must have vaccines and medicines to stay healthy.

Think and Learn

1. What jobs have dogs been bred for? _____
   guarding, hunting and herding
2. Dogs should be fed __every day__
3. Dogs need regular __exercise__
4. Every year, dogs need medical __check-ups__

234

Cat

Cats have been favorite pets for thousands of years. At first, people had cats to get rid of pests, such as mice and snakes. Cats are skilled hunters. They have keen senses, sharp claws and the ability to jump and climb. Today, most people have cats to keep them company. Cats are smart but rather independent animals. They make good pets for people who are not home often.

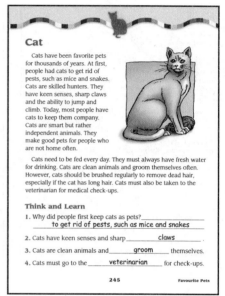

Cats need to be fed every day. They must always have fresh water for drinking. Cats are clean animals and groom themselves often. However, cats should be brushed regularly to remove dead hair, especially if the cat has long hair. Cats must also be taken to the veterinarian for medical check-ups.

Think and Learn

1. Why did people first keep cats as pets? _____
   to get rid of pests, such as mice and snakes
2. Cats have keen senses and sharp __claws__
3. Cats are clean animals and __groom__ themselves.
4. Cats must go to the __veterinarian__ for check-ups.

245

Animal Friends

Plants, animals and people must share our world. How can you be kind to our animal friends? Under each picture, write one way that you can be kind to that animal.

Be Kind to Our Animal Friends

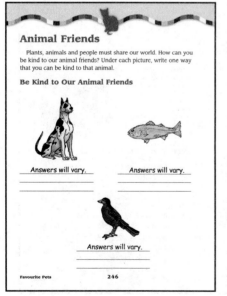

Answers will vary.   Answers will vary.

Answers will vary.

246

Rabbit

Rabbits are rodents with long ears and fluffy tails. Rodents are animals with front teeth that grow all the time. Pet rabbits must always have something to chew on. If not, their front teeth will grow too long for them to chew food normally.

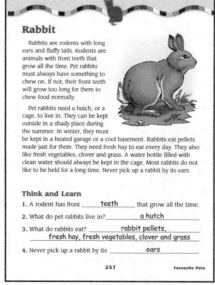

Pet rabbits need a hutch, or a cage, to live in. They can be kept outside in a shady place during the summer. In winter, they must be kept in a heated garage or a cool basement. Rabbits eat pellets made just for them. They need fresh hay to eat every day. They also like fresh vegetables, clover and grass. A water bottle filled with clean water should always be kept in the cage. Most rabbits do not like to be held for a long time. Never pick up a rabbit by its ears.

Think and Learn

1. A rodent has front __teeth__ that grow all the time.
2. What do pet rabbits live in? __a hutch__
3. What do rabbits eat? __rabbit pellets,__
   __fresh hay, fresh vegetables, clover and grass__
4. Never pick up a rabbit by its __ears__

257

Guinea Pig

A guinea pig is a small animal with a large head, short legs and small ears. They grow to 35 centimetres long and weigh about 0.5 kilograms. Guinea pigs are not really pigs. They are rodents. Rodents have front teeth that never stop growing. For this reason, guinea pigs must always have a piece of wood to gnaw on.

Guinea pigs make good classroom pets. They are easy to care for, and they don't often bite. Guinea pigs need a cage through which air can easily move. They should have food and fresh water in their cage at all times. Guinea pigs eat grain, fresh vegetables and hay. Guinea pigs are most active at night. They are quiet during the day and sleep in a burrow they make in their cage.

Think and Learn

1. Guinea pigs are not pigs; they are __rodents__
2. What is the length of a guinea pig? __35 centimetres long__
3. Why do guinea pigs make good classroom pets? _____
   They are easy to care for, and they don't often bite.
4. Guinea pigs are most active __at night__

258

Answer Key

Frog

Frogs are animals that spend part of their life in water. Some frogs live mostly in water. Other frogs live mostly on land. Almost all frogs lay their eggs in or near water. Tadpoles hatch from the eggs. Tadpoles swim and grow in water. As they grow, they change from a fishlike animal to an adult frog.

Pet frogs need a lot of care. Frogs are kept in aquariums. The kind of pet frog determines the environment in the aquarium. Some kinds of frogs live in half water and half land environments. Others live in all water environments. Still others live in all land environments. Frogs must be fed regularly. Many frogs eat live insects, such as crickets. Others eat frozen worms.

Think and Learn

1. Frogs spend part of their life in _____water_____.

2. _____Tadpoles_____ hatch from frog eggs.

3. Where are pet frogs kept? __in aquariums__

4. What do pet frogs eat? __live insects, such as__ __crickets, or frozen worms__

259   **Favourite Pets**

259

Compare and Contrast

Read about frogs and toads in the "Frogs" storybook. Then, use the Venn diagram and the facts you have learned to compare and contrast these two animals.

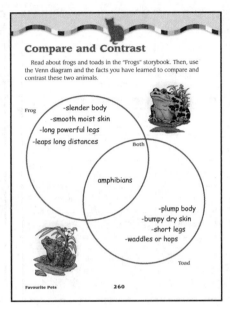

Frog
- slender body
- smooth moist skin
- long powerful legs
- leaps long distances

Both

amphibians

- plump body
- bumpy dry skin
- short legs
- waddles or hops

Toad

Favourite Pets   260

260

Classification Systems

Scientists divide all living things into major groups. Then they divide these major groups into smaller groups. And they divide the smaller groups into still smaller groups. This is called a classification system.

Your school uses a classification system, too. The whole school system includes all the schools in your area. High schools, junior high or middle schools and elementary schools make up the school system. You go to school in a certain elementary school. You are in a certain class within your school.

Think and Learn

1. Scientists use a classification system to divide __living__ __things__ into major groups and smaller groups.

2. What are the different kinds of schools that make up your school system? __Answers will vary: high schools,__ __middle schools and elementary schools__

3. What are elementary schools divided into? __classes__

Science and Animals   272   © 2000 Tribune Education. All Rights Reserved.

272

Classifying Animals

Just as your school system includes the several different kinds of schools, all of Earth's living things make up several major groups. Scientists call these major groups kingdoms. Two of the kingdoms of living things are the Plant Kingdom and the Animal Kingdom. The Animal Kingdom contains all the animals in the world.

Scientists divide each kingdom into large groups called phyla (FIH luh). Each phylum (FIH luhm) is divided into smaller groups called orders. Each class contains smaller groups called orders. In this way, scientists classify all living things on Earth.

Think and Learn

1. What do scientists call the major groups of living things? __kingdoms__

2. What are two kingdoms of living things? __Plant Kingdom and Animal Kingdom__

3. Kingdoms are divided into large groups called __phyla__.

4. Scientists divide phyla into __classes__.

© 2000 Tribune Education. All Rights Reserved.   **273**   **Science and Animals**

273

Classifying Vertebrates

Animals that have backbones are called vertebrates (VER tuh bruhts). Scientists classify vertebrates into five main groups called classes. The five main classes of vertebrates are shown below. Write the correct class name under the picture. Then, colour each of the vertebrates.

Birds have feathers and wings. Baby birds hatch from eggs.

Fish live in water and breathe through gills. Scales cover their body.

Amphibians live some of their life in water and some on land. Adults breathe with lungs.

fish

amphibian

bird

Reptiles live on land. They have dry scaly skin and breathe with lungs.

Mammals have hair on their bodies. They feed milk to their young.

reptile

mammal

reptile   fish   amphibian
bird   mammal

Science and Animals   274

274

Backbones

Animals with backbones are called vertebrates. Each skeleton below shows a different class of vertebrates. Colour the backbone in each skeleton. Then, write the class below each animal.

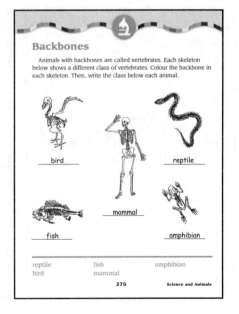

bird   reptile

mammal

fish   amphibian

reptile   fish   amphibian
bird   mammal

275   **Science and Animals**

275

Answer Key

Classy Vertebrates

Scientists group the vertebrates into five main classes. Write the name of the vertebrate class for each picture.

reptile   amphibian   fish   mammal

reptile   bird   mammal   amphibian

mammal   bird   fish   bird

reptile   fish   amphibian
bird   mammal

Science and Animals   **276**   © 2000 Tribune Education. All Rights Reserved.

276

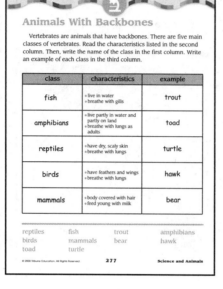

Animals With Backbones

Vertebrates are animals that have backbones. There are five main classes of vertebrates. Read the characteristics listed in the second column. Then, write the name of the class in the first column. Write an example of each class in the third column.

class	characteristics	example
fish	• live in water • breathe with gills	trout
amphibians	• live partly in water and partly on land • breathe with lungs as adults	toad
reptiles	• have dry, scaly skin • breathe with lungs	turtle
birds	• have feathers and wings • breathe with lungs	hawk
mammals	• body covered with hair • feed young with milk	bear

reptiles   fish   trout   amphibians
birds   mammals   bear   hawk
toad   turtle

© 2000 Tribune Education. All Rights Reserved.   **277**   Science and Animals

277

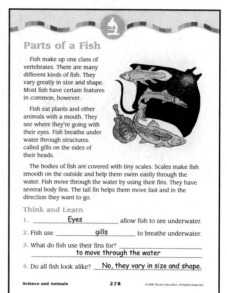

Parts of a Fish

Fish make up one class of vertebrates. There are many different kinds of fish. They vary greatly in size and shape. Most fish have certain features in common, however.

Fish eat plants and other animals with a mouth. They see where they're going with their eyes. Fish breathe under water through structures called gills on the sides of their heads.

The bodies of fish are covered with tiny scales. Scales make fish smooth on the outside and help them swim easily through the water. Fish move through the water by using their fins. They have several body fins. The tail fin helps them move fast and in the direction they want to go.

Think and Learn

1. _____ Eyes _____ allow fish to see underwater.
2. Fish use _____ gills _____ to breathe underwater.
3. What do fish use their fins for? _____ to move through the water _____
4. Do all fish look alike? _____ No, they vary in size and shape. _____

Science and Animals   **278**   © 2000 Tribune Education. All Rights Reserved.

278

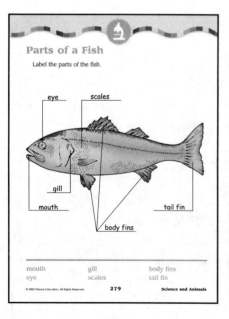

Parts of a Fish

Label the parts of the fish.

eye   scales
gill
mouth   tail fin
body fins

mouth   gill   body fins
eye   scales   tail fin

© 2000 Tribune Education. All Rights Reserved.   **279**   Science and Animals

279

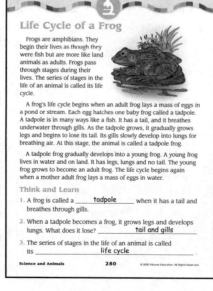

Life Cycle of a Frog

Frogs are amphibians. They begin their lives as though they were fish but are more like land animals as adults. Frogs pass through stages during their lives. The series of stages in the life of an animal is called its life cycle.

A frog's life cycle begins when an adult frog lays a mass of eggs in a pond or stream. Each egg hatches one baby frog called a tadpole. A tadpole is in many ways like a fish. It has a tail, and it breathes underwater through gills. As the tadpole grows, it gradually grows legs and begins to lose its tail. Its gills slowly develop into lungs for breathing air. At this stage, the animal is called a tadpole frog.

A tadpole frog gradually develops into a young frog. A young frog lives in water and on land. It has legs, lungs and no tail. The young frog grows to become an adult frog. The life cycle begins again when a mother adult frog lays a mass of eggs in water.

Think and Learn

1. A frog is called a _____ tadpole _____ when it has a tail and breathes through gills.
2. When a tadpole becomes a frog, it grows legs and develops lungs. What does it lose? _____ tail and gills _____
3. The series of stages in the life of an animal is called its _____ life cycle _____.

Science and Animals   **280**   © 2000 Tribune Education. All Rights Reserved.

280

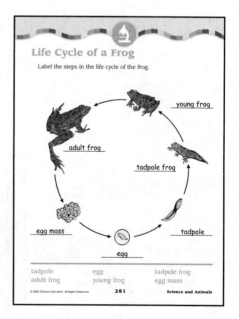

Life Cycle of a Frog

Label the steps in the life cycle of the frog.

young frog

adult frog

tadpole frog

egg mass

egg

tadpole

tadpole   egg   tadpole frog
adult frog   young frog   egg mass

© 2000 Tribune Education. All Rights Reserved.   **281**   Science and Animals

281

Answer Key

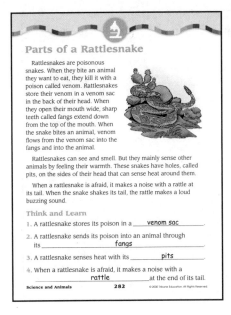

Parts of a Rattlesnake

Rattlesnakes are poisonous snakes. When they bite an animal they want to eat, they kill it with a poison called venom. Rattlesnakes store their venom in a venom sac in the back of their head. When they open their mouth wide, sharp teeth called fangs extend down from the top of the mouth. When the snake bites an animal, venom flows from the venom sac into the fangs and into the animal.

Rattlesnakes can see and smell. But they mainly sense other animals by feeling their warmth. These snakes have holes, called pits, on the sides of their head that can sense heat around them.

When a rattlesnake is afraid, it makes a noise with a rattle at its tail. When the snake shakes its tail, the rattle makes a loud buzzing sound.

Think and Learn

1. A rattlesnake stores its poison in a __venom sac__.

2. A rattlesnake sends its poison into an animal through its __fangs__.

3. A rattlesnake senses heat with its __pits__.

4. When a rattlesnake is afraid, it makes a noise with a __rattle__ at the end of its tail.

Science and Animals 282 © 2000 Tribune Education. All Rights Reserved.

282

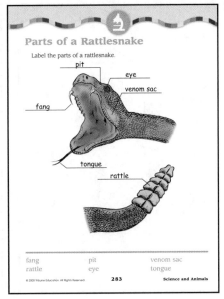

Parts of a Rattlesnake

Label the parts of a rattlesnake.

pit
eye
venom sac
fang
tongue
rattle

fang	pit	venom sac
rattle	eye	tongue

© 2000 Tribune Education. All Rights Reserved. 283 Science and Animals

283

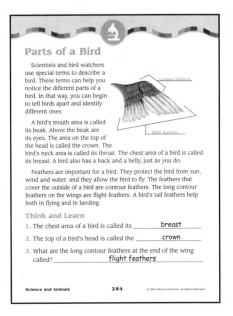

Parts of a Bird

Scientists and bird watchers use special terms to describe a bird. These terms can help you notice the different parts of a bird. In that way, you can begin to tell birds apart and identify different ones.

contour feathers
flight feathers

A bird's mouth area is called its beak. Above the beak are its eyes. The area on the top of the head is called the crown. The bird's neck area is called its throat. The chest area of a bird is called its breast. A bird also has a back and a belly, just as you do.

Feathers are important for a bird. They protect the bird from sun, wind and water, and they allow the bird to fly. The feathers that cover the outside of a bird are contour feathers. The long contour feathers on the wings are flight feathers. A bird's tail feathers help both in flying and in landing.

Think and Learn

1. The chest area of a bird is called its __breast__.

2. The top of a bird's head is called the __crown__.

3. What are the long contour feathers at the end of the wing called? __flight feathers__

Science and Animals 284 © 2000 Tribune Education. All Rights Reserved.

284

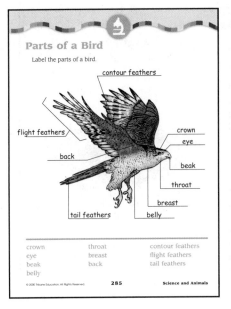

Parts of a Bird

Label the parts of a bird.

contour feathers
flight feathers
crown
eye
back
beak
throat
breast
tail feathers
belly

crown	throat	contour feathers
eye	breast	flight feathers
beak	back	tail feathers
belly		

© 2000 Tribune Education. All Rights Reserved. 285 Science and Animals

285

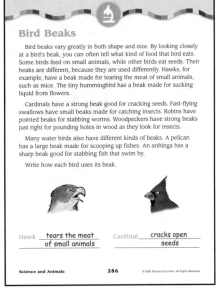

Bird Beaks

Bird beaks vary greatly in both shape and size. By looking closely at a bird's beak, you can often tell what kind of food that bird eats. Some birds feed on small animals, while other birds eat seeds. Their beaks are different, because they are used differently. Hawks, for example, have a beak made for tearing the meat of small animals, such as mice. The tiny hummingbird has a beak made for sucking liquid from flowers.

Cardinals have a strong beak good for cracking seeds. Fast-flying swallows have small beaks made for catching insects. Robins have pointed beaks for stabbing worms. Woodpeckers have strong beaks just right for pounding holes in wood as they look for insects.

Many water birds also have different kinds of beaks. A pelican has a large beak made for scooping up fishes. An anhinga has a sharp beak good for stabbing fish that swim by.

Write how each bird uses its beak.

Hawk __tears the meat of small animals__

Cardinal __cracks open seeds__

Science and Animals 286 © 2000 Tribune Education. All Rights Reserved.

286

Bird Beaks

Write how each bird uses its beak.

Pelican __scoops up fish__

Hummingbird __sucks liquid from flowers__

Swallow __catches flying insects__

Robin __stabs worms in ground__

Anhinga __stabs fish in water__

Woodpecker __pounds holes in trees to find insects__

© 2000 Tribune Education. All Rights Reserved. 287 Science and Animals

287

Everything About Animals

Answer Key

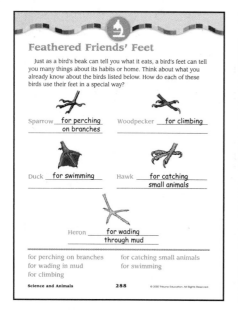

Feathered Friends' Feet

Just as a bird's beak can tell you what it eats, a bird's feet can tell you many things about its habits or home. Think about what you already know about the birds listed below. How do each of these birds use their feet in a special way?

Sparrow **for perching on branches**

Woodpecker **for climbing**

Duck **for swimming**

Hawk **for catching small animals**

Heron **for wading through mud**

for perching on branches	for catching small animals
for wading in mud	for swimming
for climbing	

288

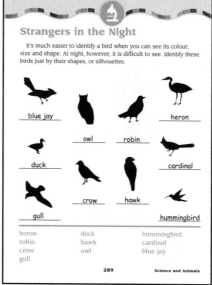

Strangers in the Night

It's much easier to identify a bird when you can see its colour, size and shape. At night, however, it is difficult to see. Identify these birds just by their shapes, or silhouettes.

blue jay

owl

robin

heron

duck

cardinal

crow

hawk

gull

hummingbird

heron	duck	hummingbird
robin	hawk	cardinal
crow	owl	blue jay
gull		

289

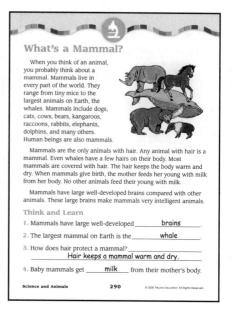

What's a Mammal?

When you think of an animal, you probably think about a mammal. Mammals live in every part of the world. They range from tiny mice to the largest animals on Earth, the whales. Mammals include dogs, cats, cows, bears, kangaroos, raccoons, rabbits, elephants, dolphins, and many others. Human beings are also mammals.

Mammals are the only animals with hair. Any animal with hair is a mammal. Even whales have a few hairs on their body. Most mammals are covered with hair. The hair keeps the body warm and dry. When mammals give birth, the mother feeds her young with milk from her body. No other animals feed their young with milk.

Mammals have large well-developed brains compared with other animals. These large brains make mammals very intelligent animals.

Think and Learn

1. Mammals have large well-developed **brains**.

2. The largest mammal on Earth is the **whale**.

3. How does hair protect a mammal?
   Hair keeps a mammal warm and dry.

4. Baby mammals get **milk** from their mother's body.

290

What's a Mammal?

Think and Learn

1. Look at the picture above. How do you know the mother is a mammal? **It has hair on its body.**

2. In the picture above, what are the babies doing that only young mammals do?
   They are drinking milk from their mother.

291

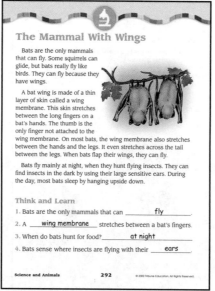

The Mammal With Wings

Bats are the only mammals that can fly. Some squirrels can glide, but bats really fly like birds. They can fly because they have wings.

A bat wing is made of a thin layer of skin called a wing membrane. This skin stretches between the long fingers on a bat's hands. The thumb is the only finger not attached to the wing membrane. On most bats, the wing membrane also stretches between the hands and the legs. It even stretches across the tail between the legs. When bats flap their wings, they can fly.

Bats fly mainly at night, when they hunt flying insects. They can find insects in the dark by using their large sensitive ears. During the day, most bats sleep by hanging upside down.

Think and Learn

1. Bats are the only mammals that can **fly**.

2. A **wing membrane** stretches between a bat's fingers.

3. When do bats hunt for food? **at night**

4. Bats sense where insects are flying with their **ears**.

292

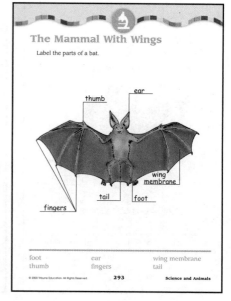

The Mammal With Wings

Label the parts of a bat.

thumb

ear

wing membrane

tail

foot

fingers

| foot | ear | wing membrane |
| thumb | fingers | tail |

293

Answer Key

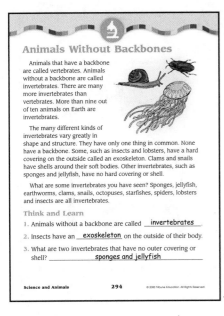

Animals Without Backbones

Animals that have a backbone are called vertebrates. Animals without a backbone are called invertebrates. There are many more invertebrates than vertebrates. More than nine out of ten animals on Earth are invertebrates.

The many different kinds of invertebrates vary greatly in shape and structure. They have only one thing in common. None have a backbone. Some, such as insects and lobsters, have a hard covering on the outside called an exoskeleton. Clams and snails have shells around their soft bodies. Other invertebrates, such as sponges and jellyfish, have no hard covering or shell.

What are some invertebrates you have seen? Sponges, jellyfish, earthworms, clams, snails, octopuses, starfishes, spiders, lobsters and insects are all invertebrates.

Think and Learn

1. Animals without a backbone are called __invertebrates__.

2. Insects have an __exoskeleton__ on the outside of their body.

3. What are two invertebrates that have no outer covering or shell? __sponges and jellyfish__

Science and Animals   294   © 2000 Tribune Education. All Rights Reserved.

294

Animals Without Backbones

Write whether each animal is a vertebrate or an invertebrate.

invertebrate   invertebrate   invertebrate

invertebrate

vertebrate   invertebrate   vertebrate

invertebrate

vertebrate   vertebrate   invertebrate

© 2000 Tribune Education. All Rights Reserved.   295   Science and Animals

295

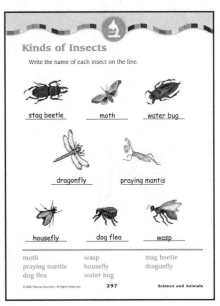

Kinds of Insects

Write the name of each insect on the line.

stag beetle   moth   water bug

dragonfly   praying mantis

housefly   dog flea   wasp

moth	wasp	stag beetle
praying mantis	housefly	dragonfly
dog flea	water bug	

© 2000 Tribune Education. All Rights Reserved.   297   Science and Animals

297

Spiders and Insects

Both spiders and insects are invertebrates. But spiders are not insects, though many people think so. If you look closely at a spider and an insect, you can see how different they are.

An insect has three main body parts. The head is in front. The chest is the next part. The abdomen is behind the chest. Most insects have wings attached to the chest. Insects also have six legs attached to the chest, three on each side.

A spider has two main body parts. The head and chest together make up one part. The abdomen is behind. A spider has eight legs attached to the head-and-chest part, four on each side. Spiders do not have wings.

Think and Learn

1. Insects and spiders are both __invertebrates__.

2. An insect has __three__ main body parts.

3. A spider has __two__ main body parts.

4. How many legs does an insect have? __six__

5. How many legs does a spider have? __eight__

Science and Animals   298   © 2000 Tribune Education. All Rights Reserved.

298

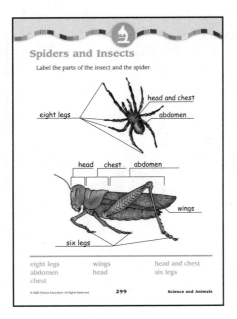

Spiders and Insects

Label the parts of the insect and the spider.

eight legs   head and chest   abdomen

head   chest   abdomen

wings

six legs

eight legs	wings	head and chest
abdomen	head	six legs
chest		

© 2000 Tribune Education. All Rights Reserved.   299   Science and Animals

299

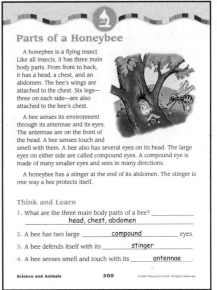

Parts of a Honeybee

A honeybee is a flying insect. Like all insects, it has three main body parts. From front to back, it has a head, a chest, and an abdomen. The bee's wings are attached to the chest. Six legs—three on each side—are also attached to the bee's chest.

A bee senses its environment through its antennae and its eyes. The antennae are on the front of the head. A bee senses touch and smell with them. A bee also has several eyes on its head. The large eyes on either side are called compound eyes. A compound eye is made of many smaller eyes and sees in many directions.

A honeybee has a stinger at the end of its abdomen. The stinger is one way a bee protects itself.

Think and Learn

1. What are the three main body parts of a bee? __head, chest, abdomen__

2. A bee has two large __compound__ eyes.

3. A bee defends itself with its __stinger__.

4. A bee senses smell and touch with its __antennae__.

Science and Animals   300   © 2000 Tribune Education. All Rights Reserved.

300

Everything About Animals

Answer Key

Parts of a Honeybee

Label the parts of a honeybee.

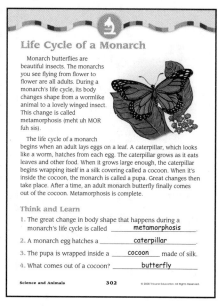

compound eye
antenna
head
chest
wings
abdomen
stinger

stinger	chest	compound eye
wings	antenna	abdomen
head		

301   Science and Animals

301

Life Cycle of a Monarch

Monarch butterflies are beautiful insects. The monarchs you see flying from flower to flower are all adults. During a monarch's life cycle, its body changes shape from a wormlike animal to a lovely winged insect. This change is called metamorphosis (meht uh MOR fuh sis).

The life cycle of a monarch begins when an adult lays eggs on a leaf. A caterpillar, which looks like a worm, hatches from each egg. The caterpillar grows as it eats leaves and other food. When it grows large enough, the caterpillar begins wrapping itself in a silk covering called a cocoon. When it's inside the cocoon, the monarch is called a pupa. Great changes then take place. After a time, an adult monarch butterfly finally comes out of the cocoon. Metamorphosis is complete.

Think and Learn

1. The great change in body shape that happens during a monarch's life cycle is called _____ metamorphosis _____

2. A monarch egg hatches a _____ caterpillar _____.

3. The pupa is wrapped inside a _____ cocoon _____ made of silk.

4. What comes out of a cocoon? _____ butterfly _____

Science and Animals   **302**

302

Life Cycle of a Monarch

Label the steps in the life cycle of a monarch.

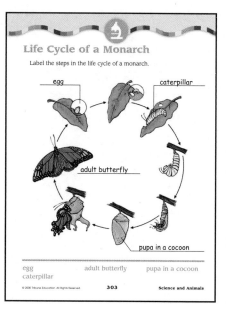

egg
caterpillar
adult butterfly
pupa in a cocoon

egg	adult butterfly	pupa in a cocoon
caterpillar		

303   Science and Animals

303

Parts of a Clam

Clams are invertebrates that live in water. A hard shell surrounds the animal's soft body. Clams can move around by using a muscle called a foot. They stick the foot out of the shell and push against a lake or ocean floor.

Clams eat and breathe by pulling water inside their shells through a tube called a siphon (SIH fuhn). Sometimes, clams bury themselves in sand for protection. To eat, they extend a siphon up to the top of the sand and suck in water.

Most of the soft body inside the shell is called the mantle. The shell is attached to the mantle. When water comes through one siphon, it passes through the clam's gills. The gills collect oxygen and bits of food from the water. The water then leaves the animal through the second siphon.

Think and Learn

1. A _____ shell _____ surrounds and protects a clam.

2. A clam moves by using its _____ foot _____.

3. How does water flow into the clam? _____
   _____ through one of its siphons _____

4. The clam's _____ gills _____ collect oxygen and food from water.

Science and Animals   **304**

304

Parts of a Clam

Label the parts of a clam.

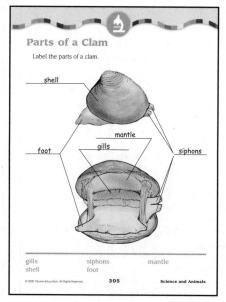

shell
mantle
foot
gills
siphons

gills	siphons	mantle
shell	foot	

305   Science and Animals

305

Animal Adaptations

Each kind of animal has characteristics that allow it to survive in its environment. For example, a fish has gills for breathing underwater. If it had lungs like mammals, a fish could not survive underwater. Any characteristic that helps an animal survive in its environment is called an adaptation (a dap TAY shun).

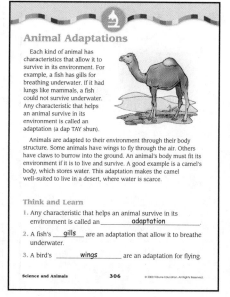

Animals are adapted to their environment through their body structure. Some animals have wings to fly through the air. Others have claws to burrow into the ground. An animal's body must fit its environment if it is to live and survive. A good example is a camel's body, which stores water. This adaptation makes the camel well-suited to live in a desert, where water is scarce.

Think and Learn

1. Any characteristic that helps an animal survive in its environment is called an _____ adaptation _____.

2. A fish's _____ gills _____ are an adaptation that allow it to breathe underwater.

3. A bird's _____ wings _____ are an adaptation for flying.

Science and Animals   **306**

306

Answer Key

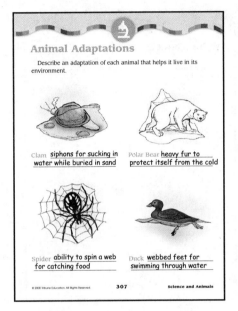

Animal Adaptations

Describe an adaptation of each animal that helps it live in its environment.

Clam **siphons for sucking in water while buried in sand**

Polar Bear **heavy fur to protect itself from the cold**

Spider **ability to spin a web for catching food**

Duck **webbed feet for swimming through water**

© 2000 Tribune Education. All Rights Reserved.   307   Science and Animals

307

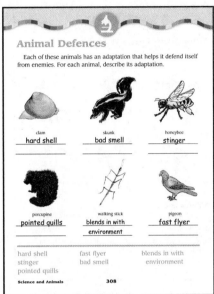

Animal Defences

Each of these animals has an adaptation that helps it defend itself from enemies. For each animal, describe its adaptation.

clam **hard shell**

skunk **bad smell**

honeybee **stinger**

porcupine **pointed quills**

walking stick **blends in with environment**

pigeon **fast flyer**

hard shell   fast flyer   blends in with
stinger   bad smell   environment
pointed quills

Science and Animals   308

308

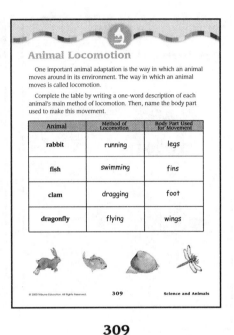

Animal Locomotion

One important animal adaptation is the way in which an animal moves around in its environment. The way in which an animal moves is called locomotion.

Complete the table by writing a one-word description of each animal's main method of locomotion. Then, name the body part used to make this movement.

Animal	Method of Locomotion	Body Part Used for Movement
rabbit	running	legs
fish	swimming	fins
clam	dragging	foot
dragonfly	flying	wings

© 2000 Tribune Education. All Rights Reserved.   309   Science and Animals

309

Food Chains

Animals need energy to stay alive. They get this energy by eating food. Some animals eat plants. Some eat other animals. And some eat both plants and other animals. Think of all the living things that feed on one another in an environment. This is called a food chain. Each living thing in a food chain is a "link" in the "chain." The energy of food passes from one living thing to another through the food chain.

The food chain shown on this page begins with underwater plants in a pond. The plants make up the first link in the food chain. A fish eats the plants. The fish is the second link in the food chain. Finally, an eagle swoops down and catches the fish. The eagle becomes the last link in this food chain.

Think and Learn

1. What are all the living things that feed on one another in an environment called? **food chain**

2. Each plant or animal in a food chain is one **link** in the chain.

3. What kind of living thing almost always begins a food chain? **plants**

Science and Animals   310   © 2000 Tribune Education. All Rights Reserved.

310

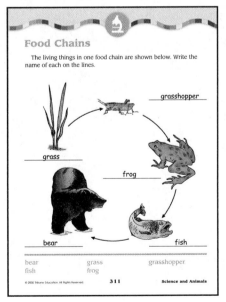

Food Chains

The living things in one food chain are shown below. Write the name of each on the lines.

grasshopper

grass

frog

bear

fish

bear   grass   grasshopper
fish   frog

© 2000 Tribune Education. All Rights Reserved.   311   Science and Animals

311

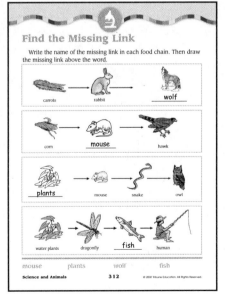

Find the Missing Link

Write the name of the missing link in each food chain. Then draw the missing link above the word.

carrots   rabbit   **wolf**

corn   **mouse**   hawk

plants   mouse   snake   owl

water plants   dragonfly   **fish**   human

mouse   plants   wolf   fish

Science and Animals   312   © 2000 Tribune Education. All Rights Reserved.

312

Everything About Animals

Answer Key

What's Its Name?

For each family group, label the members with the correct names.

buck	bull
doe	cow
fawn	calf

drake	rooster
duck	hen
duckling	chick

315 **Animal Facts and Fun**

How Long Does It Live?

Write how long each of these animals lives.

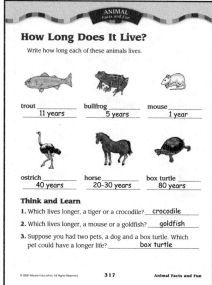

trout	bullfrog	mouse
11 years	5 years	1 year

ostrich	horse	box turtle
40 years	20-30 years	80 years

Think and Learn

1. Which lives longer, a tiger or a crocodile? ___crocodile___

2. Which lives longer, a mouse or a goldfish? ___goldfish___

3. Suppose you had two pets, a dog and a box turtle. Which pet could have a longer life? ___box turtle___

317 **Animal Facts and Fun**

Write About It

Choose an interesting animal that you have read about. Draw a picture of the animal. Then, write a paragraph that tells some fascinating facts about the animal you chose.

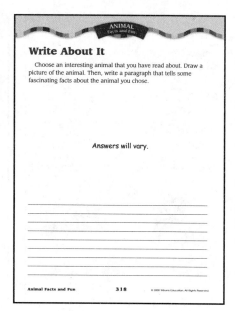

Answers will vary.

Animal Facts and Fun 318

---

315 317 318